God's Absence and
the Charismatic Presence

God's Absence and the Charismatic Presence

Inquiries in Openness Theology

ROY D. KINDELBERGER

WIPF & STOCK · Eugene, Oregon

GOD'S ABSENCE AND THE CHARISMATIC PRESENCE
Inquiries in Openness Theology

Copyright © 2017 Roy D. Kindelberger II. All rights reserved. Except for brief quotations in critical publications or reviews, no part of this book may be reproduced in any manner without prior written permission from the publisher. Write: Permissions, Wipf and Stock Publishers, 199 W. 8th Ave., Suite 3, Eugene, OR 97401.

Wipf & Stock
An Imprint of Wipf and Stock Publishers
199 W. 8th Ave., Suite 3
Eugene, OR 97401

www.wipfandstock.com

PAPERBACK ISBN: 978-1-5326-1452-1
HARDCOVER ISBN: 978-1-5326-1454-5
EBOOK ISBN: 978-1-5326-1453-8

Manufactured in the U.S.A.   MAY 9, 2017

All Scripture quotations, unless otherwise indicated, are taken from the Holy Bible, New International Version®, NIV®. Copyright ©1973, 1978, 1984, 2011 by Biblica, Inc.™ Used by permission of Zondervan. All rights reserved worldwide. www.zondervan.com

The "NIV" and "New International Version" are trademarks registered in the United States Patent and Trademark Office by Biblica, Inc.™

Scripture quotations are taken from the Holy Bible, New Living Translation, copyright ©1996, 2004, 2007, 2013, 2015 by Tyndale House Foundation. Used by permission of Tyndale House Publishers, Inc., Carol Stream, Illinois 60188. All rights reserved.

Scripture quotations marked (ESV) are from the ESV® Bible (The Holy Bible, English Standard Version®), copyright © 2001 by Crossway, a publishing ministry of Good News Publishers. Used by permission. All rights reserved

Scripture quotations taken from the New American Standard Bible® (NASB), Copyright © 1960, 1962, 1963, 1968, 1971, 1972, 1973, 1975, 1977, 1995 by The Lockman Foundation. Used by permission. www.Lockman.org

Scriptures marked KJV are taken from the KING JAMES VERSION (KJV): KING JAMES VERSION, public domain.

Scripture quoted by permission. Quotations designated (NET) are from the NET Bible® copyright ©1996–2016 by Biblical Studies Press, L.L.C. http://netbible.org All rights reserved.

New Revised Standard Version Bible, copyright 1989, Division of Christian Education of the National Council of the Churches of Christ in the United States of America. Used by permission. All rights reserved.

For my bride,
who daily shares with me the blessing of knowing God's presence
in our marriage, our home, and our ministry

Contents

Acknowledgments | xi

Introduction: God of Wonders and an Open Future | 1
    Mutable: Changeable in Experience
    Temporal: Changeable in Time
    Passible: Changeable in Emotion and Suffering
    Malleable: Changeable in Presence
    Conclusion

Part I: God's Absence

1   An Open Past and Present: "If not, I will know" | 21
    Yahweh's Investigation
    Classical Interpretation: A Closed-Minded God
    Openness Interpretation: An Open-Minded God
    An Interpretation of Radical Openness
    Yahweh's Absence from Sodom
    Conclusion

2   An Open Universe: Sin and Death as Distance | 38
    When God Withdraws His Presence
    Hamartiological Distance
    Sin and Death as True Separation from God
    Divine Suffering: A Trajectory to Hell
    Conclusion

3   Distance: Origin and Implications | 59
    Satan's Kingdom of Sin and Death
    Evil's Origin and the Competing Knowledge of Sin
    The Unpredictable Nature of Sin
    Divine Optimism
    Implications of Distance: God Sees, Hears, and Knows
    Conclusion

4   Covenant and Exile: Israel's Paradigm for Sin and Death | 82
    Covenants of Divine Presence
    The Latter Prophets and the Abyss of Exile
    The Hamartiological Distance of Israel and Judah
    The Prophets' Promise of Restored Presence
    Conclusion

5   Openness Hermeneutics: Omnipresence and the Absence of God | 103
    Exegetical Method in the Person Jesus Christ
    Divine Absence through an Incarnational Hermeneutic
    Relational Omnipresence
    Why God Isn't Obligated to Be Everywhere
    Conclusion

Part II: The Charismatic Presence

6   Salvation: Closing the Distance | 127
    Overcoming Death and Distance
    Atonement by Death or Distance?
    Forgiveness is Complete in Christ
    Ritual of Entrance: Water Baptism
    Ceremony of Presence: The Eucharist
    Conclusion: Closing the Distance

7   Pentecost: Open Expansion | 150
    Introducing an Open, Covenantal Kingdom
    Launching an Open Kingdom: Spirit Baptism
    Leading an Open Kingdom: Messiah's Presence
    Manifesting an Open Kingdom: Word, Signs, and Wonders
    Conclusion: Closing the Distance

8 Worship: Open Freedom | 168

    Introducing Charismata in an Open Universe
    Dynamic Ministry in Corinth
    Charismata's Unilateral Presence: Open Prophecy
    Charismata's Unilateral Presence: Open Tongues and Interpretation
    Charismata's Unilateral Presence: Open Miracles
    Charismata's Unilateral Presence: Open Healing
    Charismata's Unilateral Presence: Open Discernment
    Charismata's Unilateral Presence: Open Faith
    Charismata's Bilateral Presence: A Summary
    Conclusion: Closing the Distance

9 Ministry: Open Involvement | 195

    Introducing Fivefold Ministry in an Open Universe
    The Openness of Apostolic Ministry: Beyond "the Twelve"
    The Openness of Prophetic Ministry
    The Openness of Evangelistic Ministry
    The Openness of Pastoral/Teaching Ministry
    The Openness of Ministry Candidacy
    Conclusion: Closing the Distance

10 Prayer and the Coming Revival: Open Impact | 216

    The Best Possible Future
    The Openness of Prayer
    Prayer, Charismata, and the Power of Revival
    Conclusion: Showers of Revival After the Storm

Appendix: Origins of Pentecostal Tongues | 235

Bibliography | 239

Acknowledgments

There are few words worthy enough to express my utmost gratitude toward the most important theologian in my life, my mother Kristine, who has always been a mighty prayer warrior and constant in God's word.

I am indebted to David von Schlichten for his editing skills, biblical wisdom and scholarship, and many helpful suggestions to improve the manuscript.

I thank God for my fellow elders at Covenant Church East—Pat, Bonnie, Mike, and Mary—who always display utmost love for our Lord Jesus. I am so thankful for our dear friends Mike and Misty who serve God with extravagance.

I am so grateful to each of you who read the draft and offered your thoughtful comments.

Thank you, Holy Spirit, for surrounding us with so many precious people.

Introduction

God of Wonders and an Open Future

I want to first thank my courageous readers for picking up a book with such a provocative phrase as *God's Absence* in its title. Everyone knows something of a hidden God and his elusive presence in the world. We experience it every day of our lives. Yet like the psalmists who cry out, *Don't hide your face from me!* or *Where are you, Lord?*, believers often cry out in frustration while still depending on God to be near and ready to step out of the shadows to answer (Pss 10:1; 13:1; 27:9). Even in our darkest hour, the believer is privileged to experience the satisfying end to her groping for God: "Weeping may endure for a night, but joy cometh in the morning" (30:5 KJV).[1] For the child of God, absence is just presence in disguise.

Now if I were to tell you, "God is love," would you believe me? We should give serious thought to such a weighty question. You might have second thoughts if you've only ever heard, for example, that the God of the Bible is one who stringently controls a world full of hate and violence, much of which we've personally experienced. Or, that this God you serve has ordained the certain, unavoidable future demise of some of your friends and family, ultimately leaving them no choice but to remain in their miserable, depraved condition because he chose to save others instead of them.

Many of us have harbored the disturbing intuition that Satan must be some kind of puppet in God's hands, while at the same time believing that God is somehow not to blame for all the mischief, chaos, and harm done by this creature and those who abide in his kingdom of sin and death. If the world we live in exists under a God with complete, meticulous control, a

---

1. All Scripture quotations, unless otherwise indicated, are taken from the Holy Bible, New International Version, NIV.

God who knows the future in every detail and has ordained all that will be, we have no choice but to look around at the suffering and pain and question whether he really is the "God [of] love" that Scripture declares him to be (1 John 4:8, 16).

What doesn't add up is the fact that the practical, relational God we pray to and trust throughout our daily experience tends to be quite different from the God classical theologians have described to us. The God many of us have come to know in our devotions, during our worship with the believing community, or in morning prayer is one we feel confident to approach, one who hears us and assures us of his love. Yet the God of classical theism tends to be stubborn and dogmatic, ultimately closed to our input while selfishly seeking to uphold his own honor and reputation. But again, the irony is that most evangelical believers live out the Christian life as if this isn't so. We pray to God as if he really does care about what we say and really will change his mind on matters. We minister to others and serve those in need as if God really does in some way depend on us as his hands and feet. We live as if there might not be a backup plan if we fail in our sphere of influence, that God actually accepts the risk of using imperfect people to accomplish his will. We believe in our hearts that God is vulnerable in the ways he uses us to love the world.

Throughout my theological training, I was taught by many voices that God knows everything about the future, that prayers don't change God, and that God actually doesn't need people in any fundamental way, along with so many other non-relational aspects of God that fall in line with what we think of when we consider the classical view of God. This was something I never thought to question but also never heard an objection to. Yet there's something about all of this that just sticks in our craw when we size up our loving Savior with a god set on damning the world and damning our loved ones for the sake of his glory. It's challenges like these that leave so many people confused and questioning.

The exception to this picture of a dominating and domineering God has often been with liberal theologians who present a God of love and acceptance, but they do so at great cost to the authority of Scripture and the testimony of the gospel of the cross and resurrection. The cost might be a watered-down gospel, a Jesus of history who's not the Son of God, a morality without repentance, or some other defamation of God's sacred word. The choice between liberalism and classical conservatism leaves much wanting in one's theology and an impossible reconciling of the God we worship with the God of church history, but there is of course another option.

There is a third option presented by those who point to Scripture and desire to show the church a relational God who is open to a risky love

INTRODUCTION: GOD OF WONDERS AND AN OPEN FUTURE 3

because love is at the center of his existence and all his ways. When I first encountered open theism (or freewill theism), like many others, I was skeptical.[2] In many regards, I still am! But what made this journey most worthwhile was being led into Scripture to investigate the solid testimony of God's word and to find there a God who accepts the risks of loving his creatures. Over the past few decades, the church has been offered this third option for our thoughtful consideration. The openness view looks to Scripture as the final source of truth and revelation and takes seriously the descriptions, experiences, thoughts, and feelings of God that are found there. The God we serve is not only transcendent in power, presence, and knowledge but also immanent and absolutely relational! Exploring the intimate depths of God's open heart toward people, openness theology seeks to renew and revive the church's understanding of God's relationship to us. He is both Almighty God *and* capable of anger, jealousy, regret, frustration, surprise, desire, sorrow, suffering, and hope.

Looking around at the world, believers intuitively get the sense that God does not always get his way and therefore takes risks. Why else would Jesus teach us to pray to his Father, "Your will be done on earth, as it is in heaven" (Matt 6:10), if God's perfect and pleasing will is already being done everywhere? Or, are we to believe that God has two different and competing wills, one permissive and the other hidden and efficacious? For both the casual Arminian and the freewill theist, this classical Calvinist defense of two divine wills has become untenable. God's singular, consistent, perfect will can and is at times thwarted. God does not *allow* evil and suffering in the world but himself suffers at its hands due to the nature of true freedom for both humanity and angels, both fallen and unfallen. We can all be certain that the will of humanity does not always line up with the will of God.

God's blatantly obvious risk in the garden was that humans might choose to eat the fruit of the knowledge of good and evil. From the beginning it was apparent that the risks God takes are directly tied to the freedom of will he has irrevocably given to humankind. Accepting the risk, God pursues relationships with people that are of a truly personal, intimate nature, where his heart is on the line because of the possibility of rejection. Jesus summarized this grief as he looked out over Jerusalem and said with sad

---

2. I will be using the terminology open theism, freewill theism, openness theology, and the open view of God interchangeably, though they aren't always used in this way. Open theism emphasizes the relational openness of God; his heart is open to relate, respond, and rely on his creatures in a fundamentally relational manner. Freewill theism tends to emphasize the role of the creature's freedom in the world. H. Wayne House provides a rather detailed comparison between the classical or orthodox view of theism and the openness perspective; see *Charts on Open Theism and Orthodoxy*.

disappointment, "How often I have longed to gather your children together, as a hen gathers her chicks under her wings, and you were not willing" (Matt 23:37). The open theist would say that such grief is due in part to people's freedom to reject God's love. They might add that because Jesus doesn't know every detail of an open future and what every relationship holds, the divine *longing* and hopeful anticipation for closeness with his people went unfulfilled.

Openness theology teaches that God wills and longs for a loving relationship with humanity, but that immediate future is not guaranteed. God hasn't ordained every detail of the future but allows true freedom for the sake of relationship. For instance, in the face of the horrors of exile, Yahweh looked forward with eager anticipation to the future possibility that his people might turn from their wicked ways so that he could change his mind about their judgment, which was all still up in the air. The LORD said to Jeremiah, "*Perhaps* they will listen and each will turn from their evil ways. *Then I will relent* and not inflict on them the disaster I was planning because of the evil they have done. . . . *Perhaps* when the people of Judah hear about every disaster I plan to inflict on them, they will each turn from their wicked ways" (Jer 26:3; 36:3, emphasis added).[3] It's passages like this that suggest uncertainty from God. Perhaps my children will do this or that! The open theist points to such passages to support her contention that the future is not set in stone but is a future full of possibilities.

And what about prayer? Openness theology teaches that prayer makes the most sense in an open and flexible universe where the future is not yet written. When King Hezekiah became ill and was at the point of death, a prophet came to him and in no uncertain terms declared to him, "you are going to die." To avoid any confusion on the matter, the prophet added the words, "you will not recover" (2 Kgs 20:1; cf. Isa 38:1–6). But after the king cried out to Yahweh, apparently understanding the open-mindedness of God, the prophet returned with quite a different message from the LORD: "I have heard your prayer and seen your tears; I will heal you. . . . I will add fifteen years to your life" (2 Kgs 20:5, 6). But he was promised death, beyond recovery! Readers are thus encouraged not to pursue any other explanation than the most obvious, that this king's prayer changed God's mind! In an open universe, prayer not only changes you and me but also God's plans. Surely it would have been disingenuous for God to predict a death that wasn't a real and even likely possibility. This king was doomed to die,

---

3. If language means anything at all, the term *perhaps* conveys uncertainty. Regarding the divine *perhaps*, see Jer 36:7; 51:8; Isa 47:12; Ezek 12:3. Also cf. Luke 20:13.

INTRODUCTION: GOD OF WONDERS AND AN OPEN FUTURE

yet God regards a believer's prayers to such a degree that the future can be changed.

In the *Journal of Pentecostal Theology* in an article that amply demonstrates that God changed his mind about destroying his people (Exod 32:7–14), Scott Ellington opens his first section with the title, "Should Pentecostals Be Open Theists?" His answer in the end is, not yet. But Ellington remains eager to see further exploration and encourages Pentecostals to carefully "consider the implications of a relational reading of the Bible for their own theological reflections."[4] In contrast to Ellington, pentecostal minister and author C. Peter Wagner writes that "open theology is a reasonable theological deduction." Then looking at the same passage that was the subject of Ellington's article, Wagner boldly asserts, "It seems clear . . . that God actually changed his mind when Moses came down off the mountain and found the people worshipping a golden calf." Wagner observes that Moses begged God to change his mind about destroying the people, and he cites Yahweh's response from the God's Word Translation: "So the LORD reconsidered his threat to destroy the people" (Exod 32:14).[5] Based on this passage, Ellington concludes that the future may be open due to factors other than a limitation in God's knowledge, whereas Wagner believes that some aspects of the future are in fact unknown to God.

These are two differing perspectives within the same charismatic/pentecostal tradition. My own personal theological pedigree rests firmly within the tradition of charismatic theology and practice, though not strictly pentecostal. Although I believe in a post-salvation defining work of the Spirit, a second blessing, I believe "tongues" are only one of many possible evidences of Spirit Baptism.[6] Seeing that I have ultimately positioned myself within this camp, I think I have standing to introduce and respond to a slight variation of Ellington's question, namely, should Pentecostals *and charismatics* be open theists? Well, yes and no. The charismatic tradition should closely investigate and reassess our understanding of God's relationality and just how open and flexible he is in relationship. There is much to be learned from open theism and relational theology. That said, we should be careful and proceed with caution when considering whether the future of Christian clarity, ministry, and mission will be the union of the charismatic/pentecostal tradition with freewill theism and the relational interpretation of God in Scripture.

---

4. Ellington, "Who Shall Lead Them Out?," 41, 60.
5. Wagner, *Changing Church*, 154.
6. Regarding the origins of pentecostal tongues, see Appendix.

I do not intend to rehash open theism's scriptural defense nor will I lay out the theological, philosophical, and practical support for the position, all of which have been addressed by other thoughtful authors and theologians.[7] I will, however, be working from the foundation of freewill theism, the openness of the universe, and the open-mindedness of God. Though I don't agree with every conclusion taught by open theists, I am sympathetic to the relational emphasis of their theological system and remain hopeful that the church will benefit from it. Hence, I intend to give this position a fair shake in the field of charismatic theology. The content of this book will inevitably be offensive to some, appealing to others, while provocative to many in both the openness and classical camps. My intention is to make inquiry into the prospect that Scripture presents God in an even wider openness than has been considered thus far. My hope is that my presentation will stir discussion into areas of knowing and loving God and better understanding his suffering for the lost, ultimately motivating the church to pursue the nonbeliever with an even greater degree of compassionate zeal. Though I'm more than sympathetic to an open view of God, I haven't yet determined the long-term role I see it having within the church.

This introduction will briefly review key biblical themes related to the openness of God and particularly his perfect changeableness. We will proceed to review a few ways in which God is perceived to be changeable and self-limiting in experience, time, passion, and presence.

MUTABLE: CHANGEABLE IN EXPERIENCE

In an open universe, the changeableness of God's experience is most notably related to his dynamic knowledge of the future. God knows reality in terms of its correspondence to truth and what is real, so in truth the future does not yet exist except in terms of infinite possibilities, each of which are known to God. God knows what free creatures will *possibly* do in the future, but what creatures with freedom will actually do is not knowable. This is due primarily to the nearly infinite possible choices open to freewill creatures at any given moment. This is but one reason the open theist affirms that God changes in experience, because he naturally grows in knowledge particularly as people make decisions and live out the consequences of those decisions.

God's unique knowledge of the future is demonstrated in such passages as Abraham's greatest test of faith when God had asked him to offer

---

7. See Sanders, *God Who Risks*; Pinnock, *Most Moved Mover*; Boyd, *God of the Possible*; Pinnock et al., *Openness of God*; Basinger, *Case for Freewill Theism*; Hasker et al., *God in an Open Universe*.

his son Isaac as a sacrifice.⁸ At the moment of Abraham's faithful follow-through, when the knife was grasped tightly in hand and suspended over the child only seconds away from a human sacrifice, Yahweh's Messenger abruptly interrupted, announcing to Abraham, "'Do not lay a hand on the boy,' he said. 'Do not do anything to him. *Now I know* that you fear God, because you have not withheld from me your son, your only son'" (Gen 22:12, emphasis added).⁹ The Hebrew indicates that God's knowledge is inchoative or ingressive, meaning God has come to know new information. That God has learned something new seems to imply the future is not settled and that God changes in his knowledge and experience with people.

The changeableness of God and the divine desire to engage humanity and share in human experience all lead to the conclusion that our God has opened himself up to a unique divine vulnerability which includes the capacity for him to experience loss. One poignant example is found in the book of Exodus when God was preparing Moses to confront Pharaoh. The risk-taking, vulnerability of God became evident in his use of an apprehensive, imperfect messenger. Because God does not choose to use sheer power to engage the world, future plans are often at the disposal of frail human messengers. After God described to Moses the great wonders he would perform to persuade Pharaoh to let the people go, Moses' response was essentially, okay God, but what if . . . (Exod 4:1). What if Pharaoh doesn't listen? What if your plan doesn't succeed? What if they call me a liar? Then what?

The LORD's response was nothing like one might expect from a God believed to maintain both meticulous control and comprehensive foresight. Instead of rebuking Moses—how dare you question my knowledge and power!—the LORD humbled himself, acquiesced to Moses' concerns, and offered a solution to the potential problems Moses had proposed. If plan A fails, God said, then we will show them a miraculous sign, plan B. For plan B, Moses, your staff will be turned into a snake. If plan B fails, then plan C, your hand will turn leprous. The LORD was not merely acquiescing for the sake of valuing an active dialogue or give-and-take with his chosen leader, though that was surely part of it, but rather the LORD accepted Moses' concern as legitimate and agreed with the possibility of his conclusions.

8. Samuel Terrien identifies the element of risk involved in Yahweh's test: "In the context of the Hebraic theology of presence, with the absurdity of its demands, religion no longer means the ritual exchange of sacrality with a static cosmos through which man attunes himself to the life of nature but, on the contrary, the courage to face the abyss of being, even the abyss of the being of God, and to affirm, at the risk of assuming all risks, the will to gamble away not only one's ego but even one's hope in the future of mankind" (*Elusive Presence*, 83–84).

9. This was not the only time God had tested his people to learn what they would ultimately do; see Exod 16:4; 20:20; Deut 8:2; 13:3; 2 Chr 32:31.

The Lord did not predict a definite response from Pharaoh but agreed with Moses that they should be prepared with alternative actions: "Then the Lord said, 'If they do not believe you or pay attention to the first sign, they may believe the second. But if they do not believe these two signs or listen to you, take some water from the Nile and pour it on the dry ground. The water you take from the river will become blood on the ground'" (Exod 4:8–9). The possibilities denoted in the Lord's use of such language as "if" and "may" should be taken seriously as truly representative of the divine perspective; otherwise, the very integrity of his communications is suspect (cf. 33:3, 5)![10] Openness theology encourages readers to trust the veracity of ancient Scripture and rest assured God is not certain whether Pharaoh will believe the first or second signs.

In an almost humorous interchange, Moses then pleads with God not to send him at all but to instead send someone else, anybody else! God's response is that he is more than able to help Moses in this mission (Exod 4:10–12). Yet Moses pleads with him again, "Please send someone else" (4:13), so the Lord *gives in* and agrees to send Aaron. This is a supreme example of God humbling himself and changing his plans at the request of an imperfect servant. If the plans of God change, then God necessarily changes as his knowledge considers alternatives and his heart responds to the needs of his people. The God of open theism is a God of relationship.

God's openness to the future does not imply that he's ever unprepared for any imminent possibility or that he doesn't possess the wise resourcefulness to effortlessly handle any future contingencies, because he does. This passage is a microcosmic example, on a human level, that God does in fact preplan and have effective alternatives in place for accomplishing his overarching goals. This passage can be superimposed on the full revelation of Scripture, such that we can remain confident that God will one day fully establish his kingdom by using frail, imperfect human messengers to bring it about, whether by plan A, B, C, or Z.[11]

Without pressing the matter too far, one could look as far back as the beginning to see that God has always been a resourceful, plan B kind of Creator: "Now the Lord God had formed out of the ground all the wild animals and all the birds in the sky. He brought them to the man to see what he would name them; . . . But for Adam no suitable helper was found" (Gen

---

10. Regarding the divine *if*, see 1 Kgs 9:4–7; Ps 132:12; Isa 1:19–20; Jer 4:1–2; 7:5–7; 17:24–27; 22:4–5; 26:4–6; 38:17–18; 42:9–16.

11. What happens after plan Z, if plan Z should fail? The open theist should have utmost confidence in the wisdom and power of God that history would never move anywhere near plan Z.

2:19–20).¹² God not only granted Adam the responsibility of choosing a helpmate but also allowed him to reject God's numerous creative proposals. This was after God described the very situation he had brought the man into as "not good" (2:18). Regarding this *not so good* situation, literary scholar Lee Humphreys remarks, "Apparently Yahweh God judges his creative effort as not yet quite right. He has second thoughts about the human condition."¹³ This is indeed a provocative statement, yet it rings true that God did say that what he himself had made was not good.¹⁴ It seems God has accepted the necessity of his own vulnerability in his new relationship to a freethinking, foreign being, so much so that he invited this new creature's critiques into his once independent existence. Yahweh was now experiencing what it means to bring another volitional, freethinking, wise, and even critical being into his own world.

TEMPORAL: CHANGEABLE IN TIME

Because God is working with freewill creatures, people who daily make decisions that involve real alternatives, the LORD has freely and voluntarily entered into a God-world relationship that involves risk. He created the framework of the world by his design and choosing. The same world that depends on him for its existence and maintenance—it is this world that God has made himself dependent on as the meeting ground for him and his creatures. Because divine nature is faithful love, he honors his relationship with the world by experiencing the world and humanity as they truly are, a world construed of time and space.

Every narrative of Scripture implies that God has created a world that he is intimately involved in, one in which he moves about in time and space at the creature's pace: "This is what the LORD says: 'About midnight I will go throughout Egypt'" (Exod 11:4). Yahweh experiences the sequence of lives, conversations, prayers, and cause and effect relationships. Paul Fiddes affirms divine temporality, saying, "It seems doubtful whether we can speak of God's 'acting' at all unless there is some temporality in God, some

---

12. Bonhoeffer makes an interesting observation of Adam's search for a potential helpmate. He says, "God first of all forms animals out of the ground from which God has taken humankind. According to the Bible human beings and animals have the same kind of body! Perhaps the human being would find a helper who is a suitable partner among these brothers and sisters—for that is what they are, the animals who have the same origin as humankind does" (*Creation and Fall*, 96).

13. Humphreys, *Character of God*, 39.

14. Granted, the connotation may be something more like, not *yet* good, but this is not what the text says.

movement from one state of being to another."[15] Just as God experiences a future full of possibilities as just that, future possibilities, so he experiences this temporal world as it is, temporal. Do the narratives of Scripture portray a God whose home is eternity or whose home is the dimension of heaven and earth that belong to this world? Genesis records, "When he had finished speaking with Abraham, God went up from him" (Gen 17:22; cf. 35:13). The classical theologian is no longer left unchallenged to his claim that God's home is an eternity outside of the created order: "He builds his lofty palace in the heavens and sets its foundation on the earth" (Amos 9:6; cf. Mic 1:3).

Karl Barth summarizes his view on God's space this way: "He possesses and He is Himself space."[16] If there is space that is only God and of God, such as the throne of God, humanity cannot understand it apart from the creation we are born into. If such a place exists that God is occupying other than our time and space, our theology can't grasp it. Because throughout Scripture God's movements parallel the movements and pace of his creatures, we're able to see that God honors his relationship to the temporal reality of this world. Surely he does so without stepping outside of our existence to look at a panoramic view of time, what some describe as an eternal now. God knows us and we know him in terms of the created space he encounters us in, the very same space of world apart from which no revelation of inspired Scripture could come to humankind.

If we're to understand God's relationship to time, our most dependable resource is Scripture. Scripture presents a picture of God as one who experiences duration and time; he is never portrayed as distant and static but always creative, dynamic, and interacting with humanity within our world. Far from existing in some state of an eternal now, God experiences time with all the necessary nuance involved in interacting with freewill creatures. He experiences grief, surprise, regret, celebration, and dialogue, while answering prayers, loving people, and receiving love. The word of God reveals an infinite Being whose eternal nature now exists in sequence with people and their world. The LORD moves beside us, dialogues with us, awaits the future with us, experiences the hurts and ravages of time with us, and faces obstacles and challenges beside us.

Not that God is ravaged by time or in any sense worn down by it—the second law of thermodynamics need not apply with God!—but he personally experiences the pain and suffering of his creatures and our world as people live out and experience the ruining effects of time. Although philosophers and theologians alike debate whether God is one of eternal timelessness or

---

15. Fiddes, *Participating in God*, 122. See also Swinburne, *Coherence of Theism*, 225.
16. Barth, *CD* 2/1:471.

everlasting temporality, one thing is clear, that the God we encounter in the narratives of Scripture appears for all intents and purposes to be involved in current, causal, relational conversations and interactions with humanity. Our spiritual life and worship depend on this.

The eternal, distant God who at once observes past, present, and future while standing outside of the reality of our temporal existence is nowhere described this way in Scripture. As Fiddes again observes, "It has become clear, in much recent discussion, that the notion of an absolutely timeless God is a concept of Greek philosophy, replacing the biblical picture of the 'everlasting God' for whom time has meaning, but who is not trapped within it as we are."[17] Of course God is *from everlasting to everlasting*,[18] yet every human encounter with him appears as if he lives within history. Even so, because God is not flesh and blood but is spirit, he experiences this temporal world as divine Perfection, the Incomprehensible, and not as a human being. Although God is not timeless, he does indeed enjoy a vantage point we cannot conceive of.

PASSIBLE: CHANGEABLE IN EMOTION AND SUFFERING

Any vulnerability, limitation, or risk with God is one that he has voluntarily assumed and freely entered into for the duration of this age. God is nothing less than perfect freedom. In the words of philosopher Jeff Pool, "Unless God also possesses the capacity to limit the divine self in the operation of any attribute, then God cannot be unlimited in any of those respects."[19] The hermeneutic of Jesus' life and death shares this perspective from beginning to end.[20] The *kenosis* of Christ means he became the vehicle for a new ontological addition to the Godhead, the humanity of Christ's person (Phil 2:5–8). When once for millennia past the second Person of the Trinity had existed in one divine nature, he now forever exists in two, divine and human. Thus, change itself must be intrinsic to the essence of God and who God is. There is profound revelation and hermeneutical value in the *kenosis* of Jesus Christ, the self-emptying, self-limiting experience of the second person of the Trinity.

---

17. Fiddes, *Participating in God*, 122.

18. This phrase occurs multiple times in Scripture to describe God and his attributes; see 1 Chr 16:36; 29:10; Pss 41:13; 103:17; 106:48; Neh 9:5.

19. Pool, *God's Wounds*, 158.

20. See chapter 5.

The vulnerabilities of this human God become immediately apparent in the virgin birth. Jesus' birth highlights divine self-limitation but also the risk and vulnerability of becoming human in the first-century world as it was. The Mediterranean world was a hostile, hateful world environment under the political reign of King Herod who sought immediately to kill this vulnerable messianic figure (Matt 2:1–18). But Jesus' life was always an obedience unto death. How much more vulnerable could we expect God to become than to experience a mortal's birth and death? Death has always been a strange, hostile element in God's creation. Because death is a foreign element to the good that God spent six days creating, Jesus' death would have been an experience that took the divine life into unchartered territory. God is truly the risk-taking, vulnerable Lord of history.

Fiddes rightly comments, "When we think at all carefully about it, suffering must involve being changed by something or someone outside oneself. It means being affected, conditioned and even afflicted by another. A suffering God must be 'vulnerable' in the strict sense of 'open to being wounded.'"[21] Because the human Jesus was truly open to being wounded, so was God. If God suffers, and he does, then God changes; and if God changes, then he would be less than perfect if change was not internal to him. Scripture itself lays this foundation for the perfection and changeableness of God, so it is Scripture which leads us to conclude that God's essential nature involves perfect changeableness. Jesus, Son of God, who once existed in one nature, now exists in two. Furthermore, this human God died a physical death and then added a further addition to the triune identity, an immortalized resurrection body.

Divine self-limitation of personal power was God's decision regarding his relationship to the world, but changeableness itself is not God's decision because it is intrinsic to him. When God's perfect changeableness is expressed through the decision of self-limitation, the result is vulnerability, risk, and even suffering. God suffers because he chooses to open his perfect changeableness to the free experience of humanity, both as the God-human and by sharing our pain to the degree that it becomes his own. It is internal to God to suffer with those who suffer, "for we do not have a high priest who is unable to empathize with our weaknesses" (Heb 4:15). Yet this suffering was the experience of God even before Jesus became our high priest. Prior to the creation, we simply don't know what suffering God might have experienced. But once God introduced free creatures into his world, we can be certain he embraced their suffering and even rebellion as the "bearing" principal of an eternal God of longsuffering love. By his very nature, he

---

21. Fiddes, *Participating in God*, 170.

bears the sin and suffering of the many. God can never be the same again, so he should be praised for the perfect changeableness he is.[22]

MALLEABLE: CHANGEABLE IN PRESENCE

Moving on to the topic of divine presence, Karl Barth remarks that God "is everywhere completely and undividedly the One He always is, even if in virtue of the freedom of His love He is this in continually differing and special ways."[23] It's helpful here that Barth adds the element of God's freedom to our discussion. God freely and sovereignly moves in the world as his nature deems appropriate, though I'd like to expand on this. The freedom of God means he is perfectly within his rights to limit, change, enhance, or remove his presence in the world and is certainly powerful enough to do so. Any self-limitation of God is rooted in the love of God working through the freedom of God while this humility of God seeks the best for his creatures. We creatures certainly benefit from experiencing the divine presence in different and unique ways.

Fretheim and the Intensifications of Divine Presence

Helpful to our inquiry is the work of Terence Fretheim on the intensifications of God's presence, which we will take a moment to review. The world-encompassing aspect of God's presence in the created order is designated by Fretheim as God's structural or general presence (Job 38–41; Amos 9:2–6), which is the same as omnipresence. This all-pervading presence makes possible other more specific forms of the divine presence in the world and amid God's people. Those other forms can be conceived of in terms of a continuum or intensifications of God's presence, thus God is continually present but can be *especially* present at certain times.

Fretheim doesn't extensively detail the continuum of various modes of divine presence but he does provide a few examples. They include God's *accompanying presence* as he journeys with his people, the *tabernacling*

---

22. Beyond the suffering of the cross, among the greatest risks God took was opening himself up to the vulnerability of his own personal suffering from those who would reject him. But is it possible that in an open universe, prior to creation, God was not suffering? Without the existence of a preordained future, there was no fall for him to anticipate and hence no suffering for him to experience. The eventual entrance of sin and death was an unexpected anomaly, rearing its ugly head in God's good creation.

23. Barth, *CD* 2/1:470. For a summary of Barth's view on omnipresence, see Gabriel, *Lord is the Spirit*, 152–55.

presence as God chooses to dwell in an expected place of his involvement in history (e.g., ark or temple), and of course, *theophany*, the most intense mode of God's presence in the world whereby he manifests himself particularly in human form. Moreover, Fretheim points to an actual need for God's people to be met by God in specific and even tangible and personal ways. So it can also be said that God's presence is significantly affected by human need and experience.[24]

Corresponding to these intensifications of God's presence is the absence of God. Fretheim begins his section on absence by making the bold assertion that "the Old Testament language of absence (e.g., 'hide,' 'withdraw,' 'forsake,' etc.) always entails presence at some level of intensification, albeit diminished."[25] Fretheim's first remarks on the absence of God amount to the impossibility of a literal divine absence. God's presence can be diminished but never altogether removed. One purpose for my inquiry into divine absence will be to challenge Fretheim's assertion that God's hiddenness and removal in Scripture refers merely to "the loss of a certain intensification of presence" rather than "the loss of presence altogether."[26]

Taking Fretheim as a point of departure, Joel Burnett scrutinizes this language of intensification in his book *Where is God? Divine Absence in the Hebrew Bible*. Burnett says that Fretheim's notion that divine absence is only a relative matter of lesser intensification of presence "is contradicted at numerous points within the canon."[27] Burnett goes on to ask some important questions in response to Fretheim's schema of God's structural presence as a constant in creation:

> If such a conception is to take into account the whole of the canon, how does one take seriously texts like these [e.g., Pss 69:2–3; 88:3, 6–7, 14, 18; Lam 1:10; 2:3a; Hab 1:2–4] that attest to the experience of unmitigated divine absence, be it deserved or not? If the framework of structural divine presence is not just as an inference to which modern readers are privy but can be ascribed meaning for those portrayed in the biblical text itself, why do human beings and communities "within the text" so frequently entertain as a realistic scenario the possibility of God's absence? If, as Fretheim's schema implies, divine absence is largely a matter of limited human understanding, then as humans experience it, is there any difference between divine absence and the

---

24. Fretheim, *Suffering of God*, 60–65, 79. Contra Ron Highfield who denies that God's presence varies in intensities; see *Great is the Lord*, 290.
25. Fretheim, *Suffering of God*, 65.
26. Ibid., 61.
27. Burnett, *Where is God?*, 61.

perception thereof? When this possibility becomes an apparent certainty, what are the grounds for seeking an ostensibly absent God?[28]

These are indeed important questions. Burnett posits a solution by balancing Fretheim's structural presence with a "structural divine absence."[29] For Burnett, it is only the place of the dead that is truly devoid of God's presence. Burnett comments, "Even if God has access to it, the realm of death is by definition remote from the efficacious presence of the 'Living God.' . . . the Hebrew Bible presents the God of Israel as one who normally stands aloof from death and the netherworld."[30] Truly, if one definition of God's essence is eternal life, then what room is there in the divine presence for death?

In chapter 2 below, Burnett's contention of structural absence in this third realm of the dead will be brought into the center of our discussion by observing the trajectory of death as an experience that begins *while the person is still alive*. In other words, is it possible that God's unmitigated absence in the realm of death is already present in humanity's day-to-day experience by virtue of the *deathful* nature of sin? If God is distanced from death's domain, the third realm, can he also be distanced from death's domain in the sphere of personal or national sin?

The Holy Spirit's Changeable Presence

Following our brief discussion on Fretheim's structural presence and Burnett's structural absence, we can now make a more specific observation on the changeability of the divine presence. Anyone reading the Hebrew Bible can see that there are times throughout Israel's history that Yahweh manifests himself in special and unusual ways. Because Jesus Christ is the most reliable exegesis of the Godhead (see chapter 5), the humanity of Christ is possibly the most explicit example of how God's presence is manifested and experienced in a special way. Wolfhart Pannenberg makes this very point when he says "there is room for becoming in God himself" and then gives the example that God "became something that he previously was not when he became man in his Son."[31]

As goes the Son of God, so goes the Spirit in the world. Andrew Gabriel notes, "Similar to how the presence of God changes through the Son in

---

28. Ibid., 63.
29. Ibid., 64.
30. Ibid., 67.
31. Pannenberg, *Systematic Theology*, 1:438.

the incarnation, the presence of God also appears to change in the person of the Holy Spirit."[32] The Holy Spirit is naturally movement. The Spirit is dynamic breath and wind. The Spirit can be given, removed, and poured out. We intuitively get the sense that the Spirit's presence is mutable and dynamic! We conceive mental images of the Father and Son, but the Spirit remains ambiguous. Gabriel boldly asserts that "as the Spirit intensifies, the Spirit changes."[33] This suggests that God's presence changes more than just empirically but even ontologically. The Spirit's changing presence may not be merely on the level of human perception and awareness, but his world involvement may include real, dynamic, personal change. Jesus knew the perfect changeableness of the Spirit in his own life and ministry when the Spirit "descended on him in bodily form like a dove" (Luke 3:22), a beautiful illustration that combines both the perfect changeableness of the Son and the Spirit. At his baptism, Jesus' meeting with the Spirit suggests a change in God and his presence.[34]

The perfect changeableness of God's presence is necessary and useful for meeting the people of God in certain places and at certain times and filling those spaces with new life and renewed mission. Pentecost meant a unique experience of God's presence for everyone, but for the Spirit it was a personal experience of his changing presence, which he experienced when he connected with the church. Pentecost ushered in the special presence of God in a most vivid and extraordinary way, with signs confirming. Because the divine presence changes, people can truly experience it. Otherwise, an eternally static God would simply speak through the pages of dead scrolls and we would never actually experience the power of God through us to the world. Almost immediately after the pentecostal outpouring and the Spirit's occupation of the church, our mission began. Where the Spirit of the LORD is, there is liberty, mission, and liberation. The early church went out with miraculous displays of the divine presence, a presence demonstrated in perfect changeableness. They went out in the power of the *charismata* ("gifts" from God) and changed the world.

---

32. Gabriel, *Lord is the Spirit*, 156.

33. Ibid., 176. After criticizing the interpretation that only our perception of God's presence changes, Gabriel goes on to state that the language of intensifications of the Spirit's presence is merely metaphorical. God cannot be more or less in any given place but is "fully present everywhere" though in "different and changing ways in different places" (ibid., 157, 176).

34. Ibid., 159.

INTRODUCTION: GOD OF WONDERS AND AN OPEN FUTURE

CONCLUSION

Now that readers have been introduced to an open view of God and to the perfect changeableness of the Spirit's presence in the world, we are ready to move into the exciting challenge of developing a theology of both divine absence and supernatural presence from an openness perspective. In light of the possibility of divine absence, the need for a restored, manifest presence takes on even greater importance.

Just how open is our theological universe, and what would a more broadly open universe look like? In part one (chapters 1–5), we'll explore the broadness of a radically open universe. My inquiry delves into the distance that sin creates between people and the one true God under the presence and pull of death. In a radically open universe, sin can create such distance that the result is God's unmitigated absence.

In part two (chapters 6–10), further inquiry will adapt the openness of God to the Holy Spirit's mission and gifts in the church, hence the designation the *charismatic* presence (from the Greek *charismata*, gifts).[35] These ministries are intended to manifest God's presence to the world. Because the divine presence is recovered in people's lives through salvation, God can then release believers into a dynamic openness of unsurpassed power and potential to manifest his presence through Spiritually gifted lives.

One final thought before we get started: I am aware that some have considered open theism to be a theology in crisis. I would argue, however, that the open view has withstood the debate on the basis of a solid scriptural foundation. Although I designate myself a cautious observer, I will be playing devil's advocate for this system and, even more so, for a radically open universe.[36] To prepare my readers for what's to come, I'll echo Paul's heart to the Corinthian church: "If anyone is inclined to be contentious, we have no such practice, nor do the churches of God" (1 Cor 11:16 ESV).

---

35. This book's position regarding Spiritual gifts is non-cessationism, the belief that the supernatural and miraculous gifts of the first-century church continue today (e.g., tongues, prophecy, healing, etc.). Possibly the best defense to date remains Ruthven, *On the Cessation of the Charismata*.

36. In the pages to follow, I will be pursuing consistency and thoroughness in fleshing out the broad depths of openness theology. Some of the rabbit trails I will follow will not strictly conform to the theology of open theists, such as my reference to soul sleep and the idea that dead means dead in chapter 2. However, I follow such tangents because they find biblical support and have thoughtful proponents and because they provide consistency toward my overall thesis.

PART I

God's Absence

1

An Open Past and Present
"If not, I will know"

One of many positive byproducts of open theism has been to offer the church an interpretation of Scripture that reflects on an immanent, genuinely relational God of vulnerable love and intimate fellowship. This God of everlasting wisdom and infinite resources created a universe where the future is partly open and flexible, making true love and libertarian freedom possible in a world where their impact is real because the future is not set in stone. It is this compassionate, all-wise, infinitely powerful God who leads his church boldly and victoriously into a partly unknown future.

This, however, may only be part of the story. Openness theology already affirms that God is absent from the future; a real, unmitigated absence. God cannot be where he does not know, and the actual future remains unknown. Could it be, then, that an open future may also leave room for a partly open past and present as well? As you can imagine, such a thesis has serious implications for both open theism and the omni's of God.[1]

Our first enterprise will be to examine a passage of Scripture that we often gloss over without much critical analysis or giving second thought to one's presupposed hermeneutic. Our investigation begins in Genesis 18 with an important conversation between Yahweh and his servant-prophet, Abraham.

---

1. The omni's of God include omnipresence, omnipotence, and omniscience.

YAHWEH'S INVESTIGATION

Although the story of the destruction of Sodom and Gomorrah is a familiar one, what most of us remember about it is Lot's wife turning into a pillar of salt because she looked back at the home-life she left behind (Gen 19:26). Leading up to her demise was the warning of angelic visitors to flee the city because Yahweh was about to destroy it. This story has left many with an impression of God's unfeeling, wrathful, and destructive nature. With the anger of God on our minds, there are portions of the story that we tend to gloss over. But those rather ignored aspects of the story present an altogether different picture of God. The portrait is not one of a hateful, unfeeling, untouchable god but one who interacts with people, one who considers Abraham's thoughts and wishes, one who condescends and genuinely considers ideas outside of himself. For this account, we will look to Genesis 18.

Before any judgment befalls Sodom and Gomorrah, rather than a closed-minded and wrath-set Tyrant, readers are introduced to the thoughtful, open heart of God. After a divine Messenger appears to Abram (later Abraham) in Genesis 17 and is then revealed to be God himself, Gen 18:1 marks the move from using the generic title, God, to using the proper name, Yahweh. God has made himself approachable as a person! This becomes clear when Yahweh, in anticipation of executing judgment against Sodom, asks his two fellow visitors a question that exposes his own inner thoughts: "Shall I hide from Abraham what I am about to do? Abraham will surely become a great and powerful nation, and all nations on earth will be blessed through him. For I have chosen (*yada*) him" (Gen 18:17–19). Here we're given a unique glimpse into God's very own thoughts.

There are essentially three moments of internal reflection involved here. The first moment is Yahweh's internal decision to speak up about welcoming Abraham's input as his covenant partner. The second moment is when Yahweh voices that decision to the other two visitors as if to secure their agreement. Granted, if we interpret Yahweh's words exclusively as an internal dialogue, these first two moments are collapsed into one. Because these first two aspects of God's reflection are not directed to Abraham, they are likely not mere rhetoric for Abraham's benefit but point to a decision-making process within God. Hesitation might be too strong a word here, but there is an inner and then outer dialogue that reveals the value that God places on his new covenant partner; Yahweh wants to move forward with the proper consideration that this new relationship merits. Through his dialogue with the other two visitors, we see that Yahweh enters history in a profoundly personal way.

In the third moment, God approaches Abraham and shares his intentions with him (Gen 18:20–21). Yahweh's new partner, the one "chosen" and known (*yada*) to him by covenant, shares a relationship with God unique within the history of the world. The reader now sees how privileged Abraham is to join in on Yahweh's inner dialogue, the all-wise, all-powerful God. God voices his thoughts to Abraham, expecting a discussion to follow. If God isn't interested in Abraham's opinion, there would be no need to bring him up to speed. God doesn't propel his plans forward with brute force or stubborn vengeance but seeks the input of the man who would become a great and powerful nation, a man who holds power too, God-given, even God-shared power. Abraham now has a voice that impacts the direction of the nations and the world, a privilege no one before him had enjoyed.

Yahweh's two fellow messengers then start off toward the cities, leaving Abraham "standing before the LORD" (Gen 18:22). Along with many other commentators, Walter Brueggemann observes that "a very early text note (not to be doubted in its authority and authenticity) shows that the text before any translation originally said, 'Yahweh stood before Abraham.' The picture is one which agrees with . . . Abraham as Yahweh's theological instructor. It is as though Abraham were presiding over the meeting."[2] Abraham is indeed Yahweh's covenant partner and could therefore be presumptuous in his posture before him. Abraham has captured the LORD's attention, so Yahweh would in turn be attentive to Abraham's thoughts on the matter. What follows is a long discussion between Yahweh and Abraham. Because this passage should be familiar to the reader, I'm only going to cite a small portion:

> Then the LORD said, "The outcry against Sodom and Gomorrah is so great and their sin so grievous that I will go down and see if what they have done is as bad as the outcry that has reached me. If not, I will know." . . . Then [Abraham] said, "May the Lord not be angry, but let me speak just once more. What if only ten [righteous] can be found there?" He answered, "For the sake of ten, I will not destroy it." (Gen 18:20–21, 32)

This passage introduces a peculiar scenario for both classical interpreters and open theists. Even a cursory glance of the passage reveals what is easy to gloss over when one approaches the text with a closed view of God. The situation Yahweh shares with Abraham stresses that the all-knowing God himself cannot yet reach a final decision regarding judgment against Sodom and Gomorrah. He first needs to gather more information because, at this point, he simply doesn't know enough about the situation: "I will

---

2. Brueggemann, *Interpretation: A Bible Commentary*, 168.

go down and see … If not, I will [then] know." Even for Almighty God, uncertainty and questions remain.

After becoming aware of an implied impending judgment against the twin cities, Abraham entreats Yahweh to discuss with him various hypothetical situations in which Yahweh might relent altogether from his wrath. Arguing from the basis of God's own mercies, Abraham beseeches the Lord not to "sweep away the righteous with the wicked" but to spare everyone if even ten righteous people would be found there (Gen 18:23, 32). Because this is such a significant text with serious implications to freewill theism, we will spend the remainder of this chapter considering the biblical material.

CLASSICAL INTERPRETATION: A CLOSED-MINDED GOD

The classical interpretation approaches the text with the preconceived notion that God is unchanging in every respect, that God is independent and does not need human input, and that the future is closed, a future written from eternity past. Hence, Yahweh's conversation with Abraham is filled with figurative language that cannot be taken literally. Yahweh's interactions are merely a bold anthropomorphism, the weight of which may be signaled by Yahweh's appearing to Abraham particularly in human form. God already knew exactly how much evil was being committed in those cities; thus, his language of "go[ing] down" to investigate is merely rhetorical.

This talk of God moving within the world is language of accommodation, stylistic on the part of the author for the purpose of writing a quality narrative. "Go[ing] down" is basic metaphor that points to finalizing judgment. This language is intended only to draw our attention to judicial action similar to God's "let us go down" speech just prior to judging the Tower of Babel community (Gen 11:7). At Babel, God didn't mean that he was moving from one locale to another but that he was going to execute a judgment which would have ramifications felt in the world. Howard Vos takes a similar approach, stating, "'I am going down' does not imply that God's omniscience is somehow defective and that it is necessary for him to collect evidence. Rather, he will inquire in order to demonstrate to men the validity of His judgment."[3]

What about the hypothetical scenario that God might locate ten righteous persons in those cities? For classical interpreters, we're dealing here with a God of unqualified knowledge, so it's beyond question that Yahweh already knows the precise number of the righteous who are there. As the argument would go, readers should not take such language at face value

---

3. Vos, *Everyman's Bible Commentary*, 89.

but should discern a deeper purpose; Yahweh may have a hidden purpose behind this lively dialogue. Maybe he is simply positioning Abraham to mature in the face of divine presence and in Abraham's compassion for others, particularly the inhabitants of Sodom and Gomorrah. Perhaps Yahweh is merely testing Abraham's reaction as a learning experience that would benefit their relationship with each other. Because God is fixed in who he is and what he will do, it must be *Abraham* who is changing, which is something that occurs through prayer and divine fellowship. God fully understands Abraham's concern for the righteous but is in no way instructed by it. Yahweh cannot be moved in passion or swayed by argument because he already knows with eternal clarity the totality of Sodom's situation as well as Abraham's position on the matter. God chose Abraham to be in covenant with him, so this language does nothing more than point to the priority of that relationship.

Terence Fretheim critiques this perspective when he says, "One wonders if this interpretation is informed by a view of God that does not allow for consultation."[4] The classical interpretation may have inadvertently collapsed into demythologizing the straightforward simplicity of a primitive text. This demythologizing hermeneutic is applied for the sake of saving the passage from its naive primitivism. Such a hermeneutic is attempting to apply the latest in redaction, historical, textual, and narrative criticisms, but to what benefit? It may benefit readers most if we'll give ourselves a moment to take a deep breath to step back and allow the final redaction to speak for itself.

The book of Genesis was among the first books of the Bible to be compiled thousands of years ago, making Genesis 18 one of the earliest inspired accounts of theological history. Written by an author unconcerned with affecting our systematic theologies, he penned this story as one of the first inspired mediators in the flow of progressive revelation, providing us with the provocative and raw honesty of primitive transparency. The author revealed in writing what God the Spirit had revealed to him as truth, whether he was aware of any inspiring process or not. Could it be that in the hands of classical interpreters, the transparency of the text is inadvertently reduced to demythologized anthropomorphism, a humanmade convenience used to interpret passages that don't fit their theological grid?

---

4. Fretheim, *Abraham: Trials of Family and Faith*, 79.

OPENNESS INTERPRETATION: AN OPEN-MINDED GOD

An openness interpretation of this passage would differ somewhat from the classical model. In an open universe, Yahweh experiences the historical present with comprehensive knowledge. Even if there are unknowns about the future, he should be fully aware of all that's been occurring in Sodom and Gomorrah as it's occurring in the present.

At this point we need to take another step back. The openness interpretation may be an advance on the classical position, but if the reader will patiently read between the lines with me, you will see that this interpretation becomes problematic for both classical and openness interpreters. Speaking to Abraham, Yahweh reveals that in the process of his judicial investigation he intends to learn something, specifically, whether the sins of Sodom are in fact as great as the outcry suggests. He declares that he "will go down and see" (although Yahweh himself doesn't go but instead sends the other two visitors). He will also learn whether there are at least ten righteous city dwellers.

Doesn't this sound as if God not only lacks some knowledge of the future but, significantly, also of the past and present? Regarding the past, how much has the wickedness in Sodom grown over time? Regarding the present, what is the current number of righteous occupants in those cities? If God can lack knowledge of the past and present, this becomes problematic for openness theology because it violates the premise that it is only the future that remains unknown. Before we develop this thought further, I want to first consider one possible solution.

A Possible Solution: A Test of the Wicked and the Righteous?

Later in Genesis when Yahweh learns that Abraham fears him, God's growing knowledge of Abraham's heart is based on the man's resolve in both his willingness *and the act of obedience itself.* After Abraham raises his knife in willingness to sacrifice his own son Isaac, the Angel of Yahweh, God himself, intervenes and says, "Do not do anything [more] to him. Now I know that you fear God, because you have not withheld from me your son, your only son" (Gen 22:12). Through Abraham's actions, Yahweh learns that the patriarch truly fears him. Seeing that Yahweh tests people, this is one way to resolve the issue at hand. God may currently have perfect knowledge of a person's thoughts and intent, but it is only when individuals finally take action that those thoughts are confirmed. Drawing a parallel with Sodom,

Yahweh would have current knowledge of five or more righteous persons but would still need to test their final resolve just as he did with Abraham.

Because Yahweh uses tests, he could have initiated an evidentiary "test" with Sodom and Gomorrah, much like Abraham's first test. One test would involve the wicked, the other the righteous. The first test would be to determine whether the sin of those cities was as great as the outcry. Yahweh would initiate this test by sending two angelic messengers to Sodom. Upon their arrival, however, the city dwellers almost immediately fail the test by proceeding to act on their evil intentions and attempting to forcefully have sex with the two visitors (Gen 19:4–5). Through their actions, Yahweh would learn that the situation there was as bad as the outcry that had reached him. Yahweh had said if the sin was not as great, he would *know*, much like he came to *know* through Abraham's testing that Abraham did indeed fear Yahweh.

The other "test" would focus on whether Yahweh would find even ten righteous people in those cities and therefore relent on destroying them. This test would also be initiated by the angels through a warning given to Lot and his family (Gen 19:12–17). After much hesitation, however, it is only Lot, his wife, and two daughters who heed the warning. And they only do so after they're forcefully persuaded by the messengers who must literally take them by the hand to lead them out of the city (19:16)! The actions of Lot and his family would demonstrate that indeed ten righteous people could not be found there. Hence, test number two would also result in failure.

Although this *test hypothesis* does some justice to the text, it should ultimately be dismissed. Yahweh never signals readers to any special testing for those cities, nor does he inform Abraham of any such testing. When Abraham is later tested, readers are informed at the frontend that this is indeed a test: "Some time later God tested Abraham" (Gen 22:1). As for Sodom, we can conclude that Yahweh intends simply to investigate their wickedness further, just as he says he will, and to determine the number of the righteous people who are there. All of this is in response to an outcry that has drawn his attention.

AN INTERPRETATION OF RADICAL OPENNESS

At this point, openness theology might consider a most provocative solution—that the unknowns of this universe extend beyond merely the future and possibly into the past and present as well. If we find this to be the case, the current model of a merely open future would prove inadequate; rather, we may need to consider a more radically open universe. We will attempt to unravel the openness of the past, present, and future in a manner consistent with the textual evidence found in Genesis 18–19.

Yahweh Must Further Investigate

Seeing that an outcry has caught Yahweh's attention, we can assume the people crying out are not among those committing the wicked acts but are in some sense *interceding* for Sodom and Gomorrah.[5] Victor Hamilton notes that an outcry in the Old Testament "is the cry of the oppressed because of harsh treatment" and that "the clamor or cry in Scripture is the cry of those who receive, illegitimately or legitimately, brutal punishment."[6] There's little reason to believe this outcry is directed to the one true God but rather appears to be a more general, moral outcry of the innocent. Fretheim expresses the possibility that these innocents are the same people as the righteous who Abraham is concerned would be "swept away" with the wicked (Gen 18:23). Fretheim remarks, "Abraham's key question would seem to be: Should God destroy those voicing the outcry along with those who are perpetrating the injustice?"[7]

It later becomes clear that not even ten righteous people could be found there, so there weren't even at least ten righteous intercessors. We become aware of only one possibly righteous person, Lot himself, and only because the New Testament and other extrabiblical literature suggest this.[8] Rather than interceding as a remnant of the godly righteous, we have here the outcry of the suffering few. Nevertheless, it is because of this intercession that Yahweh steps in to investigate further.

It's important to observe in the textual evidence that Yahweh speaks for himself and specifies in no uncertain terms that he must gather more information: "Then the LORD said, 'The outcry against Sodom and Gomorrah is so great and their sin so grievous that I will go down and see if what they have done is as bad as the outcry that has reached me. If not, I will know'" (Gen 18:20–21). Although the grammar is straightforward, it would be acceptable to read these forms as cohortatives, *let me go down* and *let*

---

5. Earlier in Genesis the blood of Abel cries out for vengeance (4:10). Much like the blood that cries out, "the outcry against Sodom and Gomorrah" may be metonymy; i.e., the cities themselves aren't crying out but inhabitants of those cities. The source of the outcry includes at least three options: the city (figuratively), inhabitants of the cities, or others living nearby.

6. Hamilton, *Book of Genesis*, 20, 21.

7. Fretheim, *Abraham: Trials of Family and Faith*, 81.

8. On Lot's righteousness, see 2 Pet 2:7; Wis 10:6; 19:17; 1 *Clem.* 11:1; Philo *Mos.* 2:58.

me know. This reading would turn Yahweh's investigation into a proposal, which Abraham responds to by offering an alternative that focuses on the righteous instead of the wicked.[9] Either reading does nothing to deter from the implication that God is not up-to-date on the situation in Sodom. God will go down for the express reason of finding something out![10]

Yahweh doesn't say he will go down to see if what they *are doing* is as bad as the outcry, which is precisely the language we'd expect if he was looking to their present actions. Rather, he says he wants to see if what they "have [already] done is as bad . . . " (Gen 18:21). Yahweh's further scrutiny is required in order to investigate the *results* of their evil acts. He is not aware of what exactly they had *already* done because that knowledge is dependent on both the outcry, which drew his attention to it, and an investigation of the current effects of such wickedness.

Yahweh then says, "If not, I will know." What will he eventually come to know? None other than whether or not the sinfulness corresponds with the outcry. If Yahweh's knowledge of the present is exhaustive, he would already know this! If Yahweh's knowledge of current reality comprehensively includes every evil intention and every sin committed, he would have current knowledge on whether a one-to-one correspondence exists between the outcry and the sins already committed. This, however, is not the case. Fretheim draws the same conclusion in his reading of this passage, stating, "God explicitly admits the possibility of an 'if not.' For God to use 'if' language means the *future* remains open, at least to some extent. God holds out the prospect that the inquiry may issue in a verdict other than that preliminarily drawn."[11] With great respect for Fretheim's insights, it appears that more than just an open future is in play here.

Speaking of having *chosen* (*yada*) Abraham in Gen 18:19, the Hebrew *yada* has the basic meaning, *to know*. Yahweh has *known* Abraham his chosen one, but he does not *know* the situation of wickedness in Sodom. Regarding this parallel, Hamilton points out that "Yahweh knows Abraham; yet he goes to Sodom in order to know what is going on there (v. 21b). Certainty and uncertainty are placed alongside each other."[12] This uncertainly makes the most sense if the past and present are in some sense unknown. After Abraham digests Yahweh's plans for Sodom, it's significant that this is the first occasion in Genesis and the God story in which someone takes ini-

---

9. Humphreys, *Character of God*, 121.

10. Other passages that imply God comes down to find out something include Gen 11:5; 22:11–12; Deut 13:3; Pss 44:20–21; 139:1, 23–24.

11. Fretheim, *Abraham: Trials of Family and Faith*, 79, emphasis added.

12. Hamilton, *Book of Genesis*, 18.

tiative to first approach God in conversation. Abraham does this precisely because he discerns some level of doubt or uncertainty in Yahweh's tone. Had Yahweh not expressed the possibility that his investigation could have unforeseen results, Abraham would not have sensed the inkling of hope to beseech Yahweh to spare the people (Gen 18:22–32).

Abraham naturally believes his pleading with God is a worthwhile endeavor and does not assume God possesses exhaustive knowledge of the future, or the present, for that matter. It seems Abraham himself would reject at least the classical interpretation. The patriarch knows Yahweh to be sincere in what he says and does; there is nothing disingenuous in Yahweh's words. Looking deeper into this passage will assist us in seeing the validity of accepting Yahweh's conversation with Abraham at face value.

Yahweh's Embodiment

When Yahweh first approaches Abraham, he does so in human form as any embodied being would, in a body that is capable of conversation, eating, and even having his feet washed (Gen 18:4–5). Humphreys notes that "however God is present, he seems perfectly capable in partaking fully in all Abraham offers."[13] Yahweh is utilizing his embodiment to engage both Abraham and Sarah in a true give-and-take dialogue. He interacts with Abraham as one temporally limited by time and space. Because it almost sounds like a contradiction that an eternal, omnipresent God would interact in this way, readers may at first be surprised to find exactly that. Though this may not be Yahweh's usual state of existence, we should nonetheless appreciate it and not overlook its significance. Yahweh relates to Abraham as any embodied person would, choosing to reveal himself in this way both to Abraham and to us the readers. Just as in the garden when God chose in some fashion to embody himself, so throughout Scripture he frequently does the same.[14]

This theophany is significant because the temporally embodied Yahweh communicates to Abraham as a temporally limited being—not that God is limited but that he self-limits. The most reliable means we have for discerning the degree of this self-limitation is the revelation of Scripture. It is within the realm of biblical revelation that the hermeneutical battle is

13. Humphreys, *Character of God*, 116.
14. "Then the man and his wife heard the sound of the Lord God as he was walking in the garden" (Gen 3:8). I don't doubt that Yahweh was embodied in this episode and was literally heard walking in the garden. When God created the heavens and the earth, he worked for six days and then rested on the seventh, language you'd expect of an embodied being (2:1–3). I'm not suggesting that Yahweh required a body in the Old Testament, but it is significant that he often relates to people in this way.

fought. One might argue that it is only for the sake of the narrative that the author presents Yahweh both as embodied and therefore speaking as any embodied person would. This is where a bold anthropomorphism has been argued. In response, there are a few thoughts to consider.

The most prominent question might be: How far should we apply such anthropomorphism to the text of Genesis 18? The exact referent pointed to by anthropomorphic metaphor will necessarily intrude into that question—what truth or reality is this metaphor pointing to? In other words, why shouldn't we take Yahweh's words at face value? Does the context in any way suggest that we should not? Though the Visitor is an anthropomorphic portrayal, should we assume that his encounter with Abraham did not in fact occur but is rather bold anthropomorphism and possibly just an inspired voice or vision (Gen 18:1–2)? Surely we're not expected to believe that Abraham did not in fact wash the three visitors' feet, as the text describes, nor prepare them a meal that they ate, just as the text states. The presumption of anthropomorphism will not remove the difficulty of the passage but in the end may prove even more problematic.

Anthropomorphism can be confusing because it is often used to refer to at least two distinct expressions, one poetic and one historical. In the first expression, human characteristics are attributed to God, while in the second, God appears to people in human form, otherwise described as theophany. Both are anthropomorphic in nature. The latter is a literal encounter with God, experienced in time and space, presenting interaction and dialogue that speaks truthfully of God and his encounter with people. The former points to an obvious figure of speech, such as the eyes or ears of the LORD, or statements made by Yahweh, such as, "I stretch out my hand against Egypt" (Exod 7:5). Such anthropomorphism could also be applied to people: "The President of the United States stretched out his hand against terrorism." The point is not that the President or God literally extend their physical arm but that they initiate judgment.

Theophany, on the other hand, moves beyond a simple poetic anthropomorphism to an incarnational kind of revelation. Poetic anthropomorphism is not transferred to a sequence of events or a conversation within the genre of narrative but only to a description or a moment. At the point of divine movement and dialogue, theophany moves the reader beyond poetic anthropomorphism to incarnational revelation. The ultimate anthropomorphism is of course Jesus Christ incarnate, the biblical account of whom we take at face value. This anthropomorphism comes closest to the one we find in Genesis 18, God in "flesh" as it were, an embodied Visitor. We accept the incarnation as reliable revelation and have no reason, apart from classical presuppositions, rigid hermeneutics, or the illusion of trouble-free systematics, to say otherwise. What we read is what we get! This literal principle should apply to both the incarnational Christ as well as the pre-incarnation theophanies.

The confusion comes when the interpreter collapses into one these two very different ideas contained in anthropomorphism. Poetic anthropomorphism should be limited to passages of an obvious, figurative import. There is often a pithy and absurd or exaggerated quality about it, such as "the ears of the LORD" (1 Sam 8:21 KJV). Other examples like the one we find in the Abraham account should be reclassified. Otherwise, anthropomorphism can easily decline into demythologizing the text. Granted, it should be a theological given that all biblical language of the transcendent Godhead is on some level metaphor or anthropomorphic in nature, but never at the expense of assuming it no longer accurately communicates reliable truth about God. We certainly don't want to eliminate the language of anthropomorphism but rather seek to apply it accurately.

Genesis 18 was written as a theological narrative confined to the boundaries of historical truth in which Yahweh chose to reveal himself in human form. It may prove helpful for us to designate such theophany as *narrative* or *historical anthropomorphism.* In theophanic passages, we should interpret God's words and deeds no differently than those of the incarnate Christ, which occurred within an historical literalness. Even though the biblical authors were writing theologically inclined history, their words were still true to reality. In fact, many scholars describe theophany in terms of christophany, a preincarnate visitation of Christ, and would apply that understanding to our Genesis passage.[15] This interpretation would further emphasize the need to accept outright what the theophany communicates to us and just how important it is to "listen to him" (Matt 17:5).

What God says and does in an embodied state should be interpreted through the medium of the historical and human expression that Yahweh chose to utilize. In this way, readers are allowing the narrative to speak. Because Yahweh chose a humanlike body, it's through the words and deeds of a human body that he should be understood. Both his words and actions are important and reliable. Thus, there are at least three distinct classes of anthropomorphism: poetic, historical (Law and Prophets), and incarnational (Christ). We depend on the historical narratives of Scripture to relate true

---

15. Though I entertain the notion that Old Testament theophanies represent the preincarnate Christ, this idea seems to contradict or at least minimize the uniqueness of the incarnation. Scripture never describes these Old Testament appearances as the second person of the Trinity. Theophanies are just that, visitations of the Godhead, not of any particular person within the Godhead.

historical events, albeit theologically inclined history, such as the books of Genesis and Kings and Acts.

If God intended to inspire the biblical writers to accurately communicate through the genre of narrative, then no other more reliable means exists for God to tell the straightforward story of God-in-human-form interacting with humanity. Otherwise, something within the text should blatantly signal a shift to mythology (i.e., bold or extended anthropomorphism). Demythology is not a suitable hermeneutic! Rather than demythologize Yahweh's inspired word, we should understand that historical anthropomorphism is an accurate account of reality.

Accepting the accuracy of the Abraham narrative, the simplicity of the text reveals a straightforward dialogue between God-in-human-form and Abraham. Yahweh must investigate the matter further.

Matter-of-Fact Dialogue

Within the context of an historical anthropomorphic narrative, we find consistency in matter-of-fact dialogue. Just a few verses prior to their dialogue over the fate of Sodom, Yahweh talks with Abraham about his plans regarding Sarah, his wife (Gen 18:9–15). During the conversation, he reveals to Abraham that the infertile Sarah would be with child around that same time next year. Overhearing this, Sarah is unconvinced and laughs within her heart in utter disbelief, but Yahweh confronts her on it. Yahweh's rebuke not only reveals that he knows Sarah's hidden thoughts but that he also unequivocally asserts his power to bring about a promised child, making explicit to the reader that God knows the unknowable and is miraculously powerful (cf. Ps 147:5). Important to our discussion is the parallel that exists here between Yahweh's two plans, one plan for Sarah and another for Sodom. Within a few paragraphs of each other, both plans involve Yahweh's stated intentions, both plans are explained to Abraham, and both plans appear to be communicated with straightforward literalness.

Without any contextual clues to suggest otherwise, it appears to the reader that a straightforward conversation is taking place. Otherwise, if Yahweh's plans are not intended to be carried out literally as described, on what basis would Sarah have for evaluating the promise regarding her future pregnancy? Unless Yahweh is speaking literally regarding Sarah, how can either the plan for her or God's rebuke of her laughter be understood in any coherent manner? Sarah herself doesn't assume God is speaking in any figurative sense, and regarding both plans Abraham also neglects this assumption. Abraham goes on to propose hypothetical scenarios for saving the righteous because he fully believes Yahweh intends to carry out an investigation into the wicked, an assessment of the righteous, and a consequential judgment. Abraham also believes that the possibility exists to change God's mind.

As further confirmation of the literalness of the conversation, Yahweh goes so far as to rebuke Sarah for not taking his promise seriously and not trusting that he will do exactly what he says he will. Would Yahweh similarly rebuke us for not accepting his written word at face value regarding Sodom?

YAHWEH'S ABSENCE FROM SODOM

Yahweh's assertions should be taken literally because they are fulfilled, well, almost literally. Instead of going down himself, he sends his representatives, something he does throughout Scripture. When he sends the two visitors who have been accompanying him, their mission apparently includes warning any potentially righteous persons of impending doom (Gen 19:1–29). Yahweh never misleads Abraham but truly lacks knowledge on the severity of Sodom's evil, *because God is not there*. If we are to accept the text on its own merits, it's difficult to avoid the conclusion that the divine presence was removed from Sodom, along with his experiential knowledge of their situation.

Omniscience and omnipresence are a mutual necessity. As with each of God's attributes, they belong together, like spokes on a wheel. In light of Yahweh's embodied state throughout his encounter with Abraham, it makes sense that he can come and go or even avoid, withdraw, or abandon a geographical area. Yahweh is temporally and spatially limited in his encounter with Abraham, as expressed through Yahweh's own choice of words, "I will go down." If the divine absence can be attributed to anything, the prime candidate is the wickedness that consumed those cities: "Now the people of Sodom were wicked and were sinning greatly against the Lord" (Gen 13:13; cf. 18:20). So then, Yahweh was inquiring from a distance, either because his holiness compelled him so or because, in a radically open universe, creaturely freedom necessarily places that limit on him.

If the removal of God's knowledgeable presence is due to their wickedness, the matter of the fifty righteous people becomes a problem. Yahweh says, "If I find fifty righteous people in the city of Sodom, I will spare the whole place for their sake" (Gen 18:26). Because Yahweh never speaks disingenuously, his firm conviction is that he may actually discover at least fifty righteous persons, a number which is eventually reduced to ten (18:32). The most literal reading appears to assert that Yahweh does *not* know the number of righteous people. If this is true, my thesis has already collapsed on its own weight and God's knowledge is not limited solely with regard to the wicked.

I recommend we look to the activity of the two messengers to resolve the matter. Throughout Scripture, angels represent the eyes and hands of Yahweh, an extension of his authority to carry out his intended plans: "Praise the LORD, you his angels, you mighty ones who do his bidding, who obey his word" (Ps 103:20). In the context of Genesis 18–19, it should come as no surprise that the angels carry out the actions Yahweh had discussed with Abraham, investigating both the wicked and the righteous to affect both deliverance and judgment.[16] Neither Abraham nor Yahweh assume or imply this task would be accomplished by sheer divine omniscience or by simply looking into men's hearts but rather by experiential, hands-on investigation that would lead to finding the truth.

Even in their mission to discover the number of righteous people, the two messengers do not somehow move omnipresently throughout the city but go to one man. They depend on Lot to represent the best of those cities, essentially asking for his help to complete their mission: "The two men said to Lot, 'Do you have anyone else here—sons-in-law, sons or daughters, or anyone else in the city who belongs to you? Get them out of here'" (Gen 19:12). In other words, is there anyone else in this city who's associated with you? Is there anyone associated with your standing before us? Tragically, not even ten people respond to the angels' presence.

A closer look at these verses may suggest that Yahweh simply abandons his initial plan to investigate the wickedness and instead turns his full attention to locating the ten righteous people. The specific number of righteous is likely not the point. Surely if even one righteous person is found, then the cities could be spared. This, however, is not the case, as even Lot displays contemptible behavior in offering his daughters to the men of Sodom (Gen 19:8–9).

So what about the impression that God's knowledge is limited even with regard to the number of righteous persons? I would propose that the issue is not that God lacks knowledge of the righteous; rather, he is not presumptuous regarding those who might repent and turn from wickedness to

16. Although readers are only informed on what occurred within the confines of Sodom, perhaps for the sake of the narrative the angels' investigation in Sodom is representative of a similar investigation and warning brought to Gomorrah. The narrative may be limited to Sodom in order to focus on Abraham's nephew, Lot, who resided there. Nonetheless, Yahweh specifically spoke of both cities and made promises to Abraham regarding both cities. The fact that their conversation revolved around both cities is evidence that Abraham was not concerned solely with Lot's fate but with all the inhabitants of those places.

righteousness. There are numerous passages of Scripture that give individuals and nations opportunity to repent, even at the very last moment, which may shed light on what we see in Genesis 19. Scripture's overall redemptive message of proclamation and warning is specifically with a view to repentance. Hence, both the miraculous blinding of the wicked (Gen 19:11) and the verbal testimony of the angels could function as this kind of warning to the city. Throughout Scripture the hope of repentance remains central to God's purposes; this scene would be no exception.[17]

Because the two messengers visit Sodom on Yahweh's behalf, it's not a stretch to read between the lines. Anyone the messengers encounter, and in turn anyone those individuals share their encounter with (Gen 19:14), would by personal experience be faced with the decision to accept or reject the message inherent in the supernatural presence of these "divine" messengers (19:10–11, 12–13, 16–17). Hence, Yahweh had not yet determined the number of repentant righteous.

CONCLUSION

We limited our evaluation to a single episode, the Sodom cycle, which provides textual and theological evidence to suggest that an open universe has room for unknowns in the past and present, a more radical openness than first supposed. The Scripture passages that best inform us about God's nature are not found in pithy, poetic statements but in the narratives that make up the bulk of the Hebrew Bible. In the Sodom narrative, Yahweh opened up to his trusted covenant partner, Abraham. Everything in this narrative suggests we should accept their dialogue at face value. Appearing in a body, Yahweh communicated and performed actions conducive to a bodily existence, the mode of humanity. He came and went, rested under a tree, ate and drank, engaged in conversation, and even had his feet washed.

Of utmost importance, Yahweh also proposed to go down to Sodom and Gomorrah to find out whether their evil was as bad as the outcry suggested because he simply did not know. If reports were confirmed to be true, those cities would be destroyed. If readers are to trust the veracity of Yahweh's promise to Sarah regarding a child, then we should also trust the

---

17. Contrary to my conclusion, one commentator remarks, "This scene does not mention the possibility of repentance to forestall the destruction of the city, as we find in the prophetic books" (Cook, *New Collegeville Bible Commentary*, 55). In response, Scripture nowhere necessitates the need to mention the possibility of repentance for that option to exist. The redemptive arch of Scripture presupposes that God's love is not only open to repentance but always pursues it: "[God] does not want anyone to be destroyed, but wants everyone to repent" (2 Pet 3:9 NLT).

veracity of his statements regarding Sodom. In a literal fulfillment, Yahweh sent two angelic representatives to Sodom. Unable to find even ten righteous people there, they discovered that the wickedness was extreme and worthy of destruction.

Yahweh needed to conduct a more thorough investigation, but why? His conversation with Abraham revolved around wickedness and righteousness, specifically stating that Sodom's "sin [was] so grievous" (Gen 18:20). Accordingly, the circumstantial evidence points to an ontological blackout in God's knowledge of Sodom's sinful darkness. In a radically open universe, this blackout appears to apply at least within the sphere of grievous sin, where God's presence can be entirely absent. In other words, God didn't know because God wasn't there—his presence had evacuated! Divine knowledge and presence are inseparable, hence where God's knowledge is limited or restricted, so must his presence be, and vice versa. In an open universe, the future is already absent of God, so is it really inconceivable that aspects of the past and present may be as well? At least within the straightforward narrative of Sodom, it's difficult to avoid this conclusion.

There is no strong evidence in the Abraham narrative to conclude that God's knowledge is limited toward the righteous. Our theological inquiry, therefore, does not invoke a limitation of God's knowledge or presence in the lives of the righteous. The question is whether openness theology has the flexibility to include some limitations to divine knowledge and presence, past and present, as it concerns the wicked.

2

An Open Universe
Sin and Death as Distance

It is yet to be determined what degree of personal or national sin limits God. Is it sin on any level? Is it gross evil? Is it prolonged rebellion and the refusal to repent? For example, in Genesis 18 we can contrast God's knowledge and presence toward Abraham's wife, Sarah, with God's knowledge and presence toward Sodom just a few moments apart in time. Sodom's sin distanced God in a considerable way, yet Sarah's sin did not (Gen 18:9–15). Even though Sarah didn't believe Yahweh's promise to give her a child, he still knew precisely what she was thinking: "So Sarah laughed to herself as she thought, 'After I am worn out and my lord is old, will I now have this pleasure?' Then the LORD said to Abraham, 'Why did Sarah laugh and say, "Will I really have a child, now that I am old?"'" (18:12–13). Sarah's sin was not able to keep God out or hinder his thoughtful presence in her life. But very close in time to this interaction, Yahweh was to a large degree removed from the sinfulness of Sodom.

Despite God's limited knowledge of Sodom, we should not presume that any flaw or imperfection exists with God. When Almighty God delegates his authority or designs a world where even demonic authority has influence, we should not contend that our doctrine of *omnipotence* is under attack. When divine foreknowledge can't determine the exact future because it doesn't yet exist, our understanding of *omniscience* is certainly not in danger. Likewise, when the wicked are removed from God's presence in the eschaton, should we be concerned that *omnipresence* is somehow at stake? Not at all, because we are basing that eschatological situation on the word of God: "They will be punished with everlasting destruction and shut out from the presence of the Lord" (2 Thess 1:9). What if God's presence is somehow limited in this world and if his knowledge of the past and present are in some sense restricted by the darkness of sin, as with Sodom? Surely God is not internally flawed but merely conforming to the spiritual laws of his created order. Could it be that God chose to create a radically open universe in which the entrance of sin can limit him?

On the basis of Genesis 18, we cannot conclude just how far removed God can become from those engrossed in sin. In that account, God was not willfully ignorant but eventually looked more closely at the situation and confronted their depravity. So what degree of sin limits God, and to what degree does it limit him? There may not be an answer—if such distance is even possible! Nonetheless, we will pursue this line of theological reasoning in attempts to better understand divine absence. Just as the future is partly open and partly settled, there may yet be room in open theism's elaborate framework for a partly open past and present as well.

WHEN GOD WITHDRAWS HIS PRESENCE

Genesis 18 is explicit that Yahweh knew Sarah's secret thoughts (18:9-15). Scripture consistently depicts a God intimate with the thoughts of the righteous. David writes, "You perceive my thoughts from afar" (Ps 139:2). In another place, "But as for me, I am poor and needy; may the LORD think of me" (40:17). But what about the wicked? Surely God perceives the heart of the wicked, as Scripture seems to indicate. When Ezekiel confronted evil leadership, God argued that their actions did not agree with their thoughts. The LORD contended, "That is what you are saying, you leaders in Israel, but I know what is going through your mind" (Ezek 11:5; cf. Ps 44:20-21). As the leaders deceitfully spoke one thing, God could see behind the lies at what they actually thought! But how intimate is Yahweh with the depths of the sinful heart? How well does he know it and how close does he allow himself to get to it? Even though God keeps watch over "everything under the heavens" (Job 28:24), does his knowledge of a person's most hidden meditations require that he knows all thoughts at all times?

Most believers would agree that God cannot possess experiential knowledge of evil. He cannot comprehend sin in any way internal to his own thoughts and actions. Perhaps God knows the depths of the sinful heart only indistinctly, only as an empirical generalization observed from a distance. The psalmist says, "He keeps his distance from the proud" (Ps 138:6 NLT), and in the Proverbs, "The LORD is far from the wicked" (Prov 15:29). Many passages that speak of God's knowledge of sinfulness convey it in somewhat ambiguous terms, as if he was a secondhand observer: "Because your insolence has reached my ears, I will put my hook in your nose" (Isa 37:28–29). The proverbs also say, "The Righteous One takes note of the house of the wicked" (Prov 21:12; cf. Job 11:11). Although God is aware of their sin, it's as if it has reached his ears from a distance, and he observes it like one standing in the background, jotting down notes.[1]

Yahweh was not aware of Sodom's sin by firsthand knowledge but from the voice of an outcry (Gen 18:20). He was far removed from the immorality of their inner thoughts and external deeds. Such distance begs the question: When did Yahweh's thoughtful presence abandon Sodom and Gomorrah? It's important to understand God's actions toward Sodom because Scripture sets forth Sodom as a paradigm for God's righteous dealings with corrupt people and nations that came after. Being likened to Sodom and Gomorrah, the condition of those peoples and God's destruction of them is presented throughout the Old and New Testaments.[2] Among many similar voices, Yahweh declares through the prophet Amos, "I overthrew some of you as I overthrew Sodom and Gomorrah" (Amos 4:11). But is God's absence from Sodom a reliable pattern for how he deals with similar people or nations?

Although the pattern for other nations may not always be the divine absence that Sodom experienced, God's response to sin will inevitably include some degree of distance, but he never starts there. Whatever future response Yahweh has against personal or national sin, his mission has not veered from sending convicting grace to every man and woman in hopes that they might repent. Even though this activity is wrought by God's Spirit, it is accomplished primarily through human agents. Nehemiah observes, "For many years you were patient with them. By your Spirit you warned them through your prophets" (Neh 9:30; cf. 2 Kgs 17:13; John 16:7–8). When hearts are calloused and nations remain stubborn in their sin, God may still send a messenger with hope of repentance, as he did with Jonah and other prophets (Jonah 1:1–2). Scripture doesn't hesitate to point out, however, that there comes a point when God ceases to work toward temporal salvation and releases the unbelieving heart to its chosen path of rebellion (cf. Gen 6:5–7; Rom 1:21–24). We have enough examples in Scripture to know that the God of perfect, longsuffering love can eventually allow

---

1. God keeps close watch over the righteous, but the wicked are kept at a distance and even destroyed; see Pss 1:6; 11:5; 34:15–16; 145:20; 146:9.

2. See Deut 29:23; 32:32; Isa 1:9; 3:9; 13:19; Jer 23:14; 49:18; 50:40; Lam 4:6; Ezek 16:48–49; Amos 4:11; Zeph 2:9; Matt 10:15; 11:23–24; Luke 10:12; 17:28–29; Rom 9:29; 2 Pet 2:6; Jude 1:7; Rev 11:8.

individuals (Exod 8:15, 32; 9:34) and even entire nations (1 Sam 6:6) to *harden* themselves to the point of no return.³

Tragically, the wicked can become so twisted by sin that they are beyond recovery. According to Ezekiel, "For what God has said applies to everyone—it will not be changed! Not one person whose life is twisted by sin will ever recover" (Ezek 7:13 NLT). Based on the outcome of their judgment, we can safely assume that this was Sodom and Gomorrah's final fateful condition, where not even ten righteous people could be found. They were fully given over to sin, much like the world-wide evil that earlier warranted a barrage of death through the flood waters. At some point, divine tolerance ran out. This is a theme we see throughout Scripture. Ezekiel describes one of those dire instances: "I the LORD have spoken. The time has come for me to act. I will not hold back; I will not have pity, nor will I relent. You will be judged according to your conduct and your actions, declares the Sovereign LORD" (24:14). Although the LORD will often change his mind, in this case, he wouldn't.

Before the flood, when God observed that people's hearts were only bent toward evil and hopelessly lost, he changed his mind about having made humankind and destroyed everyone except eight people (Gen 7:21). Humanity was consumed with "only evil all the time" (6:5). But before this utter destruction, God made the choice to withdraw his Spirit, evidence that even God's patience wanes: "Then the LORD said, 'My Spirit will not contend with humans forever'" (6:3). In his handling of this passage, Walter Kaiser entitles his remarks, *The Holy Spirit would no longer plead with reprobates*. Kaiser asserts that sin can intensify to such a degree that God must do something about it; otherwise "evil beings would assume that there were no limits on wickedness."⁴

In the days of Noah, being a God of perfect changeableness, Yahweh's point of contact changed with regard to humanity and their wickedness. His center of contact moved from a loving, longsuffering presence that offered forgiveness to a loving, wrathful presence that brought destruction. And yes, even God's wrath is full of love. Wasn't it Jürgen Moltmann's contention that wrath is in fact injured love?⁵ Because freewill creatures can use their God-given freedom for evil rather than good, they can and often do reject God's love rather than embrace it. We are at a loss to understand when God's

---

3. Scripture designates God as an actor in hardening (חזק, *chazaq*) Pharaoh's heart (Exod 4:21; 7:3, 13; 9:12; 10:1, 20, 27; 11:10; 14:4, 8, 18). The Hebrew חזק means *to strengthen*, thus one could argue that God was merely strengthening the current resolve of Pharaoh's heart for God's own purposes.

4. Kaiser, "Pentateuch," 6.

5. Moltmann, *Crucified God*, 272.

gracious prerogative turns to wrath in response to such behavior, but the psalmist assures us that "the way of the wicked leads to destruction" (Ps 1:6). To their own destruction, people choose to distance themselves from the loving Creator. But make no mistake, flagrantly abused freedom will come to an end; God's hammer of judgment will eventually fall.[6]

HAMARTIOLOGICAL DISTANCE

During the age of the flood, of Sodom, and Babel, Almighty God wreaked judgment upon the people. But at other times, he has allowed judgment to be the natural result of what humanity brings upon itself when left to its own devices: "The violence of the wicked will drag them away, for they refuse to do what is right" (Prov 21:7; cf. Jer 44:7). It seems that in most cases judgment is the natural, self-induced consequence of sin and stubborn rebellion. A people's attitude and behavior are a good indicator that they're preparing to reap what they sow: "The look on their faces testifies against them; they parade their sin like Sodom; they do not hide it. Woe to them! They have brought disaster upon themselves" (Isa 3:9). At some point, as people choose the path of sin and continue to make one immoral choice after another, God gives them over to their lust and to the depravity of their desires (cf. Ps 81:11–12; Rom 1:24–27).

When God no longer tempers human lust, he's essentially releasing the heart into a black hole of ever increasing darkness. Though grudgingly, he necessarily removes the convicting presence of his Spirit from influencing that person's inner self any longer. This leads to a most provocative, theological consideration—that the absence of conviction coincides with the removal of the dynamics of God's presence, along with his thoughtful embrace and his powerfully influential hand. To enable a more informed discussion, we might call this three-fold removal the *hamartiological distance*. A common Greek term for sin is *hamartia*, which is the ultimate cause for any distance. The absence of the tri-partite collection of divine power, presence, and knowledge is a necessity, just as Barth wrote that the location of God's presence "includes, of course, His knowledge and power."[7] The hamartiological distance equals God's ontological, unmitigated absence.

---

6. In the Sodom narrative, God's presence was removed even before final judgment was determined. This narrative puts forward the divine movement *from absence to presence* (in judgment), *then back to absence* (in destruction). The author of Genesis 18 doesn't tell the story of how Sodom initially moved *from divine presence to absence* (in real distance).

7. Barth, *CD* 2/1:470.

Christian philosopher John Hick advanced a premise in which humanity is born into a world where there exists an *epistemic distance* between God and people, an initial ignorance of God's existence. Although an epistemic distance exists, there is never any *spatial* distance from God, which for Hick would be impossible. When we enter this world, our initial knowledge of God is necessarily limited.[8] If God's existence and presence were so obvious to humankind in all his glory and power, no one could be expected to live with any kind of non-coerced autonomy. The only reasonable human response would be to genuflect, worship, and forever serve such a glorious, awesome being—so enters the epistemic distance.

God's presence is not immediately obvious to us because the God of relationship, love, and freedom has built that freedom into every facet of his creation. Hick concludes that "the world must be to man, to some extent at least, *etsi deus non daretur*, 'as if there were no God'. . . . [God] must be knowable, but only by a mode of knowledge that involves a free personal response on man's part, this response consisting in an uncompelled interpretative activity whereby we experience the world as mediating the divine presence."[9] A world *mediating the divine presence* is one in which both general and special revelation are necessary for anyone to know God. The creation screams of him, yet apart from that still small whisper from God's Spirit, creation talks to a wall of deaf ears. People are born into a world that is "religiously ambiguous, both veiling God and revealing Him."[10]

There are few exceptions to this distance in Scripture, but one such exception is Adam and his wife. These two were not born into an apparently godless world but were handmade by the Creator and placed by him into their garden home.[11] For everyone else, the reality of distance awakens the need for faith. Faith becomes possible but also necessary. This distance

---

8. Eastern Orthodoxy holds a view that resonates with Hick. In the words of Donald Fairbairn, "God was not willing to coerce people into a relationship with him that they may not have wanted, so he did not create humanity in complete union with himself from the beginning. Rather, God created people immature, separate from him in some sense, and offered them the opportunity to use their freedom in order to attain union with him" (*Eastern Orthodoxy*, 66).

9. Hick, *Evil and the God of Love*, 317.

10. Ibid., 318.

11. According to Hick, the epistemic distance also applies to Adam, "a frail, uncertain creature living in his own world, to which God is but an occasional visitor" (ibid.). Though I appreciate the basic premise behind an epistemic distance, I depart from Hick on his mythological interpretation of Genesis and his understanding that the fall merely represents the epistemic distance or rather "the immense gap between what we actually are and what in the divine intention we are eventually to become" ("Irenaean Theodicy," 41).

is intended to be overcome through faith as the Spirit of God influences the heart through prevenient grace, which is the work of God to compel all creatures to open their spiritual eyes to him. Paul implies that even general revelation can begin to overcome this distance, stating that "since the creation of the world God's invisible qualities—his eternal power and divine nature—have been clearly seen, being understood from what has been made, so that people are without excuse" (Rom 1:20). If the testimony of creation can work against the distance, how much more can the inner conviction of God's Spirit!

I find it helpful to adapt Hick's terminology to God's own vantage point, what I have termed the hamartiological distance. In a radically open universe, it's conceivable that an epistemic distance exists not only between people and God, but one of a different kind between God and humanity. For God, this harsh distance is due to sin, the perversion of the Creator's good creation. It might prove even more helpful to describe the cause of this distance as *deathful* sin. God does not and cannot know or experience the perverseness of sin or the barrenness of death, so he maintains an epistemic distance from them. This estrangement began in the garden when Adam distanced himself from God's authority. When Adam chose to break through the protective walls of God's kingdom, he removed himself from under God's ruling hand. Adam's actions created the initial distance experienced between God and his creation. Eating the forbidden fruit represented Adam's acceptance of another authority, having disobeyed God's clear prohibition (Gen 2:16–17; 3:1, 4).

Once people remove themselves from under God's authority through the rebellion of sin, it naturally follows that God's thoughts and presence are distanced as well. The first area of distance is refusing divine authority and choosing a contrary path that leads away from his realm of protection, influence, and rule. God's original design involved humanity being under his authority, while God in turn delegated authority over creation to human agents. Yahweh loves sharing power; he always intended for people to be his vice-regents ruling over the creation, which was designated as their sphere of influence and was their responsibility to protect and care for (Ps 8:6–8). As vice-regents, humanity ruled the earth in God's place.

When Adam sinned, much of that authority was hijacked and transferred to Satan and the evil cosmic powers. Vast regions of the creation were shifted from under God's authority to "the god of this world" (2 Cor 4:4). Even the unregenerate human spirit fell under Satan's power (Eph 2:2).[12] In

---

12. The Greek of Eph 2:2 can be translated, "according to the prince of the power of the air, the ruler of/over the spirit that is now working in the sons of disobedience."

one sense, God's creation cannot be removed from his authority because the whole world is his kingdom, made up of his children: "Your kingdom is an everlasting kingdom, and your dominion endures through all generations" (Ps 145:13; cf. Mal 2:10). God's rule in this age, however, continues to be a rule *de jure* (in principal) until in the eschaton it becomes a rule *de facto* (in truth), when all things are brought into subjection to him (cf. 1 Cor 15:24–26). Until then, rejection of God's authority is quite real in the personal experience of an individual or nation.

Because God is no respecter of persons, under the old covenant those covenanted to him were no exception. Isaiah describes their rejection of the divine power when he says, "They are evil people, corrupt children who have rejected the LORD. They have despised the Holy One of Israel and turned their backs on him. Why do you continue to invite punishment? Must you rebel forever? Your head is injured, and your heart is sick" (Isa 1:4–5 NLT). Even though these are God's children related to him through covenant, they have rejected, despised, turned their backs on, and rebelled against Yahweh! After they turn their backs on the Holy One of Israel, he proceeds to warn them of their path toward perishing and utter destruction, the absoluteness of absence: "When you spread out your hands in prayer, I hide my eyes from you; even when you offer many prayers, I am not listening.... But rebels and sinners will both be broken, and those who forsake the LORD will perish" (1:15, 28).

Scripture suggests that God does not initiate any real distance, though he can ultimately reciprocate it. In rebellion against his power, people remove him from their knowledge, eventually resulting in their removal from the intimate center of his inner thoughts. Paul's letter to the Romans gives us a glimpse into the human side of this removal: "For although they knew God, they neither glorified him as God nor gave thanks to him, but their thinking became futile and their foolish hearts were darkened.... Furthermore, just as they did not think it worthwhile to retain the knowledge of God, so God gave them over to a depraved mind, so that they do what ought not to be done" (Rom 1:21, 28). Consequently, rebellion has an exponential effect. The more a person rebels against divine authority and "their minds [are] made dull" (2 Cor 3:14), the more inclined they become to keep on sinning. At that point, the words of Second Isaiah are fulfilled: "They know nothing, they understand nothing; their eyes are plastered over so they cannot see, and their minds closed so they cannot understand" (Isa 44:18). People literally distance their thoughts from God and refuse *to retain the knowledge of God* as a worthy occupation, no longer wanting to know God, which arguably results in the dismissal of God's thoughts toward them. This was evidently the case with Sodom and Gomorrah. Somewhere along the way, after the people rejected Yahweh's authority, his thoughtful presence was altogether removed, a hamartiological distance.

By now readers may be anxious to raise objections on grounds that such hamartiological distance would be too harsh a consequence for even the rebellious. But consider that this eventual divine absence is an act of grace and an expression of mercy from a relational God. If God permitted his Spirit to continue working indefinitely to influence a hardened heart, the deception and corruption of rebellious sin would only be *strengthened* with greater resolve to reject God's loving pursuit, as was the case with Pharaoh and even Israel. Regarding God's call to Israel, Hosea says, "But the more they were called, the more they went away from me" (Hos 11:2). We don't need to be reminded that the consequences of Pharaoh's increasing hardness for the Egyptian nation was more than many of them could bear, down to the death of their firstborn children (Exod 12:29)! So God is merciful, not wanting distance or the oft-inevitable death of distance to befall anyone.

Our Creator designed a world where genuine relationships exist because love is freely chosen. Creatures have the power to increasingly distance themselves from him. But the Lord still tries to reason with and constantly warn of the consequences and irrational absurdity of walking away from him: "'Your wickedness will punish you; your backsliding will rebuke you. Consider then and realize how evil and bitter it is for you when you forsake the Lord your God and have no awe of me,' declares the Lord, the Lord Almighty" (Jer 2:19). In the end, the process toward hamartiological distance is humanity's choice, a freewill decision to move away from God and continue to push him further away. This distance is not merely a matter of human perspective but creates distance from God's perspective as well. Not unlike the warning God shared with Ezekiel in his day: "And he said to me, 'Son of man, do you see what they are doing—the utterly detestable things the Israelites are doing here, things that will drive me far from my sanctuary?'" (Ezek 8:6). People drive God's Spirit and the divine presence away from them, an experience that deeply affects the heart of God as he is driven out of his home and away from his sanctuary.

When people say no to divine authority, presence, and knowledge—the hamartiological distance—sin can grow into something that even God cannot control. When God loses control of it, death is not far away. Yahweh warned Adam in no uncertain terms that the consequence of disobedience was death, which is another way of expressing an unqualified distance from God. Just as Adam was warned about the consequences of death and distance, so the hamartiological distance followed the ancestral sin. This is the ultimate logical conclusion to the path of sin, a road that always leads to death: "Rebels and sinners will both be broken, and those who forsake the LORD will perish" (Isa 1:28).

SIN AND DEATH AS TRUE SEPARATION FROM GOD

Evangelicalism has always held firmly to the conviction that sin separates people from God, but believers talk little about the full implications of the *divine* side of this separation. We are familiar with language such as redemption and reconciliation, but from God's perspective we really have little theological synthesis regarding the extent of harm done by sin to require these. What exactly does it mean that God hides his face or removes his favor? Is it only his favorable disposition that changes or special blessings that he removes? Is it merely, as Fretheim would argue, an intensification of God's presence that lessens? Yes, God's judgment is in view, but is there more we should be considering? These are all human-centered solutions, but none really consider whether God is facing an even greater tragedy and is himself the victim of a real, tangible distance. Is there possibly something more sinister and far more tragic involved, something having to do with God's experiential presence that we should consider?

When God hides his face, perhaps it's not merely an anthropomorphism for judgment but points to a true removal of the presence of his face? Isaiah speaks to Israel in the context of exile, which on a national level represents the distance of broken relationship with God. In that context, Isaiah addresses the people and declares, "Your iniquities have separated you from your God; your sins have hidden his face from you, so that he will not hear" (Isa 59:2; cf. Mic 3:4). If Sodom and Gomorrah are any indicator, then expressions like this are not always applied figuratively in Scripture. Could it be that such alarming phrases at times indicate a thorough, metaphysical *absence*?

"Where Are You?"

The idea of divine absence is not novel, especially for many who study the Hebrew Bible. Rabbi Simon Glustrom asserts that "God is never really absent from the world, and yet the [early] rabbis were prepared to accept a contradiction in speaking of the removal of His presence at those times when the individual or the group sinned against Him. . . . God cannot live together in the same environment with sinfulness. The presence of one excludes the presence of the other."[13] Sin is ultimately distance from God and from the fellowship of community life. When sin came into the world, human beings were at once brought face-to-face with a radical separation from God. After Adam ate the forbidden fruit, he and his wife heard the sound of Yahweh walking in the garden. They stayed in hiding, cowering behind the trees. The LORD God toured the garden but couldn't find the ones he knew had broken their covenant with him, a covenant of fellowship and mutual trust. Then shockingly the Creator uttered these desperate words, "Where (אי) are you?" (Gen 3:9). Most conservative commentators interpret this question rhetorically, as if Yahweh meant to say to Adam, *Why are you where you are?* or *Do you know where you are?* But what if this was humanity's first tragic taste of hamartiological distance?

Although the Hebrew word *ay* (אי) is used rhetorically in some portions of Scripture (e.g., Job 38:19, 24; Isa 66:1), any hermeneutic applied to the present text should focus on the narrative context as a primary factor in determining its meaning.[14] Later in Gen 4:9, God asks Cain, "Where (אי) is your brother Abel?" In that context, Yahweh then immediately answered his own question, bringing out the rhetorical value: "The LORD said, 'What have you done? Listen! Your brother's blood cries out to me from the ground'" (Gen 4:10). This, however, was not the case with Adam. At least for Adam, the question was real.[15] After he overheard the anxiety and alarm in Yahweh's tone, Adam spoke up from behind the bushes and closed the gap.

One might be tempted to assume God's inquiry was intended solely for Adam's own reflection, but the literal sense of the Hebrew is quite simply, *Where are you?*[16] Besides the typical kneejerk reaction to guard pre-

---

13. Glustrom, *Language of Judaism*, 171.

14. When a question is being asked in Scripture, it's important who's asking the question, whether God or a person, and in what context the question is being asked. Frequently when God was asking the question, it meant that something was wrong, which implies that some relative distance was felt (e.g., Gen 4:9). When the psalmist or another believer asked similar questions, it often meant they felt some distance in their relationship with God and were desperately seeking to close it: "Why, LORD, do you stand far off? Why do you hide yourself in times of trouble?" (Ps 10:1). For the psalmist, the task of presenting the question became an experience of presence in absence, asking in anticipation of divine response. But it shouldn't be ignored that on the human side, this distance was truly felt and therefore real to the intercessor. In a similar way, whether rhetorical or not, God is also feeling or experiencing distance when he asks questions about a person's heart condition or relationship to him.

15. For commentary that considers God's question to Adam to be more than rhetorical, see Speiser, *Genesis: Introduction, Translation, and Notes*, 24; and Humphreys, *Character of God*, 50.

16. Or, where have you gone? This interpretation is by no means novel. John Skinner commented, "The question expresses ignorance; it is not omniscience that the

conceived notions of divine omniscience, it would benefit us little in this primitive text to divest such an important query of its full force and tragic implications. The author of Genesis 3 apparently had no interest in developing a doctrine of omniscience nor of guarding it, which is also apparent in Genesis 18. Death had set in, Adam was lost, and his Creator Yahweh Elohim had sought to find and restore him.

For the first time, Adam had broken the chain of command—a dereliction of duties would be an understatement. After Adam and the woman evacuated God's protective covering, it was then that Yahweh asked the question, "Where are you?" The separation that sin and death causes between God and his creatures is radical and pervasive, more so than merely from a human perspective. Job's friend greatly misses the mark when he concludes that God is not affected by sin. Speaking to Job, he says, "If you sin, how does that affect [God]? If your sins are many, what does that do to him? . . . Your wickedness only affects humans like yourself, and your righteousness only other people" (Job 35:6–8). Job's friend was preaching a mechanical, tunnel vision approach to God, as one who blesses the righteous and curses the wicked. This so-called wisdom could not have been further from the truth! In fact, God may be the one most affected by our sin. Hence, we shouldn't ignore another possible nuance to God's search for Adam, that Yahweh was not concerned solely with Adam's physical location but also with his spiritual condition.[17] The fact that Adam was lost is indicative of the greater tragedy, that a spiritual relationship had been severed, leaving death and distance as the new reality.

Although it came as no surprise to God, it might catch us off guard to read that the immediate consequence of original sin was a hidden humanity. What was this foul blinding agent that took away God's vision of his Adam, blurring his immediate knowledge of this creature? It's strange to consider that something outside of God could overpower him, yet we should understand that God concedes to relational constrictions of freedom in this world. Furthermore, this blinding potential could also be informed by the awesome holiness of God to repel sin, a built-in distancing effect. Regardless, it appears that iniquity concealed Adam from his Creator while the wholly relational holiness of God acquiesced and accepted distance for the first time.

---

writer wishes to illustrate, but the more impressive attribute of sagacity" (*Critical and Exegetical Commentary*, 77). Cf. *Apocalypse of Moses* 8:1.

17. Rosenblatt and Horwitz assert that God's question to Adam "reverberates with innuendo. Where is man now, caught in a no-man's-land between innocence and experience, between his godlike self-image and his irrefutable animal form?" (*Wrestling with Angels*, 39).

Even though it would be hundreds of years until Adam died a physical death, God's question expounds on the significance of his warning to the man: "For when you eat from [the tree of knowing good and evil] you will certainly die" (Gen 2:17). So where had the man and his wife gone after eating the fruit? They certainly weren't dead, as would've been expected, but the deathfulness of sin had left them distant and alone. Nothing in the Eden narrative indicates they should not have died an immediate, physical death. The same language, "you will certainly die (*mowt yamut*)," appears in 2 Samuel 12 with the same implications. David is promised that his son will *mowt yamut*, and indeed he does (2 Sam 12:13–14, 18). In another passage, King Solomon promises a man Shimei that he would *mowt yamut* if he ever left the city (1 Kgs 2:37, 42). After Shimei leaves the city in search of his runaway slaves, Solomon carries out the death penalty against him (2:46).

Despite God's unconditional promise to Adam, he was nonetheless graciously merciful and allowed the man and his wife to continue to live and even bear children, the entire human race. Yahweh even gave the woman a new name, Eve, meaning *mother of all living*. Yet Adam and Eve could not remove the consequences of their sin. Death and decay ravaged the creation and they were doomed to die, which they eventually did. Death was experienced in separation, not only on the human side but even on the divine side. If separation from God does not hinder the proximity of his oft-hidden presence or his knowledge of people's thoughts and feelings, then in what sense is their true separation on the divine side of things? There was a tragic irony to Adam and the woman eating the fruit and having their eyes opened (Gen 3:5)—in that moment, God's eyes were closed.

This initial distance and separation from God was symbolically applied to the entire human race when Adam and Eve were forever banished from the Edenic presence of God, their place of worship, fellowship, and close, personal knowledge of their divine Creator. Subsequently even their son Cain, after he had sinned, was cast out of God's presence. Notice what Cain says to Yahweh: "Today you are driving me from the land, and I will be hidden from your presence" (Gen 4:14). Literally, *from your face I will be hidden*. Cain doesn't say that God will be hidden from him but that *he* will be hidden from God's view.[18] "Then Cain went away from the presence of the Lord and settled in the land of Nod, east of Eden" (4:16 ESV).

---

18. This is an example of metonymy of speech. Cain says that he will be hidden from God's face, but it's implied that Yahweh will also be hidden from Cain. The idea is that Cain is hidden from Yahweh *because* Yahweh hides from Cain.

Dead Means Dead

So far we have looked at illustrations of distance in life, but arguably the most tragic demonstration of distance is found in death itself. Prior to the eschatological day of resurrection, what if dead really means dead? Based on the biblical portrait of humanity (anthropology), we should understand the whole person to be indistinguishably body *and* soul, not the separation of one from the other at death. This psychosomatic unity of the person is the ancient Hebraic understanding and has serious implications regarding death. As Stanley Grenz concludes, "The Old Testament writers never separated the hope for eventual salvation beyond the grave from bodily existence. Hebrew anthropology could not envision life in any other form, including existence in some disembodied state."[19]

For the most part, Hebrew thought perceived even the death of the righteous as ambiguous, which we find expressed throughout the writings of the Old Testament, particularly in the Psalms and the Wisdom literature: "Whatever your hand finds to do, do it with your might, for there is no work or thought or knowledge or wisdom in Sheol, to which you are going" (Eccl 9:10 ESV).[20] The ambiguity of this *last stop* was especially the case for the wicked: "My soul clings to you; your right hand upholds me. But those who seek to destroy my life shall go down into the depths of the earth" (Ps 63:8–9 ESV; cf. Job 18:17, 21). The death of the wicked was regarded as perishing, destruction, and even the total devastation of any possible future existence, a portrayal of total loss: "Though the wicked spring up like grass and all evildoers flourish, they will be destroyed forever" (Ps 92:7). God's ultimate response to the wicked will be to "repay them for their sins and destroy them for their wickedness; the LORD our God will destroy them" (94:23). This complete destruction of the wicked was not just the belief of the Hebrew people but the prayerful expectation of the righteous. Seeking justice through divine response, the psalmist requests of God, "May you blow them away like smoke—as wax melts before the fire, may the wicked perish before God" (68:2).

Following the Solomonic tradition, in the summation of wisdom the Preacher concludes, "Who knows if the human spirit rises upward and if the spirit of the animal goes down into the earth?" (Eccl 3:21). Indeed, who does know? It is this ambiguous realm of the dead that was mentioned briefly in our introduction. Joel Burnett comments, "In death's domain, human beings are said to be cut off from the divine presence, as indicated by Ps

---

19. Grenz, *Theology for the Community*, 578.
20. See also Job 21:13; Pss 6:4–5; 88:10–12; 104:29; 115:17; Isa 38:10, 18.

6:4–5."[21] Those verses read, "Turn, LORD, and deliver me; save me because of your unfailing love. Among the dead no one proclaims your name. Who praises you from the grave?" Burnett goes on to argue that the domain of death as a place of divine absence has been the very thing that's separated the Hebrew Bible from other ancient Near Eastern religions. According to Burnett,

> Yahweh's curious distance from the realm of death in biblical tradition is one such feature distinguishing him from other known deities, including Baal. . . . the Hebrew Bible reflects a thoroughgoing concern to keep Yahweh separate from any association with the powers and realm of death. As a logical consequence, biblical reflection on this third realm of the cosmos involves a degree of "structural divine absence."[22]

Naturally death is the place of just that, death. Structurally, death remains diametrically opposed to the life of God's person and presence.

Progressing beyond the early ambiguity of the abyss as a shadowy existence for the souls of both the righteous and unrighteous dead (*sheol* in Hebrew; *hades* in Greek), Old Testament revelation eventually gave way to the hope of resurrection (Dan 12:2). But the reality of death doesn't change. Until resurrection, the destiny of both believer and unbeliever alike is a death with no temporary stops (cf. Gen 3:19; John 5:28).[23] Bodily resurrection has always been the primary hope of the church rather than an intermediate state of blissful consciousness after death.[24] Though some prefer to call this *soul sleep*, I'm hesitant to use the expression.[25] It seems this terminology might downplay the cruel reality of death, which has been and remains humanity's most unnatural and ambiguous of enemies. Regardless of the language one uses, God preserves the deceased believer for resurrection at the end of the age.[26]

---

21. Burnett, *Where is God?*, 67.

22. Ibid., 68.

23. See also Job 14:12; Ps 17:15; 30:9; 88:10–12; 146:4; Eccl 9:5–6; Dan 12:2, 13; Matt 27:52; Acts 13:36; 1 Cor 15:17–18, 22–23.

24. Jesus and Paul both point to the body's resurrection as the believer's hope for a future beyond death; see John 5:28–29; 6:39–40, 44, 54; 11:24; Acts 24:15; 1 Thess 4:13–18; 1 Cor 15:51–54.

25. For a defense of the doctrine of soul sleep, see Grenz, *Theology for the Community*, 573–598; and Thielicke, *Death and Life*. A few historical proponents of soul sleep include Pope John XXII (1249–1334), John Wycliffe (1320–84), William Tyndale (1494–1546), Anabaptist Michael Sattler (1490–1527), and Martin Luther (1483–1546).

26. A few prevalent passages raised in objection to soul sleep include Jesus' assurance to the thief on the cross, "Today you will be with me in paradise" (Luke 23:43),

The misdirected hope of an interim spiritual body before the resurrection is reminiscent of the serpent's lie in the beginning: "'You will not certainly die,' the serpent said to the woman" (Gen 3:4). On the contrary, we will and we did and we do, "for dust you are and to dust you will return" (3:19). The distance of death is possibly the most powerful symbol to illustrate the loss of fellowship and community most naturally associated with God's loving presence. As powerful a symbol death may be, however, the believer does not experience God's actual distance in death. Paul is clear that for him, and by extension for every believer, "to die is gain" (Phil 1:21). John says it like this: "Then I heard a voice from heaven say, 'Write this: Blessed are the dead who die in the Lord from now on.' 'Yes,' says the Spirit, 'they will rest from their labor, for their deeds will follow them'" (Rev 14:13). In death, every believer will still "be with Christ" (Phil 1:23), safely surrounded by his thoughtful, loving presence. The Christian is no longer held captive by a "fear of death" (Heb 2:15) because after we die, whether we're conscious of it or not, we remain under the protection and safety of the divine presence until the resurrection: "For this God is our God for ever and ever; he will be our guide even to the end" (Ps 48:14).

If we are going to make any sense of the possibility of a real, unmitigated divine absence, it will emerge in the idea that sin is humanity's temporal experience of death. Death means distance and separation; thus, it is a death-filled, lethal sin that produces real distance between God and his creatures.[27] Are we to imagine that separation is merely the violation of a righteous standard that needs satisfied or punished? Is it merely God's awareness of a forensic offense that leaves him with an obligation to forgive? If so, does he truly experience any real distance from people, and what would that separation feel like for him? From the human perspective, people may feel this distance in a life of hopelessness and loss, but what about the suffering of God? What about the distance he feels?

If hamartiological distance is real, it's because sin does not merely illicit God's disappointment or injure a legal obligation. Scripture portrays sin as something that radically separates God from humanity; this distance is felt and experienced by God in the most profound and personal ways. The break in relationship even affects his desire to be loved, but any possible love from his creatures disappears in the distance. If distance means suffering for God, then death and divine absence mean the most profound suffering.

---

the parable of Lazarus and the Rich Man (Luke 16:19–31), and Moses' appearance on the Mount of Transfiguration (Matt 17:1–8). For passages relevant to both sides of the debate, see 1 Sam 28:7–15; Eccl 12:7; Mark 12:26–27; John 8:56; Acts 7:59–60; 2 Cor 5:8–10; 12:2–4; Phil 1:21–23; Eph 4:8–10; 1 Thess 4:16; 1 Pet 3:19–20; 4:6.

27. See Beck, *Slavery of Death*.

DIVINE SUFFERING: A TRAJECTORY TO HELL

When deathful sin curtails the thoughtful, powerful presence of God, the result is hamartiological distance. We might describe this distance as experiential, temporal death leading to physical, eternal death. Because death is separation and distance from God, the ultimate distance will be eternal separation and permanent distance in hell. Such eternal destruction, not just for individuals but for multitudes, could only be fully felt by the Maker who knows them best and created them for relationship. This trajectory of distance may be the cause for all of God's suffering.

When people or nations abandon God, it's often followed in Scripture by the reciprocity of divine rejection: "They abandoned the God who made them and rejected the Rock their Savior. . . . The Lord saw this and rejected them" (Deut 32:15, 19). Although God appears to respond in kind, such reciprocity may not be entirely a matter of divine choice. Burnett notes, "If God's absence from death's realm is a function of the structure of the cosmos, then might other instances of divine absence likewise be inherent to creation?"[28] We answer in the affirmative. Even though the Lord does not "take any pleasure in the death of the wicked" (Ezek 18:23; 33:11), the structure of the cosmos will eventually demand it.

In reciprocity, the Lord abandons the wicked to the trajectory that will eventually end at the gates of hell itself. But God is not to blame. Again, Burnett observes, "In the Hebrew Bible, God's presence or absence in the realm of death is presented not so much as a matter of clear-cut divine choice—the Hebrew bible is fairly mute on this note—as it is Israel's experience of its God." He then concludes that "some aspects of divine absence are a matter of neither divine punishment nor divine failure but rather are built into creation, at least at the level of human understanding of God."[29] Regardless of divine choice in the matter, the hamartiological distance and the progressive separation of the lost will be finalized in eternal judgment. According to the Apostle Paul, "They will be punished with everlasting destruction and shut out from (*apo*) the presence of the Lord and from the glory of his might" (2 Thess 1:9). The Greek preposition *apo* describes movement *away from*. The essence of this is captured well by the New Living Translation, which describes those lost souls as "forever separated from the Lord." Hence, hamartiological distance in time is a foretaste of this final judgment away from the presence of God forever, the temporal reality eventually parlaying into the eternal.

---

28. Burnett, *Where is God?*, 75.
29. Ibid., 75, 76.

The unrepentant have positioned themselves on a trajectory to hell, the opposite of relationship with God, the total undoing of that relationship. Where else could the rejection of God's love lead, especially if it is ultimately sin's dimension of unlove that distances people from God? As Michael Lodahl points out, "*Sin* is a term that may be identified with any falling short of God's ideal for us: a life of love."[30] This unlove, this transgression against God's perfect law of love, primarily surfaces in our interactions with other people. Listen to Yahweh's word to Ezekiel regarding Sodom: "Now this was the sin of your sister Sodom: She and her daughters were arrogant, overfed and unconcerned; they did not help the poor and needy. They were haughty and did detestable things before me. Therefore I did away with (*sur*) them as you have seen" (Ezek 16:49–50). It was concrete acts of unlove—arrogance, lack of concern, and not helping the poor and needy—that led to God finalizing Sodom's trajectory. In the Hebrew, the language that God "did away with them" literally means he *removed them* (*sur*) from life, so Sodom's trajectory was fulfilled.

Now what if divine suffering is defined by distance and a person's trajectory to hell runs parallel to God's suffering? Perhaps the suffering of God's heart is proportionate to his distance and separation from the creatures he loves. This would mean that hamartiological distance equals maximum divine suffering. Hence, God's experience is real because the distance is real. This may be the most profound tragedy of eternal death—the divine experience of permanent separation. To illustrate this divine calamity, the prophet of Lamentations shares God's heart when he describes his feelings in the face of death: "This is why I weep and my eyes overflow with tears. No one is near to comfort me, no one to restore my spirit. My children are destitute because the enemy has prevailed" (Lam 1:16). Much like this prophet's experience, God too must grieve terribly when the enemy of death and distance has prevailed.

After the end of the age, when God's kingdom is fulfilled, he will no longer confront sin as he did with Sodom. He will also no longer have knowledge of lost souls and have to bear that crushing burden. Those souls will be lost forever, along with God's tearful memory of them, just as the sins of believers are forever forgotten and removed from his recollection (Isa 43:25). Referring to the false prophets in Jeremiah's day, the Lord declares that due to their deceitful rebellion he will cast them out of his presence and forget about them: "I will surely forget you and cast you out of my presence" (Jer 23:39). While this language may to some degree involve a Semitic figure of speech, the reader is left with the emphatic impression of a broken

---

30. Lodahl, "Sin in Relational Perspective," 37, emphasis original.

relationship without future resolve. This means no less than a lack of familiarity and intimacy and ultimately distance.

The next verse in Jeremiah reads, "I will bring on you everlasting disgrace—everlasting shame that will not be forgotten" (Jer 23:40). Although the Lord has declared that the person will be forgotten, her sin and disgrace never would. Hell will be an eternal realm wherein the lost have what they've always wanted, an existence without God. Yet it's questionable whether what they have can even be called an existence; it will be a state of isolated consciousness, devoid of the vigilance of life.[31] In heaven, believers will have no personal knowledge of them but will be aware that there are *others* out there who abide in some state of existence or possibly non-existence. Without any personal familiarity, believers will know that there are people on the outside who have chosen sin and disgrace away from God and his kingdom.

Because of the horrifically appalling seriousness of hell, we should consider the possibility that the eschatological absence for lost people will *not* include unending, conscious torment.[32] After all, we serve a God of extravagant love, not sadistic torture. What would be the greater distance: to be annihilated and no longer exist, or to exist (and I use that term lightly) somewhere in God's creation but forever separated from him?[33] Perhaps those wicked souls will be completely destroyed in the "fires" of hell, an absolute distance—truly and utterly dead.[34] Jesus himself says, "Do not be afraid of those who kill the body but cannot kill the soul. Rather, be afraid

---

31. For a similar description of hell, see Boyd, *Satan and the Problem of Evil*, 338–57.

32. Those who believe in eternal, conscious torment point to the following passages for support: Matt 13:42; 22:13; 25:41, 46; Mark 9:43–48; Luke 16:23–24; 2 Thess 1:9; Rev 14:9–11, 19:20; 20:10, 15. The most compelling are the passages in Revelation, but we must be cautious when interpreting such highly figurative language surrounded by imagery that is certainly symbolic.

33. The idea of *conditional immortality* (annihilationism) is conducive to the concept that *dead means dead*. Conditionalists teach that the human soul is not inherently immortal; only God is immortal (1 Tim 6:16). We are all destined to die unless God grants the gift of eternal life (Rom 6:23). The ungodly *perish* in death and are consumed by the fires of hell (Ps 80:16), leaving open the possibility of varying degrees of punishment before the person is annihilated. Apart from divine life, there is absolute loss, the end of life. This annihilation is described as eternal punishment in the sense of being *permanent* (Jude 1:7). The testimony of Scripture seems to indicate that the soul/body is mortal and destined to die/perish unless God imparts eternal life; see Gen 37:35; Lev 17:11; Pss 6:5; 146:4; Isa 10:25; 66:24; Mal 4:1–3; Matt 7:13; 13:40–42; Luke 20:35–36; John 11:25–26; Rom 2:7; 1 Cor 15:22, 50, 53; Phil 3:19; 4:3; 2 Tim 1:10; Heb 10:39; Jas 4:12; 2 Pet 2:6; 3:7; Rev 20:14.

34. For a biblical defense of annihilationism, see Crofford, *Dark Side of Destiny*; Pinnock, "Conditional View," 135–66; Fudge, *Fire that Consumes*; and Gregg, *All You Want to Know About Hell*, 195–214.

of the One who can destroy both soul and body in hell" (Matt 10:28).[35] On some level, their shame "will not be forgotten" in the everlasting consciousness of both God and his saved people (Jer 23:40).

Now regarding those who escape this trajectory of doom, the psalmist describes God as keeping his distance from sin while also seeking to distance his people from it: "As far as the east is from the west, so far has he removed our transgressions from us" (Ps 103:12). This distance is only ever resolved when the sinner turns to God for salvation, at which time the LORD removes the guilt of their sin. If sin is not distanced from God through forgiveness applied to the sinner, then God has no choice but to distance both sin *and sinner* from himself in eternal death, as far as the east is from the west. The choice belongs to you whether it will be your sin that's forever banished from his presence or your person too. At the end of the age, the LORD will declare unto the wicked, "Depart from (*apo*) me, you who are cursed, into the eternal fire" (Matt 25:41). In another place, "I never knew you. Away from (*apo*) me, you evildoers!" (7:23). These will be forever "shut out from (*apo*) the presence of the Lord" (2 Thess 1:9).

CONCLUSION

In our endeavor to explore deeper implications of openness theology, I have coined the phrase hamartiological distance to describe the situation in which the LORD's intimate knowledge, personal presence, and immediate authority become absent from the rebellious who continue in their sin. This proposal is no more drastic than other unprecedented claims of open theism. Granted, it's almost unthinkable that God could suffer such distance from his creatures, but in a radically open universe, the possibility is quite real. After the first sin, the LORD groped for Adam in partial disbelief, asking, "Where are you?" Though the man and his wife were hidden for only a short time, they were forever banished from the garden, and their son Cain was also later banished from God's presence. We can't know when God steps away from someone's life nor the extent to which this occurs, but in an open universe, the human race has inherited this legacy of distance.

If we are going to make sense of the possibility of divine absence, we should consider that sin is humanity's temporal experience of death. The trajectory of deathful sin in this life parlays into eternal destruction in hell in the next. One degree of death gives way to another degree of death. If

---

35. Too numerous to list all of them here, there are dozens of Scripture verses that describe the destiny of the wicked as *destruction* or *perishing*, which implies an absolute end to their existence; e.g., Pss 37:20; 78:38; 145:20; John 3:16; 10:28.

God's suffering is defined by his experience of those who have distanced themselves, then their death impacts the heart of God in the most profound way. We also discussed the possibility that death is a real encounter for the believer. If believers are not afforded the luxury of a spiritual rest stop on the way to resurrection, we will linger in death until Jesus returns to establish his kingdom and defeat the last and greatest enemy, death itself.

3

Distance
Origin and Implications

What exactly is this awful reality the Bible calls sin? We know that its presence lives within every human being and that people have sinful thoughts and perform sinful actions, but there's not a single theologian who can point us to a metaphysical conclusion on the matter. If sin could consist of something, its substance would surely be death. Sin is a foreign *other* to God's good creation; among other things, sin is deceitful, unpredictable, and destructive. As such, it could not originate with God and didn't even originate with people, but its origin lies with Satan. Because of such terrible beginnings, sin's ultimate victim and greatest impact is against God.

In the previous chapters, we were introduced to the possibility that an open universe can involve real distance between God and his creatures, a radical experience of separation and divine suffering caused by sin and eventuating in death and eternal destruction. If God's thoughtful, authoritative presence can indeed be removed from the lives of the wicked, what we are calling the hamartiological distance, and because sin is central to this distance and God's unspeakable suffering, it will help our study to look deeper into the origin and nature of the sin that creates such striking distance. We will then seek to clarify some implications of distance as we evaluate various passages of Scripture that point to God's knowledge of sin.

SATAN'S KINGDOM OF SIN AND DEATH

When Satan used the serpent to approach the woman in the garden, this incursion was the first act of war against God's good creation.[1] This strategic maneuver was Satan's attempt to gain ground after losing much in what can perhaps be described as a prehistoric battle over heaven and earth. We aren't aware of the extent of Satan's authority in Eden, but we cannot ignore the Creator's hand in permitting this evil presence into his good creation in the form of a serpent. We can be certain, however, that Yahweh's presence significantly limited this dark presence in the world. Only in a radically open universe might we posit that Satan was banished to a remote corner of the earth, isolated and unmonitored, only to use his distance away from Yahweh as a tactical advantage to invade the garden. Warfare is real in this world; Satan's attacks are not divinely controlled *or permitted* but are truly hostile.[2] Thus, the LORD can honestly say, "If anyone does attack you, it will not be my doing" (Isa 54:15).

It is highly unlikely that Satan's prehistoric domain, however limited it was, still extended to the tree in the garden or even to the garden itself. The text simply says that "the LORD God had planted a garden in the east, in Eden," and then quite generically, "in the middle of the garden were the tree of life and the tree of the knowledge of good and evil" (Gen 2:8, 9). The authority over all aspects of the earth, the garden and everything in it, were not granted to Lucifer but to humanity to both rule and protect this new environment (cf. 1:26, 28; 2:15). In fact, didn't God have the serpent in mind when he charged Adam/humanity to "[rule] over all the creatures that move along the ground" (1:26) and then reiterated the same responsibility in Gen 1:28?

We can speculate that before Satan's fall he was granted authority over the whole world, much like Adam's charge over the "new" creation.[3] When

---

1. Wis 2:24 makes the very first association of the serpent with Satan. Some have described the serpent as supraterrestrial.

2. Warfare between God and Satan can only be real if the threat is real. Satan's dominion has always presented a real threat to God, evidenced by Yahweh's later reaction to the "kingdom" that humans were building on a plain in Shinar, later named Babel: "But the LORD came down to look at the city and the tower the people were building. 'Look!' he said. 'The people are united, and they all speak the same language. After this, nothing they set out to do will be impossible for them!'" (Gen 11:5–6 NLT). Yahweh is clearly concerned that humanity could seize power that would elevate the threat.

3. Some scholars propose that the "chaos" and the formless, void, and dark conditions of the world in Gen 1:2 provide a glimpse into the earth's conditions *after* Satan's fall. Proponents of this "gap theory" speculate that there were two creations, one for the angelic community in Gen 1:1 and another for human beings after the angelic conflict in Gen 1:2, when the earth *became* formless and empty. Some passages to consider

God created the heavens and the earth, Satan still roamed about freely and eventually ended up in the garden. It appears he was aware in Eden that his freedom was irrevocable for the time being and that the duration of that freedom would continue until a future, undisclosed time. Although an historical, irrevocable freedom is evident from the fact that Satan hadn't yet been imprisoned, there remains a future sentence to be carried out against him at the end of the age (Matt 25:41). When he invaded the garden, Satan took full advantage of Adam's epistemic distance from God, even inciting humanity's emancipation from their Creator, which seems central to the woman's lust for knowledge. She wanted to be "like God" instead of dependent on him, a knowledge that she interpreted as independence (Gen 3:5).

Adam and his wife sought to accelerate their conformity to godliness by taking over their own sanctification through emancipation. What could have motivated this rebellion? What was it about that *tree of knowing good and evil* that so tempted them? They were already vice-regents over the creation, ruling in God's place. To know good and evil didn't imply they were previously devoid of a conscience, nor could it have meant they couldn't already exercise moral judgments. God had already empowered them to make ethical decisions and to display utmost discernment and care over his creation. Even pride doesn't appear to have been the primary motivation. Rather, the temptation of a new wisdom meant *being more like God* than they already were, having already been made in his image. It meant emancipation from God's ruling hand, ultimately replacing the need for divine presence and guidance in their lives. It was emancipation from the manifest presence of Yahweh! They replaced the Edenic presence of God with the illusion that they themselves would be a god present in the world.

Regarding the tree of the knowledge of good and evil, Gerhard Von Rad remarks that eating its fruit includes "knowledge of all things and the attainment of mastery over all things and secrets, for here good and evil is not to be understood one-sidedly in a moral sense, but as meaning 'all things.' By endeavoring to enlarge his being on the godward side, and seeking a godlike intensification of his life beyond his creaturely limitations, . . . man stepped out from the simplicity of obedience to God."[4] Tragically, humanity's self-centered pursuit of godliness resulted instead in their mortality and death, the exact opposite of Satan's promise that Adam and the woman would be living gods renewed in knowledge.

---

include Isa 14:12–20; 45:18; Jer 4:23; Ezek 28:11–19 (esp. v. 13, "You were in Eden, the garden of God"). This view seems to add too much modern sophistication to an otherwise primitive text. In defense of the gap (or restoration) theory, see Boyd, *Satan and the Problem of Evil*, 313–17; and Boyd, *God at War*, 100–113.

4. Von Rad, *Old Testament Theology*, 155.

Naturally there was a considerable distance between God and Satan after Satan's fall. This was implied in Yahweh's words to this evil creature at the celestial council in Job 1:7, where God asked him, "Where have you come from?"[5] The adversary's presence at the council was at least unusual, if not unexpected, so God requested a report on the independent activities of a rogue angelic agent. More than that, God's question reflects the possibility of hamartiological distance between him and Satan. Satan no longer yielded to the Lord of Hosts as his Creator and King, which is implied in Satan's actions, carrying out his own marching orders throughout the earth. When Satan absconded from a divinely authorized path of angelic activity, the subsequent distance extended throughout their relationship, a hamartiological distance.

Although the question of Satan's whereabouts may have been purely rhetorical, it nonetheless alludes to the distance first experienced by Adam when God asked him, "Where are you?" Scripture then says, "Satan went out from the presence of the Lord" (Job 1:12). Satan exited the divine presence and returned to his godless path! What is more telling is that once this adversary again returns to God's presence, Yahweh asks him the very same question: "And the Lord said to Satan, 'Where have you come from?'" (2:2). Satan continues to act independently of the Lord! And once again, "Satan went out from the presence of the Lord" (2:7).

Based on personal experience, Satan would have known that rebellion would result in an unexpected distance between humans and their Maker. Satan's attack was another tactical maneuver designed not only to remove Adam and the woman from fellowship with God, but also to create the possibility for people to experience hamartiological distance. This distance was necessitated by deathful sin, on the one hand, and by the faithful holiness of God on the other. God's holiness is the guardian attribute over the love and fellowship he shares with his creatures. Just as Satan had been cast out of heaven and away from the immediate presence of God (cf. Isa 14:12; Luke

---

5. Boyd argues that the adversary (*the satan*) in Job is an evil figure and not an angel in good standing. He says, "Some distinction between the 'sons of God' who regularly form God's council and the *satan* seems to be implied here." When Yahweh questions the adversary's whereabouts, Boyd suggests "it is natural to read in this an element of surprise on Yahweh's part, and an uncontrolled dimension to the *satan's* activity." Moreover, the adversary's questions about Job "reflect no concern for the genuineness of Job's piety." Rather, he "is calling into question Yahweh's wisdom in the way he orders his creation." Boyd continues, "There is something sinister about the eagerness of the *satan* to destroy Job.... This does not appear to be an angel who is simply intent on following God's orders. When he carries out his own destructive desires, he clearly does it with excessive thoroughness (1:13–19; 2:7–8)" (*God at War*, 146–47, emphasis original throughout).

10:18), so after Eden both Satan *and* humankind were distanced from God's thoughtful presence and pleasure.

Later, the prophet Isaiah would reflect on just how much humanity's stubbornly sinful ways separate them from a holy God: "But your iniquities have separated you from your God; your sins have hidden his face from you, so that he will not hear. . . . Our offenses are ever with us, and we acknowledge our iniquities: rebellion and treachery against the LORD, turning our backs on our God, inciting revolt and oppression, uttering lies our hearts have conceived" (Isa 59:2, 12–13). Those Israelites not only separated themselves from God but also followed faithfully in the footsteps of the serpent who previously *incited revolt and oppression*. They too were now *uttering lies* like Satan, "a liar and the father of lies" (John 8:44). Yahweh also said to Isaiah, "I was enraged by their sinful greed; I punished them, and hid my face in anger, yet they kept on in their willful ways" (Isa 57:17; cf. 1:5). As with Satan, even after rebellion drives people away from the divine presence and they begin to feel its harsh consequences, they nonetheless continue along the same self-destructive path. Moreover, when Satan and Israel preach revolt and emancipation, it never ends with freedom but always ends under Satan's rule.

Through that crafty serpent, Satan introduced humanity to his own kingdom of sin and death, a kingdom of demonic authority and presence. When the woman chose the competing wisdom of the serpent and his "crafty" logic (Gen 3:1), she exalted the authority behind his words and person over and against Yahweh God. In this way, she ultimately chose the presence (i.e., relationship) of an other-than-God. Not only did the serpent promise the woman she would *know* something new, but he also went so far as to imply that she would *become* something new, being "like God." Even her eyes would become something new and would "open" up! In this process of becoming, the change essentially involved relocation from one kingdom to another, which Col 1:13 calls the kingdom or "dominion of darkness." Satan never elaborated on the details of his alternate kingdom, and he certainly didn't mention that the woman would not reign in this kingdom in the way she had imagined. He also failed to mention that in this alternate kingdom, he would be the one reigning over her! As far as the woman was concerned, she would be emancipated and free. The tragic irony was that, in the end, she was ruled by the creation instead of ruling over it.

When people reject divine authority, they're ushered out of the kingdom of light and into this domain of darkness. In Satan's oppressive realm, he enters into relationship with sinners more personally than even God can know them. Because divine knowledge is always relational, God cannot familiarize himself with sin or sinner. Jesus said it like this: "You belong to your father, the devil, and you want to carry out your father's desires" (John 8:44). In the process of withdrawing one's self from God's thoughtful reveries, they instead consume Satan's thoughts as he works within them (Eph 2:2). So it could be said of that person that "Satan has so filled your heart" (Acts 5:3) or that "Satan entered into him" (John 13:27). It could also be said that Satan would stand at their right hand, representing a close relationship: "Let Satan stand at his right hand" (Ps 109:6 KJV). Anyone who can assist Satan in his mission becomes a priority. Thus, John warns us, "Do not be like Cain, who belonged to the evil one" (1 John 3:12).

Satan has always been obsessed with destroying the King of humanity's kingdom while using people to do it. He deceived Adam and the woman by masking the lethalness of their sin, luring all of humanity into his own deceitful kingdom. The human race is now blatantly aware of the heinous consequences of the deception because we certainly aren't ruling as gods over kingdoms. Instead, humankind has inherited an oppressive kingdom of misery and death. The realm of sin is the kingdom of Satan, so everyone who sins must be redeemed from the presence and power of that kingdom.[6]

A greater tragedy of this warped kingdom is the effects it has on the rest of creation. In a radically open universe, the utter darkness of sin results in pockets of divine absence throughout the cosmos, as with Sodom and Gomorrah. Such darkness cannot be separated from Satan and his sinful kingdom. Satan's kingdom is exalted in those *godless regions of undisturbed evil*. The godless regions are analogous to the desolate and waste places we see throughout Scripture. They eventually become regions of waste and loss because of the wickedness of their inhabitants: "All its land is brimstone and salt, a burning waste, unsown and unproductive, and no grass grows in it, like the overthrow of Sodom and Gomorrah, Admah and Zeboiim, which the LORD overthrew in His anger and in His wrath" (Deut 29:23 NASB).[7] In the end, all such kingdoms will be destroyed. Yahweh himself declares, "Surely the eyes of the Sovereign LORD are on the sinful kingdom. I will destroy it from the face of the earth" (Amos 9:8).

---

6. Regarding that redemption, the hope for victory over the adversary is found early on in Genesis 3. According to James Payton, "The emphasis is not on curse but on grace to the undeserving.... Even though [Adam and the woman] would die (Gen 3:19), God would not leave his image-bearers in the serpent's thralldom: God promised a deliverer who would ultimately destroy the work of the serpent (Gen 3:15)" (*Light from the Christian East*, 110). I would add that God ultimately overcomes sin and death by a cosmic victory that includes defeat of the serpent, the "god of this world" (2 Cor 4:4). This cosmos-encompassing, sin-defeating victory occurred at the cross and through the resurrection of the Lord Jesus, the subject matter of chapter 6.

7. Regarding the godless regions of undisturbed evil, see Job 12:23–25; 15:27–28; Ps 69:25; Isa 33:8; 34:10; Jer 12:10; Ezek 15:8; 36:4; Joel 3:19; Mic 7:13.

EVIL'S ORIGIN AND THE COMPETING KNOWLEDGE OF SIN

Not only did sin bring about a false sense of independence from God, but it also created a competing knowledge against divine understanding. Once the first people ate from the tree of knowing good and evil and seized upon that new knowledge, the new mind necessarily competed with and even challenged God's knowledge. Adam and his wife essentially had the choice between "the mind of Christ" (1 Cor 2:16) and the "carnal mind" (Rom 8:7 KJV), and they chose the latter. The carnal mind is totally contrary to the mind of God. The deadly sin that resulted arose out of the neutral seat of the will that God had created within them, a clean slate so to speak. And not merely a clean slate but a slate engraved with God's goodness and the goodness of his creation. The will is an empty vessel waiting to be filled, so God filled it with everything needed for healthy self-esteem and mutual respect, including authority to rule, the love of relationship, and yes, even freedom for maximum enjoyment of life.

Perhaps Satan could have tempted Adam for an eternity without affect, and Adam could have continued to internally entertain that thought forever. But once Adam *acted* on the temptation and ate the fruit, sin entered and a knowledge was acquired that God intended to remain outside the heart, the knowledge of everything good and evil, a knowledge no longer filtered through the divine presence. This was the first time humanity saw the world without receiving that information through their wise Creator. But God was not to blame! Yahweh is responsible for their choice only as the author of true freedom for both humans and angels. He created the human capacity for choosing evil but not the underlying lust toward it. The potential for lust arises out of the misuse and abuse of that freedom. This is a mystery in evil's origin.

Yahweh's creation was good, as was all that he created. He is not the author of evil nor can he tempt anyone to sin (Jas 1:13). There is absolutely no darkness in the divine nature (1 John 1:5) and "no wickedness in him" (Ps 92:15; cf. Deut. 32:4). Sin could not originate with God but solely within the will of human beings.[8] Reformed scholar Henry Bavinck provides a helpful summary on the mysterious origin of sin, writing, "*God most certainly created human beings to be capable of sin; he willed the possibility of sin. How that possibility became a reality is, however, a mystery. Sin defies explanation; it is a folly that does not have an origin in the true sense of the word, only a*

---

8. Anselm, *Cur Deus Homo* 2.2.

*beginning."*⁹ In another place Bavinck adds that *"because in its own existence it has no real right to exist, sin is a riddle, a mystery."*¹⁰

Because we know that the Creator of all things is perfectly good, holy, and loving, and desires only the highest and best for humanity, the true origin of sin is almost impossible to explain. Because we are bewildered by its mystery, it's tempting to posit at least by analogy the self-creation of sin, which we must nonetheless reject for a number of reasons. First, sovereign creative power does not exist outside the will of God, which is sufficient enough to explain it away. Second, Scripture never suggests sin is a quantitative substance or anything consisting of *stuff* that could be created. For sin to have its own stuff would require a creator, and Yahweh certainly did not create it. To no avail we resign ourselves to the somber reality that sin and death exist, but we have no grasp of it whatsoever, except for the single hint of a crooked evil that lingered around an ancient slithering serpent. Hence, we turn our attention to Satan and that mysterious serpent that lurked in the garden. Gerald Bray concedes that "the evil we experience is not self-generated but has been brought upon us by Satan, who has seduced us into joining his rebellion."[11]

In light of Satan's role in all this, perhaps sin is the *uncreated privation* of God's created good, a startling result of Satan's seduction. God could not have created or authored sin, but sin strangely resembles a perverted distortion of the freewill he did create. Again, Bavinck provides some helpful comments: *"Christian theology has always rejected all substantive notions of sin. Sin as a no-thing can only be a privation or corruption of the good. The idea of sin as privation, however, is incomplete; sin is also an active, corrupting, destructive power."*[12] Fiddes adds that God allowed

> something strange and alien to emerge from God's own creation. There is something that God has not planned, something to be confronted, something therefore to be suffered. . . . the implication not always drawn is that if evil issues from creation through the freewill of the creatures, it is something that *happens* to God; it *befalls* God. The Creator does not make it, and so has to endure it. God takes the risk in creation that non-being will emerge, and suffers its impact.[13]

---

9. Bavinck, *Reformed Dogmatics*, 3:28, emphasis original.

10. Ibid., 3:126, emphasis original. Regarding sin as mystery in variety, see ibid., 3:145–46.

11. Bray, *God is Love*, 345.

12. Bavinck, *Reformed Dogmatics*, 3:126, emphasis original.

13. Fiddes, *Participating in God*, 166, emphasis original.

Sin is not a substance or entity but both a privation and a destructive power. We acknowledge that sin arose not by God's creative authorship but out of the freewill decisions of both Satan and humanity. Even though its origin remains a mystery, if nothing else we can confidently affirm that God is not the author of sin and evil but in fact suffers because of it. God suffers the existence and distance of sin.

Prior to the fall, the Creator fellowshipped with that innocent couple and shared his perfect, holy knowledge with them, a knowledge full of wisdom and truth. In turn they shared their knowledge with him, which must have brought great pleasure and enjoyment to their relationship. This fellowship of shared knowledge was not the knowledge of the good-evil but the knowledge of God all-in-all. The Creator experienced Adam's knowledge and creativity firsthand. He experienced the thrill of hearing Adam conceive and *create* a dimension of newness to the divine creation when Adam named the animals, an experience that was new even to God. Yahweh eagerly stood by to "see what [the man] would name them" (Gen 2:19). Experiencing this extraordinary event must have filled God with joy and anticipation as he listened and watched his own creature involved in an act of creating! In naming the animals, Adam exercised authority over them while also exercising his creative potential. Even after such wonderful exchanges of creative imagination, while experiencing a relationship with his Creator on so many levels, the man and woman still exchanged God's inspiring knowledge for the pseudo-wisdom of a *crafty* serpent. Rather than pursuing the glory of God to bridge the gap of epistemic distance, they extended that distance and lost their way in an otherwise good creation.

After the man and woman ate of the fruit and sin was realized, the Godhead observed, "The man has now become like one of us, knowing good and evil" (Gen 3:22). For humankind, the issue of the carnal mind and its carnal knowledge was not merely knowing or distinguishing between good and evil, but it was also internally permitting, knowing, and adopting evil into the fundamental mind of the inner person. Ever since the fall, the knowledge of evil flows over into humanity's knowledge of good, leaving all hope of a pure, ethical goodness in the dust. Rather than a person's knowledge flowing directly from God's presence, as it did before the fall, good and evil are now filtered through a mortal mind. Just as the fruit was eaten and internalized, so humans have accepted and internalized the deepest possible knowledge of sin, owning it as the basis and drive behind every thought.

Shortly after the fall, it could be said that the thoughts and deeds of all people were "only evil all the time" (Gen 6:5). The human nature is now wholly informed by sin; now the fleshly, perishable, mortal nature is the location "where sinful passions are aroused."[14] Adam and the woman chose to replace divine knowledge of the world and themselves with a knowledge made up of evil as well as good. Their sin involved not merely an act of disobedience in eating the fruit but an intrinsically acquired knowledge of evil that embedded itself within their world and would now find expression through their mortal nature.

The devastation to Yahweh's good creation was so great because sin—a death-filled sin—became the separation God had promised when he assured the first humans they would die. This deathful sin reacts with such tainted distortion to the divinely good creation that it becomes a virtual blinding agent to the "eyes" of God. Among the greatest tragedies of all human history is that God suffers because of sin. On the day Adam ate, the separation and distance of death was realized, deathful sin corrupted the creation, and the hamartiological distance became a new, dark reality. This awful idea of sin originated with Satan, which is about as far as our theological reflection can take us.

THE UNPREDICTABLE NATURE OF SIN

There are two levels of choices people must make when confronted with temptation, which are often collapsed into one. The first is the choice to sin, and the second is the choice to hide. The first man Adam is evidence of this. As with Adam, people voluntarily and willingly remove themselves from under God's watchful and protective care, severing not just some but every intimate tie. The pattern is simple: A person sins and hides himself from God, but God comes looking and aggressively pursuing. Jesus succinctly describes God's pursuit when he says, "Suppose one of you has a hundred sheep and loses one of them. Doesn't he leave the ninety-nine in the open country and go after the lost sheep until he finds it?" (Luke 15:4). This parable reveals the heart of God! Just as we would pursue something precious to us, how much more does the heavenly Father? Despite God's aggressive pursuit, many choose to embrace the distance and stay in hiding. Even though guilt and the conviction of sin warn them of distance, they ignore the warnings because at its core, sin is profoundly irrational. One might say, sin is *deadly* irrational, overwhelmingly so.

Paul summarizes the irrationality of sin like this: "I do not understand what I do. For what I want to do I do not do, but what I hate I do. . . . As it is, it is no longer I myself who do it, but it is sin living in me" (Rom 7:15, 17). Without entertaining a debate over Paul's view of sin in Romans 7, I

---

14. Beck, *Slavery of Death*, 9. See Romans 7–8.

want us to consider just one implication: When human beings act contrary to what they desire, they are experiencing the unpredictable nature of sin. It's a puzzling statement for Paul to suggest that he was no longer the one committing the act, saying "it is sin living in me," but it illustrates the point. If in some sense the individual ceases to act and sin takes over, the dictates of sin prove to be unpredictable. Perhaps Paul is simply saying that sin has introduced a powerful influence over humanity, which may be the case, but that influence has dramatically changed the original, pure, and even predictable intent God created people to possess.

The quality of unpredictability is always relative and not at all limited to sin but is also a feature of goodness and innocence. Before the fall, Adam's innocence involved predictability in the sphere of doing good, but that predictability did not negate creativity, imagination, and novelty. Because the predictability of Adam's innocence was not boring or lacking in creative beauty, it was relatively unpredictable in its expression. Good is in essence predictable but quite varied in its expressions. Adam lived within the predictable sphere of creative love and every joyful novelty one can imagine in the Edenic paradise. Even though this man's creative imagination was a joyfully welcomed experience for the Creator, sin and death replaced unpredictable beauty with the manipulation and deceitfulness of a divided heart. The deceitfulness of sin marred the beauty of humankind's predictable love.

The beauty of Adam's spontaneous imagination degraded into the sphere of impulsive corruption, yet God knew the risk he was taking in granting his creatures unrestricted creative freedom. Fiddes comments that "when evil is defined as non-being it emerges from God's creation through creaturely freewill, as something strange to God.... In the humble act of creation, God freely chooses to be open to the hurt that will befall, *with its unpredictability. God willingly faces something unknown and alien on the journey of love for the sake of creation*."[15] Because God faces something alien and unknown in the face of evil, is it possible that sin is not only irrational and impulsive to people but also unpredictable to God? What if sin created a situation within human nature that is at times unpredictable and even unknowable to the divine gaze?

Per openness theology, a person's future choices are somewhat unpredictable due to libertarian freedom, the ability to choose between alternatives without being bound even to one's personal desire. Moreover, if every choice a person makes limits his future choices, there still exists a wide range of rebellious decisions to be made. Due to the absurd and irrational nature of sin, free choices can be considerably unpredictable. Nonetheless,

---

15. Fiddes, *Participating in God*, 175–76, emphasis added.

the unpredictable nature of sin certainly doesn't keep the Almighty from predicting the full range of a person's *possible* choices and actions, something God is always prepared for in advance. God doesn't always expect the decisions and paths people take, but he remains hopeful for good or better things. God, who is love, always hopes (1 Cor 13:7)! Even so, a person's choices, especially choices rooted in sin, can at times surprise God or stir deep regret. We would be naive to think God is ever caught off guard or without an appropriate response, but he can be disappointed or even shocked by the choices people make.

The unpredictability of sin led to God's deep regret over creating human beings (Gen 6:6). It led to God changing his mind about Eli's family ministering before him. The language there is even as strong as God going back on his promise: "Therefore the Lord, the God of Israel, declares: 'I promised that members of your family would minister before me forever.' But now the Lord declares: 'Far be it from me! Those who honor me I will honor, but those who despise me will be disdained'" (1 Sam 2:30). Sin's unpredictability also led to God expressing grief and sorrow over making Saul king (15:11, 35). It led to God believing that Israel would repent even though she didn't (Jer 3:7). It led even to Christ choosing a disciple who would ultimately betray him (John 13:2).[16]

One could argue that it was human freedom that led to God's regret in each of these examples. True enough, but sin adds still another layer of unpredictability. When God personally experiences grief, regret, and even disappointment, the bewildering unpredictability of sin is a primary reason. In drastic situations, God can remove much of the unknowns by further investigating the matter, as with Sodom. But even after a full investigation, our wise and holy God falls short of exhaustive, definite knowledge because it's beyond the grasp of the divine nature to *know* sin. Habakkuk is familiar with this truth, declaring, "Your eyes are too pure to look on evil; you cannot tolerate wrongdoing" (Hab 1:13). But even if an exhaustive investigation of sin was possible, libertarian freedom guarantees a certain unpredictable future.

At its core the motivation behind sin is deceit, a lie that replaces God's truth with a false reality (Gen 3:1, 4–5; 1 Tim 2:14). This deceitfulness of sin and its irrational contradiction to the loving ways of God are what make it so impulsively manipulative. Foolishly, a person deceived by this darkness could themselves attempt to deceive even God! Time after time this was the

---

16. There is a question as to when Jesus knew that Judas was going to betray him, though John tells us he knew "from the beginning" (John 6:64). It is likely Jesus knew from the moment he chose Judas as a disciple, but he also likely sought Judas's repentance and redemption throughout their time together.

case in God's dealings with his people, even when he expected otherwise: "*I thought, 'After she has done all this, she will return to me.'* But she did not return, and her faithless sister Judah saw this.... But despite all this, her faithless sister Judah has never sincerely returned to me. *She has only pretended to be sorry.* I, the LORD, have spoken!" (Jer 3:7, 10 NLT, emphasis added). The deceived heart can be so convinced of its own cunning that it believes it can somehow pull one over on God! So God is left to grieve in disappointment while people walk away feeling vindicated that they've fooled him again.

Prior to the fall, God knew the thoughts of the man and his wife with flawless knowledge and clarity. He was aware of the "chaos" that existed in the world before they were created (Gen 1:2), and he even anticipated the deceptive environment that the serpent would introduce into their garden home (3:1). It follows that a good God would not set anyone up to fail, so he must have remained optimistic that the innocent couple would be victorious over temptation. But we know all too well that it wasn't long before that hope was utterly disappointed. Perhaps this is because a radically open universe keeps the door open for an ontological distance to exist between God and sin and even a degree of unpredictability and the unknown.

DIVINE OPTIMISM

When God created Adam and his wife, how could we deny that he intended anything less than to share the most personal relationship with them for all time? The loving triune fellowship created persons outside their circle to share in the beauty and bliss of an intimacy the Trinity alone had enjoyed for an eternity beforehand. God now pursues every human being with the vigilance of a lover who from the eternal past had been making preparations for his bride. Scripture describes the Spirit of the triune Oneness as yearning jealously for us (Jas 4:5). Yahweh will go to the greatest lengths to make a people his very own, to have a bride set apart solely to him and for him.

Our great God has always enjoyed the fellowship of a community of three distinct yet united persons, together experiencing the delightful wonder and newness of true love. Scripture declares that *God is love*, one of the only statements in Scripture on God's inherent being (1 John 4:16). God's love never grows old or becomes commonplace but always enjoys the heights of bliss and the nostalgia of what we think of as new love. Despite all that, the only way to honor divine love was to create beings who could derive their greatest pleasure from sharing in its supremacy. This was God's good pleasure. He wanted that relationship to be so personal that he embodied himself when he appeared to the man in the garden (Gen 2:15, 19; 3:8). When Yahweh took on a body, he made their interaction personal. He must have believed the man could derive the greatest benefit from enjoying a person-to-person relationship with a Creator who appeared in a consistent human form.

God not only created humanity innocent and good but also provided them with an ideal environment. He gave them such a satisfying, body-oriented relationship and such fulfilling responsibilities that he foresaw the *unlikelihood* that they would disobey him and fall into sin.[17] In light of other inspired passages of Scripture, this proposal is not only logical but biblical. The Creator's sentiment could have been much like his later attitude toward elect Israel. Under much less ideal circumstances than the nearly perfect conditions of Eden, God's thoughts toward Israel were optimistic: "Surely they are my people, children who will be true to me" (Isa 63:8). The LORD's tone resounds with optimism! Surely, surely, surely because they are my people, they will remain true and faithful. This optimism was of course disappointed. In Eden, God planted something pure within Adam and his wife, not unlike the new work he sought to produce in Israel, yet things didn't turn out as he had planned: "Yet I planted you a choice vine, wholly of pure seed. *How then have you turned degenerate and become a wild vine?*" (Jer 2:21 ESV, emphasis added). Yahweh's tone is one of confusion and frustration; he is perplexed that the good thing he initiated didn't grow into the beautiful vine he was expecting!

But what else could he have done? We could say that God had made preparations for his bride throughout the eternal past, so it wasn't for lack of trying. Yahweh solemnly declares, "What more was there to do for my vineyard, that I have not done in it? When I looked for it to yield grapes, why did it yield wild grapes?" (Isa 5:4 ESV). This is what we might call divinely perplexed. Why did this happen? How could this have possibly occurred? What else could I have possibly done that I didn't already do? God is saying

---

17. One might argue that in light of what philosophers describe as transworld depravity, what I am proposing here is improbable. Transworld depravity has been a popular topic among philosophers in the debate over whether God could have brought about the best of all possible worlds. The premise is that in whatever truly free world God could have created, humanity would inevitably sin. In terms of my proposal and the unlikelihood of sin in the garden, my response would be that the logic behind transworld depravity does not guarantee that our first parents would sin nor even their children or children's children. What it does properly highlight is that both the capacity and mystery of sin are real possibilities in any truly free world. For creatures to possess true libertarian freedom, God must remain open to the possibility of disobedience and be prepared for the worst. Even so, transworld depravity is not a necessity. Rather, it emphasizes the very real risk God had to take in creating a world of free creatures.

here that he did everything he could for the best possible outcome, but Israel still rebelled.

Working with such flawed creatures, the divine heart was always optimistic, expecting more from Adam and from Israel: "I myself said, 'How gladly would I treat you like my children and give you a pleasant land, the most beautiful inheritance of any nation.' *I thought you would call me 'Father' and not turn away from following me'"* (Jer 3:19, emphasis added). God reflects here upon the unexpected. I thought, I hoped, I was optimistic, but you let me down. How much more should this have been his expectation in Eden? Yet tragically there was not victory for Israel or in the garden. God saw that all of his creation was good, including the man and his freedom, yet the mysterious fall still occurred (Gen 1:31).[18]

God had embraced such optimism for humanity's future that he never pre-planned a place of punishment for potentially rebellious people but rather an "eternal fire prepared for the devil and his angels" (Matt 25:41). This is apparently plan B for those who reject the love of God and choose that fate. It was likely after Satan's fall that God prepared this eternal fire for him. Just as God anticipated humanity's victory, he may have had good reason to expect victory from his angels. Notice Gerald Bray's comments regarding Satan's fall: "Did God know when he created Satan that he would turn out this way? This is a question impossible to answer. By giving his angels freewill, God created the possibility of rebellion, but that can hardly have been his intention. The angels were meant to use their freewill to enjoy eternal fellowship with God."[19] Indeed, it's hard to believe God ever intended the fall of humans or angels.

After being warned, Adam must have known in no uncertain terms that death meant distance from God. Adam always had a choice; in fact, he wielded the power to distance God! He chose to eat the fruit, he chose to die, and he chose to accept a foreign knowledge that competes with and even replaces the knowledge of God. Adam's choice was irrational to say the least, though not unthinkable. God was prepared for the worst even though

---

18. One might argue that my proposal more resembles philosophical speculation than theological reflection. In response, it is only the classical foreknowledge position that would demand that God ordained the fall, based on presuppositions of divine knowledge. Scripture nowhere addresses the matter other than to inform readers that all God had made was in fact *good*. We should be able to assume that God's assessment was a metaphysical absolute—it really was good! The only thing that wasn't good was corrected, and God gave Adam a helpmate to bring about an even more ideal existence. If God is truly good, who himself is the very essence and definition of pure and perfect love, shouldn't our theological assumption be that God would give humans the advantage to remain without sin in an ideal relationship with him?

19. Bray, *God is Love*, 347.

he was expecting better;[20] nonetheless, something about sin led to an unexpected outcome. In a moment it became true that "the heart is deceitful above all things and beyond cure. Who can understand it?" (Jer 17:9). Sin was a foreign invader into humanity's innocence, adding to the soul a combination of the essentially absurd and irrational, resulting in the arbitrary and unpredictable nature of sin. It's an irrational, vulgar contradiction that lives within us. Even in their innocence, our first parents committed the first act of sin, acquiring at that moment a proclivity that is now the common experience of every member of the human race (Rom 5:12).[21] Their first sin brought about spiritual and physical death for all people universally because we all inevitably sin. The mortal nature is now forever inclined toward ungodliness.[22]

Pantheism, the belief that God is literally made up of everything and everything is God, must be rejected for the biblical description of sin and creation which are exclusively *not* God. The world is distinctly separate from the divine presence and as such exists outside God, while he takes note of all things. The sin-filled corruption of the mortal nature is foreign to the mind of God, so much so that people and nations can be depicted as *ungodly* (Pss 36:1; 43:1), the opposite of divine nature. This ungodliness is the undoing of the image of God in people.

The corruption of sin brought about a unique situation to the triune Godhead, who always existed in the company of perfect holiness. Yahweh wants to share that fellowship with his creatures, but it remains woven into the fabric of the universe that he cannot intimately know any ungodliness.

---

20. Being prepared for the worst, Rev 13:8 records that God's Son was slain from the foundation of the world (cf. Acts 2:23; 1 Pet 1:19–20). This translation is debatable, however. Most translations appear to follow the NASB: " . . . everyone whose name has not been written from the foundation of the world in the book of life of the Lamb who has been slain."

21. The discrepancies by scholars over the nature of sin go on and on. Some teach that the guilt deserving of eternal punishment is inherent in our nature at the moment of birth, while others teach that guilt is imputed after an age of accountability when the first intentional sin is committed. Still others would not use the language of sin-nature, as if sin were an entity, choosing instead to emphasize acts of sin. Some prefer to discuss our fallen state in terms of human nature, sin being our overall disposition. Still others prefer mortal nature, which is necessarily weak but not inherently sinful. Regardless, in our human or mortal nature, apart from the Holy Spirit, people are inclined to think and act contrary to the heart of our Creator. Pelagianism teaches that people can overcome sin through their own efforts, while the mainstream Christian position has always been that people require the overcoming grace of God's Spirit.

22. Ian McFarland summarizes the importance of distinguishing between sin and the fall, tracing the origins of the western doctrine of original sin; see "The Fall and Sin," 140–59.

Only after salvation can it be said of anyone, "But now that you know God—or rather are known by God" (Gal 4:9). God had previously "destroyed the world of ungodly people" and now awaits "the day of judgment, when ungodly people will be destroyed" and the ungod of creation is done away (2 Pet 2:5; 3:7 NLT). Until then, he remains at a strange distance, quite strange for One who only ever knew relationship.

IMPLICATIONS OF DISTANCE: GOD SEES, HEARS, AND KNOWS

Having looked at the origin of sin and distance, we'll clear up some implications of divine absence. Based on the groundwork from Genesis 18, God can eventually remove his presence, influence, and consideration from the wicked, the hamartiological distance. This doesn't mean that God is ignorant of the thoughts and plans of the wicked, only that the divine presence *can* withdraw at some point along their trajectory toward the second death.

Throughout the Old Testament's progress of revelation, there are numerous passages that affirm that God is constantly keeping his eye on the thoughts and deeds of the wicked. Although for a season they may feel like there aren't any consequences, no hurtful act will ultimately go without divine justice. If I were to suggest that God does not see or hear what the wicked are up to, there would be little difference between that and the multitude who have convinced themselves that they can get away with anything.

Wicked People Presume Divine Ignorance

There is a healthy sampling of passages from the Prophets, Psalms, and Wisdom literature that demonstrate the twisted perspective that God is ignorant of evil. This is a false projection arising from the aloofness of the wicked. For some, Yahweh never enters their thoughts; he's not an option in their self-made religion: "Will those who do evil never learn? They eat up my people like bread and wouldn't think of praying to God" (Ps 53:4 NLT). Others have deluded themselves into the comfort of believing there will be no consequences to their actions, that God is nothing more than a myth or possibly just too weak to carry out justice or avenge the suffering. As for the wicked, "He says to himself, 'God will never notice; he covers his face and never sees'" (10:11). "Yet they say to God, 'Leave us alone! We have no desire to know your ways'" (Job 21:14). "They say, 'How would God know? Does the Most High know anything?'" (Ps 73:11). "Yet you say, 'What does God know? Does he judge through such darkness?'" (Job 22:13).

Despite the foolishness of accusing God of being ignorant, uncaring, or incapable, God is always faithful to warn the wicked and rebellious. First Isaiah records this warning: "Woe to those who go to great depths to hide their plans from the LORD, who do their work in darkness and think, 'Who sees us? Who will know?'" (Isa 29:15). Second Isaiah resonates with the same message, saying, "You have trusted in your wickedness and have said, 'No one sees me.' Your wisdom and knowledge mislead you when you say to yourself, 'I am, and there is none besides me'" (47:10). Isaiah warns the people of their self-deception, ensuring that God does in fact see and know what they're up to. Inherent in this message is also the warning for them to see the error of their ways and repent. The psalmist speaks similarly and says, "When you did these things and I kept silent, you thought I was exactly like you [and didn't care]. But I now arraign you and set my accusations before you" (Ps 50:21). The wicked clearly project their own apathy upon the heart of God, but they will be held accountable.

Even so, the wicked are aware that justice is not always swift, which breeds even greater complacency, apathy, and indifference. They will eventually learn that their aloofness and smug disregard for the divine presence has not duped God. When Job spoke up to his friends, he offered a reasonable conclusion to God's elusiveness toward the wicked. Job said, "He may let them rest in a feeling of security, but his eyes are on their ways" (Job 24:23). Zephaniah too speaks conclusively for Yahweh when he says, "I will search with lanterns in Jerusalem's darkest corners to punish those who sit complacent in their sins. They think the LORD will do nothing to them, either good or bad" (Zeph 1:12 NLT). But Yahweh is not ignorant of humanity's wickedness, and their victims will get justice.

Righteous People Lament the Elusive Presence

The delay of divine retribution often leaves the people and prophets of God with the sense that God is not only distant or absent but has also abandoned justice altogether. Frequently we find this complaint, even a lamenting accusation against God's integrity in this area. No doubt born out of frustration and the impatience of mortality in the face of suffering, the prophets aren't shy about bringing their accusations before God. Habakkuk questions how there can be such violence, yet Yahweh seems to do nothing about it: "How long, LORD, must I call for help, but you do not listen? Or cry out to you, 'Violence!' but you do not save?" (Hab 1:2).

In the psalter we frequently find this charge brought against God. The psalmist beseeches Yahweh to see and remember the offense of the wicked as well as the suffering of the people, as if these things had slipped his mind: "Remember how the enemy has mocked you, Lord, how foolish people have reviled your name. . . . Rise up, O God, and defend your cause; remember how fools mock you all day long. Do not ignore the clamor of your adversaries, the uproar of your enemies, which rises continually" (Ps 74:18, 22–23). God is asked to see and remember, but he is also asked to hear, as if he's been aloof to the activities of the wicked as they afflict the righteous: "Don't you hear the uproar of your enemies? Don't you see that your arrogant enemies are rising up?" (83:2 NLT).

When the patience of the psalmist finally runs out, he demands justice and gives God the reason why: "Lord, it is time for you to act, for these evil people have violated your instructions" (Ps 119:126 NLT). Despite the fear or harshness we may detect in many of these prayers, pleas and groanings like this are ultimately uttered by a believing remnant. This remnant held on to the profound conviction that God can not only be sought after but actually found. Isaiah preaches this truth in the form of endorsing the faithfulness of even an elusive divine presence, while extending a warning to the people: "Seek the Lord while he may be found; call on him while he is near" (Isa 55:6).

The Lord Affirms His Knowledge

In general, we often elevate the proverbial tradition of the Hebrews and its poetic descriptions above clear narratives that imply that God is *not* always everywhere. We may read a pithy statement such as, "'Do not I fill heaven and earth?' declares the Lord" (Jer 23:24), and we instinctively elevate its interpretive value above other passages like Gen 18:33, which says, "When the Lord had finished his conversation with Abraham, he went on his way" (NLT). Unlike pithy, proverbial statements, it is narrative descriptions like this latter example that dominate the biblical material and emphasize a spatial limitation of God.[23] Nevertheless, we can't avoid those pithy statements that declare the knowledge and presence of God throughout a world of sinners. We'll briefly look at one such example.

Despite the frequent denial of the wicked, Yahweh emphatically declares to the prophets that he does indeed perceive their actions: "'Who can

---

23. See Gen 4:16; 11:5; 17:22; 18:21; Exod 11:4; 20:24; 25:8; Num 23:15; Deut 33:2; 2 Sam 7:6; 1 Kgs 19:11–12; Job 1:12; 2:7; Pss 9:11; 10:1; 74:2; 76:2; Isa 24:23; 37:14; Hos 11:9; Joel 3:17; Jonah 1:3, 10; Hab 3:3; Zech 8:3.

hide in secret places so that I cannot see them?' declares the LORD. 'Do not I fill (*malak*) heaven and earth?' declares the LORD" (Jer 23:24). This has been among the more popular passages in support of divine omnipresence. Jeremiah makes a twofold declaration, the second explaining the first. First, God does *see* the wicked who try to hide. Second, this is because God *fills* all of creation throughout the heavens and earth. Yahweh *sees* everywhere because he *fills* everything. What might this look like in an open universe? Since Yahweh fills everything, so to speak, must this refer to omnipresence? Or, is it possible Jeremiah is saying there's not a single place in all of creation that God cannot go to find those who try to hide?

This passage and others like it do not inevitably lead to the conclusion that God exhaustively sees all things and pervades all spaces at all times. For instance, even humanity is said to fill (*malak*) the earth (Gen 1:28; 9:1), as well as the fish who fill (*malak*) the sea (1:22; cf. Num 11:22; Ezek 47:10). It would be absurd to assume people fill every square inch of the earth or that fish exhaust the sea. Notice the prophet Habakkuk's remarks: "God came from Teman, the Holy One from Mount Paran. His glory covered the heavens and his praise filled (*malak*) the earth" (Hab 3:3; cf. 2:14). It's evident that God's glory is on display in the creation, so the praise that results from it is said to *fill* the earth, but only in the sense that people throughout the world are praising and honoring God. Likewise, when Jeremiah says that Yahweh fills heaven and earth in Jer 23:24, it's because the LORD has assured his prophets that no enemy can ultimately hide from his justice.

It has long been the comfort of the righteous remnant that God is watching the good and the evil with a view to eventually making all things right. The general assessment has been that God is taking note: "Surely he recognizes deceivers; and when he sees evil, does he not take note?" (Job 11:11). Beyond this general consensus, the LORD himself also frequently declares his attentiveness with a view to just judgment and to righting wrongs. Yahweh reinforced to the prophet Jeremiah that people can maintain their confidence that he is in fact watching: "My eyes are on all their ways; they are not hidden from me, nor is their sin concealed from my eyes" (Jer 16:17). Yahweh also said, "I have listened attentively, but they do not say what is right. None of them repent of their wickedness, saying, 'What have I done?'" (8:6).

As the LORD watches, he is not always elusive and difficult to lay hold of. He often actively watches people's actions while calling to them over and over again to repent and draw near to him: "Has this house, which bears my Name, become a den of robbers to you? But I have been watching! declares the LORD. . . . While you were doing all these things, declares the LORD, I spoke to you again and again, but you did not listen; I called you, but you did not answer" (Jer 7:11, 13). Isaiah shares the same perspective: "For I called but you did not answer, I spoke but you did not listen. You did evil in my sight and chose what displeases me" (Isa 65:12). The Lord is watching and he sees the evil that is done, but he repeatedly calls and is often met with a negative response. Knowing the Lord is watching, the people still choose contrary to his desires. A similar thought is echoed a few passages later in Isaiah: "So I also will choose harsh treatment for them and will bring on them what they dread. For when I called, no one answered, when I spoke, no one listened. They did evil in my sight and chose what displeases me" (66:4).

In stark contrast to the wicked, the Lord always keeps his eye on the righteous: "The Lord watches over all who love him, but all the wicked he will destroy" (Ps 145:20). The psalmist also testifies that Yahweh keeps watch over the deepest things of the heart, saying, "If we had forgotten the name of our God or spread out our hands to a foreign god, would not God have discovered it, since he knows the secrets of the heart?" (44:20–21; cf. Job 31:4). Yet quite remarkably, even the darker secrets of the heart and the common faults of believers do not distance us from Yahweh. The psalmist says, "You, God, know my folly; my guilt is not hidden from you" (Ps 69:5; cf. 17:3). This is a given, which also reinforces the idea that God can and does look upon sin to a certain degree. In fact, he even sees his people's unknown or unintentional sins; otherwise, the psalmist couldn't pray, "Forgive my hidden faults" (19:12). Being aware of our day-to-day follies, Yahweh graciously seeks to expose those thoughts and behaviors in order to keep his people close to him. The psalmist affirms that all our faults and failures are laid bare to the redemptive radiance of God's presence: "You have set our iniquities before you, our secret sins in the light of your presence" (90:8).

Despite God's best efforts to keep his people close, we know all too well the tragedy of Israel. As the Lord kept watch, there came a point when her sins totally consumed her righteous kingdom, turning the kingdom of God into a kingdom of sin: "'Surely the eyes of the Sovereign Lord are on the sinful kingdom. I will destroy it from the face of the earth. Yet I will not totally destroy the descendants of Jacob,' declares the Lord" (Amos 9:8). Even though God kept his eye on Israel for her highest good, he eventually had to destroy the sinful element within her.

The Prophets Know

God is not the only one who sees. The prophets frequently observe what the wicked are doing and present those deeds to the Lord. It appears here that the psalmist has observed visible acts when he says, "Lord, confuse the wicked, confound their words, for I see violence and strife in the city" (Ps 55:9). The psalmist also at times goes so far as to declare the *hidden* thoughts of the wicked, much like Yahweh does: "They encourage each other in evil plans, they talk about hiding their snares; they say, 'Who will see it?' They plot injustice and say, 'We have devised a perfect plan!' Surely the human mind and heart are cunning" (64:5–6; cf. 36:4). This is quite a remarkable observation for the hymn writer to describe the secret thoughts of the wicked in this way, yet we never once assume he possesses exhaustive knowledge. He can speak in generalities because actions naturally follow thoughtful planning. Without being omniscient, the psalmist often describes what's taking place within the hearts of evil people: "O Lord, rescue me from evil people. Protect me from those who are violent, those who plot evil *in their hearts* and stir up trouble all day long" (140:1–2 NLT, emphasis added). If frail mortals can declare the secret thoughts of people distant from them, how much more can Almighty God?

While both God and prophet are observing the wickedness around them, at times God alerts the prophets to particulars. There is a general understanding God gives his people, such as in the psalter: "I have a message from God in my heart concerning the sinfulness of the wicked: There is no fear of God before their eyes. In their own eyes they flatter themselves too much to detect or hate their sin" (Ps 36:1–2). For others, the Lord is more specific. Just as Yahweh had conducted an investigation in Sodom and Gomorrah to know the degree of evil that was there, he also asks his prophet to go and investigate: "And he said to me, 'Go in and see the wicked and detestable things they are doing here'" (Ezek 8:9). In another place, Yahweh is curious if the prophet is aware of the conduct of the leadership, so he brings this to the prophet's attention: "He said to me, 'Son of man, have you seen what the elders of Israel are doing in the darkness, each at the shrine of his own idol? They say, "The Lord does not see us; the Lord has forsaken the land"'" (8:12; cf. 11:2; 14:22).

It appears that Yahweh and his prophets can both be aware of the thoughts and deeds of the wicked, especially with a view to judgment (Jer 17:10; 32:19).

CONCLUSION

In our venture into a radically open universe, we have proposed a number of considerations for open theism. Although the essence of sin remains a mystery, our best efforts trace its origin back to Satan. More than anyone else, this rogue angelic agent played a crucial role in releasing evil's darkness into God's good creation. After experiencing his own separation from the Creator, he must have had some understanding of what distance would mean for the human race. Because Lucifer is truly free and his exploits cannot be blamed on a divine puppet master, his seductive influence brought about unexpected results. This creature's demonic kingdom has unleashed incalculable devastation upon the world, leaving dark pockets of hamartiological distance throughout the cosmos. I have described those areas as *godless regions of undisturbed evil*, like Sodom and Gomorrah.

When Adam and the woman gave in to temptation, they became slaves to Satan's oppressive kingdom of sin and death. Yahweh had hoped for better things from our first parents, just as he later expected more from his chosen people Israel. But despite God's perfect wisdom, the entrance of sin and death brought with them a sway over the human heart which was foreign to this creation. Thus, God experiences the unpredictable nature of sin, leaving him at times disappointed in humanity and regretful over his decisions.

After an overview on the nature and origin of sin and distance, we clarified some implications of distance and specifically what it's not. God is not ignorant and does not stand aloof to humankind's wrongdoing. Wicked people may presume they're getting away with something, but God takes note of all that is happening in the world. To a certain degree, Yahweh knows, sees, and hears what the wicked are up to but largely as a secondhand observer to their sin. The righteous grieve the elusive presence, but rest assured God is near and willing to respond. Yahweh gives his prophets insight, and they too make it a point to draw his attention to wrongdoing and injustice. Although the wicked misinterpret the longsuffering of the Lord, they will not escape his ultimate justice.

4

Covenant and Exile
Israel's Paradigm for Sin and Death

It has been quite a tragic portrayal investigating the depths of divine absence and the hamartiological distance. The godless regions of undisturbed evil sound more like something from a horror movie rather than a theology class. It's almost too dismal a topic to consider the possibility of such a deathly existence devoid of God's presence.

If openness theology finds a place for such a terrible doctrine, we may be tempted to conclude that such distance could never touch us and our spirituality, surely not our religious families, churches, or Christian heritage. We may resign the hamartiological distance to a few maliciously evil characters on the plain of history, such as a Hitler or Stalin. Nevertheless, the most vivid, historically longstanding portrayal of divine absence is found right in the middle of God's family with his daughter Israel. The biblical paradigm for hamartiological distance isn't most notably located among pagan nations, such as Sodom and Gomorrah, but with God's own chosen people. The best Old Testament illustration of distance is found in Israel's entry into the abyss of exile.[1]

COVENANTS OF DIVINE PRESENCE

As we investigate exile as Israel's paradigm of sin and death, we will first look briefly at the covenants of the Old Testament, which reveal God's commitment to defeat distance and promote his presence in the world. We will

1. Cf. Brueggemann, *Introduction to the Old Testament*, 268.

then turn our attention to Israel's failure to maintain covenant faithfulness and the resultant exile away from her land and temple. This is the national, historical picture of hamartiological distance.

Yahweh's Covenant with Noah

The worldwide devastation of the flood brought about the finality of death's distance to all the wicked people of the world. After the flood, even though people's hearts didn't change, God's dealings with them certainly did. Yahweh was determined to raise up a faithful remnant. Determined to remain faithful to his creation, he looked at his plan thus far. Perhaps he started by taking into account the expectations he had for humanity back in the garden. He would certainly have evaluated the downturn of wickedness and the utter devastation caused by his worldwide flood. But he then refused to go down that path again, deciding that a similar divine response would be too costly. Perhaps his conclusion wasn't so much in response to his judgment on the world but to the hope he found in one faithful man, Noah. Faithful Noah had become God's sole representative remnant:

> Then Noah built an altar to the LORD and, taking some of all the clean animals and clean birds, he sacrificed burnt offerings on it. The LORD smelled the pleasing aroma and said in his heart: "Never again will I curse the ground because of humans, even though every inclination of the human heart is evil from childhood. And never again will I destroy all living creatures, as I have done.... I establish my covenant with you: Never again will all life be destroyed by the waters of a flood; never again will there be a flood to destroy the earth." (Gen 8:20–21; 9:11)

Because of one man's faithfulness, a singular remnant voice, Yahweh looked down on mortal humanity and concluded that he would not give up on it, despite the distance caused by human thoughts being *evil from childhood*. This is one of many commitments God made with people in the form of a covenant.

An important nuance of the covenants is the reality that God holds himself accountable. Yahweh sought to reduce the worldwide distance by holding himself accountable to people, calling Noah out of the world and inviting him into a future full of hope and promise. Because the entire world would come through Noah's lineage, he represented the whole human race before God. The Noahic covenant meant that God made himself accountable to humankind in accordance with a visual reminder, the warfare *bow* of cascading colors that he had placed in the sky. The rainbow is forever a sign that Yahweh will not bring a similar warring devastation upon people again; he is not at war with creation but at war with distance. The formality of God's oath with Noah informs humanity that we too are privileged to hold him accountable.

Is it possible that, in light of the flood, Yahweh's experiment proved more devastating than he first imagined? Rather than allowing the distance to once again grow *ad infinitum*, he made a covenant with Noah and then later with Abram and his descendants. The covenants made with Noah, Abram, Moses, and David were all unilateral, promissory oaths, depending largely upon God's faithfulness rather than people. God would not destroy the earth but would remain committed to the betterment of people and their world.

Yahweh's Covenant with Abram

After his promise to Noah, God *cut a covenant* with Abram the Semite, promising salvation and blessing to the nations through this man's descendants.[2] God did not give up on the nations but offered to display to the world his faithful intentions toward an undeserving nation, Israel. He wanted to demonstrate fairness and justice toward that nation, exhibiting faithfulness by destroying the distance caused by the sinfulness of even those chosen vessels. The first four books of the Pentateuch tell the story of God's faithfulness to reduce the distance, presenting him in terms of Creator and Covenant-keeper.

"The LORD had said to Abram, 'Go from your country, your people and your father's household to the land I will show you. I will make you into a great nation, and I will bless you; I will make your name great, and you will be a blessing. I will bless those who bless you, and whoever curses you I will curse; and all peoples on earth will be blessed through you'" (Gen 12:1–3). "You will be a blessing" can also be translated as an imperative, *Be a blessing!* In other words, *Abram, follow me, reverse the distance, and be a blessing!* After Yahweh reiterated these promises in Genesis 15 and assured Abram that he would indeed bless him by giving him a land, we could say that Abram had the audacity to question Yahweh's faithfulness when he asked, "Sovereign LORD, how can I know that I will gain possession of it?" (15:8). Only an open-minded God would expect his creatures to engage him so forthrightly, even condescending to Abram to offer him the reassurance that

---

2. See Gen 3:15; 12:1–3; 13:14–17; 15:4–5; 17:4–8, 19; 18:18–19; 22:17–18; 26:3–4; 28:14–15; 35:12.

he sought. This early Genesis account teaches readers that Yahweh is a most approachable God.

The ritual of animal sacrifice that transpired gave Abram confidence that God would defeat Abram's enemies, a story line acted out as Abram chased away the "birds of prey" that came down on the carcasses (Gen 15:9–11). After falling into a deep sleep of "dreadful darkness" that likely represented the Hebrews' imminent slavery in Egypt, Yahweh verbally assured Abram of both deliverance and the punishment of their enemies (15:12–16). Finally, in a drama of epiphanic presence that consisted of a "smoking firepot with a blazing torch" passing through the animal carcasses, Abram was reassured that none other than God's presence would go with his people as they fought for the promised land (15:17). So it was that "on that day the LORD made a covenant with Abram" (15:18), a unilateral, promissory oath. This covenant was in the background of the Sodom cycle when Yahweh shared his plans with Abraham and listened to him, and so it was said that God *knew* him (18:19).

The essence of this covenant was an alliance consisting of Yahweh's promise that he would be present with Abram and his people. This was the first time in history that God made a promise of his presence, linking his presence to a people and a land. Any distance felt by this people in this land would also be felt and experienced by God in the most profound of ways. Yahweh volunteered to enter into solidarity with Abram's descendants, which meant his own vulnerability as a father to his new children. This new relationship is fleshed out throughout the prophetic books: "For the LORD has spoken: 'I reared children and brought them up, but they have rebelled against me'" (Isa 1:2). God himself had raised these children, so he had high hopes for them. Yet even with the best intentions and the very best efforts of a divine father, the children were still prone to rebel. Nonetheless, God had covenanted to be their father and ours.

Second Isaiah points to a divine empathy that motivates Israel's heavenly Father to deliver his people when they are suffering: "In all their distress he too was distressed, and the angel of his presence saved them" (Isa 63:9). It was quite literally the divine presence that delivered and eliminated the distance that came between God and his people. And why was this so? Zechariah tells us, "This is what the LORD Almighty says: 'I am very jealous for Zion; I am burning with jealousy for her'" (Zech 8:2). Because of God's heart as Creator and Covenant-keeper, he won't give up on his people. Notice the language Hosea uses to express this same thing: "How can I give you up, Ephraim? How can I hand you over, Israel? How can I treat you like Admah? How can I make you like Zeboyim? My heart is changed within me; all my compassion is aroused" (Hos 11:8). Truly their covenant-making, covenant-keeping God experienced the profoundly intimate depths of this covenant relationship with his people. Hosea goes so far as to say that God's "heart is changed" and his emotions stirred. This prophet was given insight into the very heart of God! Thus, Hosea can conclude on behalf of Yahweh, "I will not carry out my fierce anger, nor will I devastate Ephraim again. For I am God, and not a man—the Holy One among you. I will not come against their cities" (11:9). The prophet assures us that God would remain committed to his covenant people and never completely destroy them.

Regarding covenant, Lawrence Boadt observes, "Israel recognized that the covenant was a gift from Yahweh and an honor for them and not the other way around. God freely chose to bind himself to this people, but not blindly no matter what they did in return." Boadt continues, "Most of all, he will be present whether it is a time of prosperity or of failure, for he has laid claim to this people as his own."[3] The divine presence had never before been so intimately involved with any people group upon the earth, which changed the moment Yahweh called Abram. This partiality of divine presence was at the heart of Yahweh's covenant with the patriarchs. The hymn writer understood this when he spoke of God's commitment, saying, "He has revealed his word to Jacob, his laws and decrees to Israel. He has done this for no other nation; they do not know his laws" (Ps 147:19–20; cf. Deut 4:7–8).

Even with God's undivided attention, the people would not comprehend the reality of divine presence as much as the reality of absence.[4] This was brought out very early in Israel's worship, even before a tabernacle was erected. We see it in the travels and worship of Jacob. Jacob dreamed of a stairway to heaven that revealed the angelic presence that would accompany him along his way, a presence that represented God's own. Scripture says, "When Jacob awoke from his sleep, he thought, 'Surely the LORD is in this place, and I was not aware of it.' He was afraid and said, 'How awesome is this place! This is none other than the house of God; this is the gate of heaven'" (Gen 28:16–17). Jacob was completely caught off guard by God's elusive presence! Not only was Jacob ignorant that God was at Bethel, but he also lacked a general awareness of an omnipresent deity. Scripture says that he was not aware of it! One might say that Jacob, whose name was later changed to Israel (35:10), represented a common ignorance of presence among the Israelites. Such ignorance would be perpetuated as long as the

---

3. Boadt, *Reading the Old Testament*, 175.

4. Terrien says as much: "For fifteen centuries the recurrent motif of divine nearness is historically limited to a few men. The sense of presence is persistently compounded with an awareness of absence" (*Elusive Presence*, 28–29).

divine presence was restricted to places and structures, whether altars, tents, temples, or Mount Zion.

Yahweh's Covenant with Moses

Yahweh had finalized an ultimate distance by the worldwide devastation of the flood and then the lesser devastation at Sodom. Even though this movement from worldwide to individual cities demonstrated a reduction in divine judgment and destruction, Yahweh still sought to further minimize the negative impact of distance by establishing a covenant with Abram, the father of nations. This covenant was quickly tested, as observed by Stephen the first martyr of the church. Stephen recounts how God responded to the cry of the Israelite people, similar to his response to the outcry that arose from Sodom and Gomorrah. Using heavily anthropomorphic language, Stephen relates God's history with the Hebrew man, Moses:

> "I have indeed *seen* the oppression of my people in Egypt. I have *heard* their groaning and have *come down* to set them free. Now come, I will send you back to Egypt." [Moses] was sent to be their ruler and deliverer *by God himself, through the angel* who appeared to him in the bush. . . . He was in the assembly in the wilderness, *with the angel who spoke to him* on Mount Sinai, . . . But our ancestors refused to obey him. Instead, they rejected him and in their hearts turned back to Egypt. They told Aaron, "Make us gods who will go before us. As for this fellow Moses who led us out of Egypt—we don't know what has happened to him!" . . . But God *turned away from them* and gave them over to the worship of the sun, moon and stars. (Acts 7:34–35, 38, 39–40, 42, emphasis added)

After 400 years of enslavement to Egypt, the groaning of Yahweh's covenant people captured his attention, so he looked down and *saw* and *heard* their outcry. He then decided to *come down*, first to appear to Moses and then to rescue his people. Then on Mount Sinai, because of the golden calf the people had made, there was an immediate test of the covenant renewal which Yahweh had initiated by presenting Moses with the Decalogue (or Ten Commandments). It was through this test that readers are introduced to the highly significant role of a covenant mediator. In the absence of Moses their mediator, the people assumed the absence of God and created their own gods to replace him.

Covenant holds God accountable but not without the help of a mediator who is acquainted with God's heart and understands the necessity of covenant faithfulness. In response to the golden calf, Yahweh fully intended to destroy all the people and fulfill his covenant promises through Moses alone. God went so far as to ask Moses to "leave me alone" so that his wrathful anger could "destroy them," knowing that if Moses failed to intervene, God indeed would have finalized their distance into death's abyss (Exod 32:9–10). But instead of destroying the people, the "whole world" of Israelites, Moses was able to persuade God to keep them alive: "Then the LORD relented and did not bring on his people the disaster he had threatened" (32:14). This was certainly not the last time Yahweh relented from destroying his people solely in response to a covenant mediator.[5]

Through covenant, Yahweh had taken his stand in human history to reduce the distance between him and the people of the earth. That distance involved more than sin and death, even the Hebrew notion of sickness and disease as encroaching forms of death: "He said, 'If you listen carefully to the LORD your God and do what is right in his eyes, if you pay attention to his commands and keep all his decrees, I will not bring on you any of the diseases I brought on the Egyptians, for I am the LORD, who heals you'" (Exod 15:26). In his discussion on covenant, Boadt captures this same sense: "God pledges himself to be Israel's personal protector and helper, not only against foreign enemies, but against sickness, disease, and chaos as well."[6] God sought to eliminate distance from every facet of life, promising to attach the presence of his anti-distance to a chosen people.

Under Moses, God provided the people with an elaborate system of law and priesthood. The priesthood was intended to subdue the distance through atoning sacrifice. This truth was symbolically transferred to temple worship and brought out especially in the categories of cleanness and uncleanness, particularly in the book of Leviticus (see chapters 1–7). Regarding uncleanness under Moses' law, T. D. Alexander writes that "people who willfully ignore God's commands, decrees, or laws are a source of uncleanness and defile all that they touch. *Their actions both distance them from God and bring them further under the domain of death.*"[7] To subdue such distance, the law was given in addition to the priesthood to outline God's expectations for his people and to provide descriptive warning of the consequences of disobedience, which was ultimately the distance of exile (Lev 26:14–46; Deut 28:15–68). Seeing that Israel's unfaithfulness could result in exile or even death, it was obvious God's temporal covenant faithfulness was not something to be taken for granted: "The LORD will also bring on

---

5. See Num 14:1–20; 16:16–27, 41–50; Deut 9:18–21.

6. Boadt, *Reading the Old Testament*, 175.

7. Alexander, *From Paradise to Promised Land*, 212, emphasis added.

you every kind of sickness and disaster not recorded in this Book of the Law, until you are destroyed.... Then the LORD will scatter you among all nations, from one end of the earth to the other" (Deut 28:61, 64). Despite God's desire to be their Healer, the chosen people always had the choice to distance him and bring disease and death upon themselves.

The law and the priesthood were means to help ensure the divine presence would remain within their nation. Moses maintained the firm conviction that Yahweh's presence must abide with the people for his promises to be fulfilled and for the Israelites to possess the land. Even though God had historically revealed himself in the form of an angel or messenger, during a conversation with Moses he distinguished between himself and the angel, saying, "I will send an angel before you and drive out the Canaanites, Amorites, Hittites, Perizzites, Hivites and Jebusites. Go up to the land flowing with milk and honey. But I will not go with you, because you are a stiff-necked people and I might destroy you on the way" (Exod 33:2-3). The open-mindedness of God becomes blatantly transparent in this passage. Yahweh voices genuine concern over the real possibility that he might become provoked and destroy the people along the way! Hence, there is a negative dimension of feeling and emotion to God's open heart.

Notice Israel's response: "When the people heard these distressing words, they began to mourn and no one put on any ornaments. For the LORD had said to Moses, 'Tell the Israelites, "You are a stiff-necked people. If I were to go with you even for a moment, I might destroy you"'" (Exod 33:4-5). They grieved over the possibility that God would send someone other than the divine presence to go with them. This response implied that it was in fact possible for a messenger other than God to accomplish a mission on his behalf, while God himself remained absent from the process altogether. Yahweh never once challenged this assumption! Yet he finally, if not grudgingly, submitted to Moses' request and reassured him with these words: "My presence will go with you, and I will give you rest" (33:14). Yet even after such confident reassurance, Moses still wasn't satisfied but reminded Yahweh of his ongoing concern: "Then Moses said to him, 'If your presence does not go with us, do not send us up from here'" (33:15).

In keeping covenant with an earthly people, Yahweh condescended to a not so ideal situation among the people, particularly tabernacle worship. Not only was this context restrictive of the divine presence but it also reeked of the stain of animal blood with its overtones of slaughter, death, and distance. The heart of God was in one sense misrepresented by a violent context, while the presence of God was closed off to a select few from among priests and Levites. Although Yahweh accepted the mutilated sacrifices of the tabernacle, his presence there was fleeting and obscure. Michael

Hundley comments, "The nature of his presence in his dwelling remains a mystery. His true form and location remain hidden. Although he presumably rests between the cherubim, his whereabouts between appearances are unclear. The ambulatory nature of the theophanic elements hints that he may come and go."[8] As long as the Israelites worshiped in portable tents or even in the temple Solomon later erected, God's presence would remain elusive and largely ambiguous.[9]

Yahweh's Covenant with David

This brings us to the Deuteronomist history and Israel's trajectory into exile. It is commonly recognized by scholars that the book of Deuteronomy and the Former Prophets (Joshua, Judges, Samuel, Kings) "stood as a *single literary piece* written from a *single interpretive angle* as a commentary upon the destruction of Jerusalem in 587 and as a meditation upon the ensuing crisis of exile."[10] The theological interpretation of history presented in these books tells the story of Israel's deliverance from Egypt only to end up on a trajectory into the abyss of exile. Israel's exile remains the most vivid historical analogy of hamartiological distance.

From the outset, the Deuteronomist identifies the crisis of presence and makes explicit Israel's choice between presence and absence: "See, I set before you today life and prosperity, death and destruction.... But if your heart turns away and you are not obedient, and if you are drawn away to bow down to other gods and worship them, I declare to you this day that you will certainly be destroyed. You will not live long in the land you are crossing the Jordan to enter and possess" (Deut 30:15, 17–18). It becomes apparent here that the intensity of God's warning has changed somewhat since the garden. The "certainly die" for Adam's disobedience is replaced with the more hostile, you will "certainly be destroyed."

During the premonarchical era, the primary point of contact for the divine presence—priest and prophet—was hindered by the corruption of those offices (e.g., 1 Sam 2:12–17, 22–25). The resultant situation for the nation is reflected in 1 Sam 3:1, which says, "In those days the word of the LORD was rare; there were not many visions." Although there were still a few people like Hannah and Samuel who were obedient to Yahweh and pursued

---

8. Hundley, *Keeping Heaven on Earth*, 50.

9. Regarding this transitory period in Israel's history, Terrien remarks, "The nomadic motif of movement through space emerges as a symbol of openness to the future" (*Elusive Presence*, 73).

10. Brueggemann, *Introduction to the Old Testament*, 104, emphasis original.

the promise of his presence, the corruption of those offices displayed a failed relationship with God that dramatically affected the nation. They stifled the divine presence and muffled the prophetic evidence of that presence.

Possibly the most dramatic analogy of God's absence in this time period came when the Philistines captured "the ark of the covenant of the LORD Almighty, who is enthroned between the cherubim" (1 Sam 4:4). If the ark was for all intents and purposes the location of God's enthronement, then it could be said that this vulgar Philistine army captured God! The evidence was that "the Israelites were defeated and every man fled to his tent" (4:10). By analogy, the sinful condition of Israel resulted in the loss and removal of God's presence. This scenario is reminiscent of Moses' concern that God's presence must always go with the people in order for them to remain in his rest. Moses knew that without the divine presence the result could only be defeat (Exod 33:12-17). Hence, God's presence could be *captured* and taken away from the nation when her sin welcomed defeat from physical and spiritual enemies, who in this case were the Philistines.

Within the corpus of Deuteronomist history, Yahweh introduced a further development to his everlasting covenant; namely, the addition of a king who would forever be enthroned. This was accomplished through God's everlasting covenant with King David and his descendants (2 Sam 7:10-16). Unlike the defeat the Israelites experienced at the hands of the Philistines and the loss of the Ark-presence of God, under this renewed covenant "wicked people will not oppress them anymore, . . . I will also give you rest from all your enemies" (7:10, 11). Contained in this covenant renewal was the promise of an eternal kingdom and the assurance of the king's presence with his people (7:16). This kingdom would be the royal sphere of the divine presence, a kingdom for the king's people, the children of Israel (7:10).

Once the Abrahamic, Sinaitic, and Davidic covenants were in place, God was covenanted to a people of the earth in a promissory relationship of longsuffering, faithful love. It wasn't that Yahweh hadn't always possessed the virtue of such persevering love, but now the nations would see it uniquely on display through the Hebrew people. God's presence in the world became connected to and known through a particular people and a particular place: first the patriarchal prophets, then his judges, then his kings and the tabernacle of Zion, and finally through all the prophets of Israel. In a particular place among a particular people, God made his name known and manifested his glory. Although it's strange to think the divine presence could be restricted to a temple or land (2 Sam 7:6), Yahweh nonetheless limited his presence by making Israel his primary point of contact to the world (1 Kgs 8:59-60).

Deuteronomy and the Former Prophets provide a detailed explanation of Israel's exile, demonstrating that the reason for exile was Israel's sin and her failure to maintain covenant faithfulness as outlined in God's law (Deut 28:15–68). Despite Israel's failure, however, the covenants were working to reduce the distance: "But the LORD was gracious to them and had compassion and showed concern for them because of his covenant with Abraham, Isaac and Jacob. To this day he has been unwilling to destroy them or banish them from his presence" (2 Kgs 13:23).

THE LATTER PROPHETS AND THE ABYSS OF EXILE

The Assyrian captivity in 722 BC and Israel's exile to Babylon in 587 BC stand together as history's most graphic, long term analogy of death and the hamartiological distance. The prophets spoke to both northern and southern kingdoms. During the Babylonian Age, Jeremiah described the horrific situation with Judah in the north: "And there at Riblah, in the land of Hamath, the king of Babylon had them all put to death. So the people of Judah were sent into exile from their land" (Jer 52:27 NLT). Because of unfaithfulness to the covenants, the people of Judah found themselves on a trajectory of distance, resulting in death and exile. The conditions of exile were dreadfully grim, reversing the blessing of presence that God sought to share with the world through this nation. But as horrible an experience as the Babylonian invasion was, Yahweh declared to Judah that the distance of death was preferable to the conditions of exile: "Wherever I banish them, all the survivors of this evil nation will prefer death to life, declares the LORD Almighty" (8:3).

The covenant people were meant to enjoy the land of promise under the personal arm of divine presence, being a light to the world rather than defeated by darkness. Even though Israel's land and temple were intended to be headquarters for displaying God's presence to the world, God sadly had this to say of his people: "See how all of you are following the stubbornness of your evil hearts instead of obeying me. So I will throw you out of this land into a land neither you nor your ancestors have known, and there you will serve other gods day and night, for I will show you no favor" (Jer 16:12–13). The language of distance is undeniable. Exile meant casting the people of promise out of and away from the national perimeter of God's presence, power, and privilege.

Despite Israel's rebellion and ongoing discipline and distance, Yahweh continually warned his people, saying, "Take warning, Jerusalem, or I will turn away from you and make your land desolate so no one can live in it" (Jer 6:8). In the Hebrew, "I will turn away from you" is literally the anthropomorphic phrase, *lest my soul departs from you*, where God is said to have a soul that can abandon the people! In this passage, the crisis of divine presence causes the land's desolation. This theme is present throughout Jeremiah: "When the Lord could no longer endure your wicked actions and the detestable things you did, your land became a curse and a desolate waste without inhabitants, as it is today" (44:22).

The land was representative of Yahweh's presence on earth. Just as Yahweh abandoned the land, so the people were forced to leave the place that once reflected his presence: "'No one will live in it; both people and animals will flee away.... As I overthrew Sodom and Gomorrah along with their neighboring towns,' declares the Lord, 'so no one will live there; no people will dwell in it'" (Jer 50:3, 40). The land and temple were abandoned without any trace of God's favorable presence, much like Sodom and Gomorrah before her. Symbolically, the heart of God was so affected by this that the very center of his presence, the sanctuary, was no longer a place of God-presence but a place of false-God-presence: "She saw pagan nations enter her sanctuary—those you had forbidden to enter your assembly" (Lam 1:10).

Notice the strong language used throughout Jeremiah of this crisis of presence in the face of exile:[11]

> I will thrust you from my presence, just as I did all your fellow Israelites, the people of Ephraim. (7:15)

> Then the Lord said to me: "Even if Moses and Samuel were to stand before me, my heart would not go out to this people. Send them away from my presence! Let them go!" (15:1)

> Therefore, I will surely forget you and cast you out of my presence along with the city I gave to you and your ancestors. (23:39)

> [The false prophets] prophesy lies to you that will only serve to remove you far from your lands; I will banish you and you will perish. (27:10)

> You expect to fight the Babylonians, but the men of this city are already as good as dead, for I have determined to destroy them in my terrible anger. I have abandoned them because of all their wickedness. (33:5 NLT)

---

11. See also Jer 6:21; 9:21; 10:15; 12:17; 15:7; 16:13; 27:15; 28:16; 32:31.

> It was because of the Lord's anger that all this happened to Jerusalem and Judah, and in the end he thrust them from his presence. (52:3)

The language of divine absence for a wicked people could not be clearer! They are said to be sent away from God's presence, forgotten and cast out of his presence, removed from the land and banished, destroyed and abandoned, and thrust out from his presence. Jeremiah 33:5 provides the clear reason for all this: "I will hide my face from this city because of all its wickedness," a hamartiological distance. Indeed, Yahweh had thrust an entire nation out of his presence and into exile.

This crisis of presence further elevated the importance of a remnant of prophets to function as covenant mediators. Yet Jeremiah observed that even God's prophets, the chosen channels of divine presence like Moses, had distanced themselves from Yahweh. Jeremiah even compared these rebels to Sodom and Gomorrah! "These prophets are as wicked as the people of Sodom and Gomorrah once were. . . . Have any of these prophets been in the Lord's presence to hear what he is really saying? Has even one of them cared enough to listen?" (Jer 23:14, 18 NLT). Jeremiah highlights the root cause of the downfall of these prophets—they had not been in the Lord's presence! They distanced themselves because they did not care enough to observe the revelatory *presence* of God.

Perhaps the prophet who describes the most literal depiction of distance and the crisis of presence is Ezekiel: "Therefore, as I live, declares the Lord God, surely, because you have defiled my sanctuary with all your detestable things and with all your abominations, therefore I will withdraw" (Ezek 5:11 ESV). Seeing firsthand the devastation of divine withdrawal, Ezekiel was deported to Babylon in the 597 BC exile under Johoiachin (1:1–3). The wickedness of the people was such that God could not abide with them, yet Yahweh declared that things were going to get much worse! The Lord told Ezekiel, "Son of man, do you see what they are doing—the utterly detestable things the Israelites are doing here, things that will drive me far from my sanctuary? But you will see things that are even more detestable" (8:6). Ezekiel makes this extremely personal when he describes the impact upon God's very soul, speaking of both the northern and southern kingdoms: "So she discovered her whoredoms, and discovered her nakedness: then my mind (*nephesh*, soul) was alienated from her, like as my mind (*nephesh*) was alienated from her sister" (23:18 KJV).

Referring to the writings of Ezekiel, Burnett observes that "in keeping with classic temple theology . . . Yahweh speaks of the envisioned temple as the place of God's earthly habitation."[12] The temple as Yahweh's habitation is significant because Ezekiel chapters 10 and 11 provide a literal portrayal of distance when God's glorious presence forsakes and departs from it. In those chapters, we see God's progressive movement away from the temple, a vivid portrayal of the hamartiological distance. In Ezek 10:4, the "glory" (*kabowd*) of God moved out to the threshold of the temple. Then the *kabowd*-presence followed the cherubim, an angelic presence, to the east gate of the temple (Ezek 10:19). The final increase of distance was the departure of the *kabowd* altogether: "Then the cherubim, with the wheels beside them, spread their wings, and the glory (*kabowd*) of the God of Israel was above them. The glory (*kabowd*) of the LORD went up from within the city" (11:22–23). Hence, the naive notion that God's presence would indiscriminately remain in their temple, the "Zion theology" of the day, was forever refuted (e.g., Mic 3:11).

THE HAMARTIOLOGICAL DISTANCE OF ISRAEL AND JUDAH

"For Jerusalem has stumbled, and Judah has fallen, because their speech and their deeds are against the LORD, defying his glorious presence" (Isa 3:8 ESV). While observing the testimony of the prophets, we discover numerous passages that point to distance: the hiding of God's face, exile, banishment, being driven away, divine withdrawal, defying his presence, etc. It becomes tempting then to reduce all such language to metaphor or anthropomorphic jargon that indicates nothing more than an ambiguous judgment or divine disapproval. We mustn't forget, however, that the Hebrew people were not merely sent away from their land, but in many cases, they perished and experienced physical death—they were literally destroyed! Are we somehow expected to believe that death and destruction are also mere metaphors and that those who have failed at life and are destroyed in death have somehow managed to remain in God's presence beyond the grave? This would be quite a hard pill to swallow. The principle of the psalmist applies throughout Old Testament Scripture to the nations and to Israel: "Those who are far from you will perish; you destroy all who are unfaithful to you. But as for me, it is good to be near God" (Ps 73:27–28). Illustrated most poignantly by exile, death is the final hamartiological distance.

Even Mount Zion was not beyond the same fate as Sodom and Gomorrah who first experienced God's distance, and then his presence in judgment, and finally the ultimate distance in death. The psalmist says, "As the mountains surround Jerusalem, so the LORD surrounds his people both

---

12. Burnett, *Where is God?*, 156. See Ezek 43:1–9.

now and forevermore.... But those who turn to crooked ways the Lord will banish with the evildoers" (Ps 125:2, 5). In other words, Israel is no exception! Even if we focus on Psalm 139, one of the most quoted passages in support of omnipresence, the psalmist also contrasts those who are present with others who are distant: "Where can I go from your Spirit? Where can I flee from your presence?" (139:7). Shortly after affirming nearness and presence for himself and others like him, the psalmist reflects upon the necessary distinction caused by the crisis of presence and observes, "If only you, God, would slay the wicked! Away from me, you who are bloodthirsty!" (139:19). The psalmist speaks as God, stepping into God's shoes and desiring that God bring about the final distance ("slay") of the wicked. The psalmist personifies this divine action in himself when he declares to the bloodthirsty, *away from me!*

If one wonders whether God's response to Israel is far removed from the distance and fate suffered by Sodom, we should remember that it was Yahweh who brought the charge against his own special people, saying their punishment was actually "greater than that of Sodom, which was overthrown in a moment without a hand turned to help her" (Lam 4:6). During the Assyrian Age in the eighth century BC, Yahweh also said to Israel, "'I overthrew some of you, as when God overthrew Sodom and Gomorrah, and you were as a brand plucked out of the burning; yet you did not return to me,' declares the Lord. 'Therefore thus I will do to you, O Israel; because I will do this to you, prepare to meet your God, O Israel!'" (Amos 4:11–12 ESV). What an ominous warning—prepare to meet your God! In other words, the divine presence is coming, but it's coming to destroy you.

Without making any critical distinction between Israel/Judah and Sodom/Gomorrah, Yahweh doesn't hesitate to highlight the grim similarities when speaking to the Hebrew nation. Ezekiel reveals God's thoughts on this:

> Your younger sister, who lived to the south of you with her daughters, was Sodom. You not only followed their ways and copied their detestable practices, but in all your ways you soon became more depraved than they. As surely as I live, declares the Sovereign Lord, your sister Sodom and her daughters never did what you and your daughters have done. Now this was the sin of your sister Sodom: She and her daughters were arrogant, overfed and unconcerned; they did not help the poor and needy. They were haughty and did detestable things before me. Therefore I did away with them as you have seen. (Ezek 16:46–50)

This *doing away with them* was nothing less than their final destruction in death. Yet God's own peculiar people in Judah are said to be "more depraved than they"! The people of Judah would not escape the same fate of the cities that Abraham had warned centuries before.

Indeed, for greater sins there is greater distance. Sodom and Gomorrah were never considered worshipping capitals of the world for the one true God, as Israel and Judah were. So how much more grave is the situation when we read that "the Lord has rejected his altar and abandoned his sanctuary" (Lam 2:7)? Or, when speaking of covenant people, we hear God say, "I was angry, so I punished these greedy people. I withdrew from them, but they kept going on their own stubborn way" (Isa 57:17 NLT)? Before we presume that the Lord is unjust or unfair in hiding his face and allowing himself to be driven from his sanctuary, Second Isaiah reminds us that it is in fact the people's sins and their initiative in turning their backs on God, which results in such distance:

> Surely the arm of the Lord is not too short to save, nor his ear too dull to hear. But your iniquities have separated you from your God; your sins have hidden his face from you, so that he will not hear.... Our offenses are ever with us, and we acknowledge our iniquities: rebellion and treachery against the Lord, turning our backs on our God, inciting revolt and oppression, uttering lies our hearts have conceived. (Isa 59:1–2, 12–13)

We should also note that the Lord's work in banishing the rebellious was not carried out indiscriminately at the nation as a whole with innocents carelessly suffering along with the wicked. Whenever possible, the focus remained on individual responsibility and consequences. Notice the individualized language used by Zechariah:

> This is the curse that is going out over the whole land; for according to what it says on one side, every thief will be banished, and according to what it says on the other, everyone who swears falsely will be banished. The Lord Almighty declares, "I will send [this curse] out, and it will enter the house of the thief and the house of anyone who swears falsely by my name. It will remain in that house and destroy it completely, both its timbers and its stones." (Zech 5:3–4)

Whenever possible, Yahweh's banishing distance was directed toward individuals rather than the community, such as thieves and those who swear falsely and even farmers who go out to tend their flocks but have neglected their God: "When they go with their flocks and herds to seek the Lord, they will not find him; he has withdrawn himself from them" (Hos 5:6).

Even though the Lord's heart is always to relieve and deliver the innocent, the destructive nature of evil often negatively impacts innocent bystanders. God himself is always affected, but there are also disastrous repercussions that spill over into the lives of innocent people as well. Who can be more innocent than children, yet Hosea speaks for Yahweh when he says, "Even if they rear children, I will bereave them of every one. Woe to them when I turn away from them!" (Hos 9:12). This may sound harsh, but it is in fact a warning that can be avoided: *Woe* to the people of God!

THE PROPHETS' PROMISE OF RESTORED PRESENCE

While the prophets were bystanders experiencing the nation's hamartiological distance as an historical reality, they sought to balance their message of warning and destruction with a word of hope for renewal and restoration. Isaiah said, "No one calls on your name or strives to lay hold of you; for you have hidden your face from us and have given us over to our sins" (Isa 64:7). When Yahweh turns away from sin, he consequently hides his face from the people he works so hard to reach, simultaneously giving them over to the consequences of their sins. Speaking on behalf of the nation as covenant mediator, Isaiah beseeched the Lord, saying, "Do not be angry beyond measure, Lord; do not remember our sins forever. Oh, look on us, we pray, for we are all your people" (64:9). Isaiah's immediate response to God's actions was the only responsible action for Israel; namely, a repentance that begs the Lord to eliminate the distance by once again looking upon his people.

Besides warning Israel of the tragic consequences of exile, the writings of the prophets also present the hope of restoration and the return of God's presence. The return of divine presence would coincide with the return of the exiles. Distance for the nation of Israel was just for a season so that the chaff could be separated from the wheat. Zechariah attested to this when he declared God's word to the sixth-century people of Judah, saying, "Though I scatter them among the peoples, yet in distant lands they will remember me. They and their children will survive, and they will return" (Zech 10:9). Although many would continue in their rebellion to their own destruction, there was always a remnant of those who would remember and repentant.

While the prophets remained hopeful that a repentant remnant would ultimately prevail, there was nonetheless an encroaching concern that the Israelites could bring about their final destruction. Speaking two centuries before Zechariah, Hosea said of the people of Israel, "But the more they were called, the more they went away from me. They sacrificed to the Baals and they burned incense to images. . . . Will they not return to Egypt and will not Assyria rule over them because they refuse to repent?" (Hos 11:2, 5). It was because of trends of rebellion and refusal like this that it was always a real concern of the prophets, just as it had been with Moses, that Yahweh may once and for all destroy this rebellious people.

Ezekiel, another sixth-century prophet who interceded as covenant mediator, cried out to the Lord, saying, "While they were killing and I was left alone, I fell facedown, crying out, 'Alas, Sovereign Lord! Are you going to destroy the entire remnant of Israel in this outpouring of your wrath on Jerusalem?'" (Ezek 9:8). Reminiscent of the days of Moses, this was a legitimate concern shared by the prophets because time and again God had argued for the utter annihilation of his people. Only a few centuries before Ezekiel, the prophet Zephaniah spoke a devastating word from Yahweh that resembled the judgment of Noah's day, using language indicative of destroying both Israel and Judah and all the wicked nations of the world: "'I will sweep away everything from the face of the earth, when I destroy all mankind on the face of the earth,' declares the Lord. 'I will sweep away both man and beast; I will sweep away the birds in the sky and the fish in the sea—and the idols that cause the wicked to stumble'" (Zeph 1:2–3). Yahweh wanted to destroy the wicked and the source of their temptation! Nonetheless, among others, the prophet of Lamentations maintained the assurance that "no one is cast off by the Lord forever" (Lam 3:31; cf. Lev 26:44).

The prophets spoke doom, but they also understood that Yahweh's greatest burden was to return to his temple and to the land of the people he had chosen for himself. Among the greatest promises of Scripture, Yahweh told Ezekiel,

> I dealt with them according to their uncleanness and their offenses, and I hid my face (*panim*) from them. Therefore this is what the Sovereign Lord says: I will now restore the fortunes of Jacob and will have compassion on all the people of Israel, and I will be zealous for my holy name. . . . I will no longer hide my face (*panim*) from them, for I will pour out my Spirit (*ruach*) on the people of Israel, declares the Sovereign Lord. (Ezek 39:24–25, 29)

The face (*panim*) of God is the Hebrew equivalent for the overall presence of God, as is the case in other Old Testament passages (Gen 3:8; 4:16). Through the eloquence of Hebrew parallelism, Ezekiel described the restoration of the divine presence in terms of another dynamic, personal metaphor—namely, a renewed outpouring of God's Spirit (*ruach*).

Ezekiel anticipated not only a renewal of God's Spirit but also a return of God's glory. After God's glorious presence departed from the temple in Ezekiel 11, the prophet predicted his certain return: "Suddenly, the glory of the God of Israel appeared from the east. The sound of his coming was like the roar of rushing waters, and the whole landscape shone with his glory.... And the glory of the LORD came into the Temple through the east gateway. Then the Spirit took me up and brought me into the inner courtyard, and the glory of the LORD filled the Temple" (Ezek 43:2, 4–5 NLT). Brueggemann summarizes this return of God's glorious presence, contrasting it with the ultimate punishment of divine absence: "The dramatic return of YHWH's glory in 43:1–5, a glory now permanently secured for the temple in 44:1–3, is the decisive antidote to the departure of YHWH's glory in chapters 9 and 10. Thus, the supreme punishment of YHWH, in priestly purview, is *absence*; the supreme resolution of crisis in priestly purview is restored cultic *presence*."[13]

Although Ezekiel described God's restored presence in terms of glory, he was also hopeful for the more relational dimension of personal encounter with the Spirit: "Therefore prophesy and say to them: 'This is what the Sovereign LORD says: My people, I am going to open your graves [of exile] and bring you up from them; I will bring you back to the land of Israel.... I will put my Spirit in you and you will live, and I will settle you in your own land'" (Ezek 37:12, 14). Ezekiel was explicit in predicting such future hope, and he wasn't the only prophet talking about restoration—Isaiah and others were speaking the same promises centuries earlier. More than a century before Ezekiel, the prophet Isaiah spoke on behalf of Yahweh, saying, "'In a surge of anger I hid my face from you for a moment, but with everlasting kindness I will have compassion on you,' says the LORD your Redeemer" (Isa 54:8). A contemporary of Isaiah, Amos also declared from the LORD, "I will bring my exiled people of Israel back from distant lands, and they will rebuild their ruined cities and live in them again. They will plant vineyards and gardens; they will eat their crops and drink their wine" (Amos 9:14 NLT). Hosea, another eighth-century prophet, echoed a similar thought: "After two days he will revive us; on the third day he will restore us, that we may live in his presence" (Hos 6:2).

Combined with this message of hope, there was a nuance of expectation within the prophets, not for another covenant, but for a new kind of

---

13. Brueggemann, *Introduction to the Old Testament*, 203, emphasis original. Even though God's presence was secured in the temple, it was also secured away from the people (Ezek 44:1–2). Until the future outpouring of God's Spirit, his presence would continue to be restricted solely to the prince: "Only the prince himself may sit inside this gateway to feast in the LORD's presence" (44:3 NLT).

covenant altogether, the renewal of the human heart. Ezekiel spoke of this when he said, "I will give them an undivided heart and put a new spirit in them; I will remove from them their heart of stone and give them a heart of flesh" (Ezek 11:19; cf. 36:26). The prophet Jeremiah was given a similar message from the LORD, saying, "'The days are coming,' declares the LORD, 'when I will make a new covenant with the people of Israel and with the people of Judah. . . . This is the covenant I will make with the people of Israel after that time,' declares the LORD. 'I will put my law in their minds and write it on their hearts. I will be their God, and they will be my people'" (Jer 31:31, 33). These prophets looked forward to a dramatic resolution to the problem of distance, one that deals intrinsically with the rebellious and sinful heart. This renewal would become the unique occasion for the people to truly possess God's presence and for God to know and possess them. Jeremiah added, "'No longer will they teach their neighbor, or say to one another, "Know the LORD," because they will all know me, from the least of them to the greatest,' declares the LORD. 'For I will forgive their wickedness and will remember their sins no more'" (31:34). In other words, Yahweh looked forward to a time when the hamartiological distance would be abolished!

Promises were made and hope was being restored within the nation, but by the end of the fifth century BC, the prophets stopped speaking altogether. Cold silence settled into the land for four hundred years leading up to the fulfillment of such promises. Four hundred years was plenty of time to question their distance from Yahweh and whether he would remain absent forever.

CONCLUSION

Yahweh instituted and committed himself to certain covenant commitments to overcome distance and guard his presence among the people of the earth. Both sides of the covenant, God and people, can hold one another accountable to its terms. The Noahic covenant protected the entire human race from another worldwide exile into the flood of death. Yahweh's covenant with Abram committed the divine presence to a specific people and land. God's covenant with Moses sought to protect the Hebrew people from the abyss of national exile through law and atonement. Lastly, the Davidic covenant was the promise and premier of an eternal kingdom where the people of God would dwell in the presence of a Davidic king forever.

Despite God's commitment and gracious promises, Scripture displays the utter failure of the Israelites to remain faithful to God under those covenants, ultimately resulting in their exile both in the eighth and sixth centuries BC. With Israel's entry into the abyss of exile, the national paradigm of sin and death, we observe an unparalleled illustration of distance in the Old Testament. God's chosen people weren't given any special treatment because no one is exempt from hamartiological distance! Sodom and Gomorrah weren't alone in this; even God's chosen nation had experienced the divine withdrawal and the ultimate distance of death. Jeremiah describes the nation's distance in nearly exhaustive fashion. Because of the people's sin, they are described as being sent away from God's presence, forgotten and cast out, removed from the land and banished, destroyed and abandoned, and entirely thrust out from the presence of Yahweh. In Ezekiel chapters 10 and 11, God's glorious presence departs from the temple but not without promise of return in chapter 43.

In a radically open universe, this national paradigm of hamartiological distance is the most vivid, historically longstanding portrayal of divine absence. As graphic as it was, with many Israelites displaced and even killed, God's patience had not run out. God always looked for a repentant remnant to return to the land, which would usher the return of his presence. More than that, there was still a message of renewal throughout the prophets. Within that message was the promise of a renewed covenant of the heart.

Before we move on to part two and explore new covenant salvation in an open universe, we'll conclude our examination of a radically open universe by taking a closer look at our hermeneutic and its impact on the doctrine of omnipresence.

5

Openness Hermeneutics
Omnipresence and the Absence of God

It's important to evaluate the appropriateness and credibility of my inquiry thus far. Although I won't delve deeply into method, the church community has a responsibility for respectful dialogue when approaching the issues of hermeneutics and the contours of any exegetical or theological method. Fundamentally, the development of sound theological method involves the "mutual correction and mutual enrichment of the partners in the conversation."[1] What makes practicing theology such a difficult and daunting task is that the Bible contains *many* theologies, not just a single theological scheme, as well as many methodologies on how we might come to best understand the material. As inconvenient as this might sound, a scriptural, practical hermeneutic mustn't be as complicated as we often make it.

Our first task is to recognize that no single, general hermeneutical method could be adequate for interpreting Scripture. Scripture is not just "another book,"[2] but divinely inspired doctrine, history, prophecy, warning, hymn, poetry, visitation brought to us through individual perspectives and church-wide testimony, faith, reasoning, and experience. Scripture was written by men centuries apart, even continents apart, and especially worldviews apart. In their own respective contexts, the authors approached the task of communicating divine truth from their own unique perspective and with their own unique purpose for the task at hand. Hence, our method may

---

1. Migliore, *Faith Seeking Understanding*, 15.
2. Jowett, "On the Interpretation of Scripture," 482.

need to change from book to book or even from one section of a book to another! Those of us who accept this daunting task are left with an arrogant undertaking. Our assignment remains beyond us, yet we push forward, at times having to stop in our tracks just to take a moment to laugh at ourselves. As Michael Hundley puts it, "Divine Presence, like divinity itself, is difficult to explain, much less envision, as one must describe in human terms what by definition transcends them. Such a quest remains an effort to grasp the ungraspable."[3] In the end, we can all agree that "theology is the foolish attempt to speak about God, the ultimate mystery, who is beyond the grasp of all human categories."[4]

Although there are numerous approaches to biblical interpretation, many would agree that we must begin with the literal or plain meaning of the text. This is, of course, easier said than done. But again, we should not allow ourselves to drown in an overly complicated process. We will see how Jesus Christ and the incarnation are the most reliable hermeneutic for understanding God's presence and knowledge in the world. We will conclude with a brief discussion on what I have termed *relational omnipresence*. As you can see, our study has moved from questions of divine knowledge to questions of divine presence.

EXEGETICAL METHOD IN THE PERSON JESUS CHRIST

God's own words and actions should be the most reliable factor of any biblical study. First and foremost, the most direct and conveniently packaged revelation of God is found in the person of Jesus Christ. Jesus Christ is the true and reliable "image of the invisible God" (Col 1:15). Because the essence of God did not always include human nature, we conclude by Jesus' appearance that God does in fact change: "Who, being in very nature God, did not consider equality with God something to be used to his own advantage; rather, he made himself nothing by taking the very nature of a servant, being made in human likeness. And being found in appearance as a man, he humbled himself . . . " (Phil 2:6–8). These mysterious statements proclaim that God does indeed change. Jesus having "made himself nothing" thereby entered into change. Jesus who "humbled himself" thereby experienced change.

One of the most profound revelations of God in Christ Jesus is the divine self-limitation whereby Almighty God assumed the humble role of a servant. By becoming a man, the Godhead did not experience merely a

---

3. Hundley, *Keeping Heaven on Earth*, 39.
4. Inbody, *Faith of the Christian Church*, 20.

change in appearance, a belief held by the Gnostics and other heretics, but an undeniable change in essence. The ontological makeup of the Trinity became something it was not before. At least to our knowledge, this is the most radical change that has occurred with God. But there is also a continual, perfect changeableness related to God's knowledge and experience. This change does not imply that the *character* of God's nature in any way changes because "God is faithful" (1 Cor 1:9; 2 Cor 1:18) and will always remain true to the ultimate standard of love. His practical changeableness occurs in relationship with his creatures, as he seeks out, interacts with, responds to, and even blesses and judges people.

God's perfect changeableness is best understood in the context of love because divine love enjoys experiences of its own, even longing to receive and experience the reciprocal love of free creatures. There should be no doubt that our loving God "is really related to his creatures, where 'really related' means that it makes a difference to God how things are with the creatures."[5] In Jesus Christ, believers "do not have a high priest who is unable to empathize with our weaknesses" (Heb 4:15). We should take seriously such a statement about the ability of Jesus, and therefore of God, to be affected by and enter into our individual experiences.

Indeed, God is *most moved* by the experiences of a world full of people he has chosen to relate to. Not only are his actions appropriate in response to what happens to human beings throughout history, but he also feels, experiences, and reacts to our pain and struggles as well as our joys and pleasures. Yet God does not experience divine schizophrenia! In effortlessly perfect and all-powerful knowledge, he is more than capable of feeling and experiencing a divine empathy for billions of different human emotions and experiences all occurring at any given moment throughout the world: "Great is our Lord, and abundant in power; his understanding is beyond measure" (Ps 147:5 ESV).

The epitome of the vulnerable love of God is Jesus Christ crucified. If there is an exegetical rule available to theologians from the pages of Scripture, it is that Jesus Christ is the most reliable *exegesis* of the eternal Godhead, the One who explains God: "No one has ever seen God, but the one and only Son, who is himself God and is in closest relationship with the Father, has made him known (*exegesato*)" (John 1:18). Because Jesus is the unique one, closest to the Father's heart, "himself God," there is no more reliable exegete to reveal God to us. Jesus Christ, who suffered at the hands of his own creatures, experienced change that involved God's own pain and suffering. Jesus who died a physical death thereby experienced change in

---

5. Hasker, "An Adequate God," 216.

his humanity and another kind of change in resurrection when he was then exalted to the right hand of the Father. Jesus reveals that God does change and is not at all insecure or threatened by his perfect changeableness.

Related to changeableness, self-limitation is an important quality of God's humility. He makes himself vulnerable in areas of his own self-expression that are otherwise powerful and limitless. Applying this to Jesus Christ, we see divine limitation experienced in God's knowledge of the future. Regarding the timing of the end of this present age, Jesus declared, "But about that day or hour no one knows, not even the angels in heaven, nor the Son, but only the Father" (Mark 13:32). Perhaps even more telling are the questions Jesus posed to the Father before and during the crucifixion. Leading up to the cross, Jesus inquired of God, "Father, *if* you are willing, take this cup from me; yet not my will, but yours be done" (Luke 22:42, emphasis added). Later from the cross Jesus cried out, "My God, my God, *why* have you forsaken me?" (Mark 15:34, emphasis added). Neither of these statements can be reconciled with a God of exhaustive foreknowledge. Seeing that Jesus Christ is the epitome of changeableness in God, through him we have a better frame of reference for interpreting and understanding the changeableness of God throughout Scripture.

"And Jesus grew in wisdom and stature, and in favor with God and man" (Luke 2:52). As a human being, Jesus grew older and wiser. His changeableness as a human being does not in any way diminish the accuracy of his representation of the Godhead. If the human template within the created order did not match the eternal nature of God with a special predesigned compatibility, then God could not have become human! That people have truly been made in God's image is one of the highest truths to embrace. If we are to begin to know what it means to be human, we must reflect upon God himself (theomorphism) and his ultimate revelation to humanity, the person of Christ. Jesus is the exact representation and perfect expression of the Godhead, which proportionately includes his humanity as a necessary component in our comprehending God. Although God is uncreated, the best way to know him is through his creation. God is everlasting, yet his temporal expression in Jesus Christ is the most accurate representation of him. Jesus is what humanity was intended to be before the fall. It was never human nature that was offensive to God's representation in the world, but death and mortality that were later added to our nature. Human nature became mortal nature.

The humanity of Christ is essential revelation for our knowledge of God. The unknowable, transcendent glory is not ultimately what makes God divine but his loving, relational, self-sacrificial nature revealed in the person of Christ. Jesus' entire ministry focused on the priority of relationship and self-giving. He sought relationship within every socio-economic stratum of society, with the poor and the rich alike. Relationship is everything to Jesus, so he maintained the divine relationship even in his death by his dependence upon the Father and the Spirit (Heb 9:14). Jesus is the final revelation to humanity to sufficiently disclose the nature of God.

Our theological method begins with Jesus Christ as the lens through which we arrive at any systematic presentation of Scripture. However, not all biblical interpreters will agree on how to apply this, just as Migliore remarks, "Differences in theological method reflect fundamental differences in understandings of revelation and the mode of God's presence in the world."[6] Just as Jesus Christ is the foundation of any proper theological method, we must look finally to him for a better understanding of the mode of God's presence in the world.

DIVINE ABSENCE THROUGH AN INCARNATIONAL HERMENEUTIC

Now that we have been introduced to an exegetical method in the person of Jesus Christ, we should ask the question, *Does the exegetical factor involving Christ and his experiences provide us an avenue or justification for divine absence in the world?* In response, two questions will need to be answered. The first: What does the incarnation contribute to our understanding of God's spatial locale? The second: Does the cross event depict God's real distance from sin when the Father forsakes his Son?

Incarnation and the Localized God

As for the first question, the incarnation speaks volumes. The ultimate test of the internal and ontological life of God is revealed in salvation history as it involves the triune economy. More specifically, it's revealed through the economic function of Jesus Christ in the world. If the economy of the tri-unity of God in salvation history (Father Creator, Son Redeemer, Spirit Renewer) is an accurate depiction of God's eternal ontological existence, so also through a unique expression in the person of Christ are we able to discern the internal nature of God.

The incarnation reveals to the world once and for all that it is eternally within God's ability *and nature* to locate himself spatially in one place and not another, if he so chooses. God is perfectly capable of limiting his own

---

6. Migliore, *Faith Seeking Understanding*, 14.

presence, since this was precisely the decision made with regard to the incarnation. The Apostle Paul recognized that the incarnation was an event of time and place for the Godhead: "But when the set time had fully come, God sent his Son, born of a woman, born under the law" (Gal 4:4). The Son, begotten and not created, eternally generating from the Father, was born. It was within *time* that Jesus arrived locally, that God was localized, *born* into a world *under the law*. Of course, the world cannot contain deity because he fills everything, but unless we are pantheists, the incarnation leads us to a satisfying conclusion. God is not limited to *fill* the world by means of an exhaustive, all-encompassing presence. He retains the prerogative for his presence to *fill* our world in a less exhaustive but nonetheless adequate and plentiful way. This was true in the person of Christ when the day arrived that infinite God was born into the world he created.

Jesus never once acted independently but always in sync with both Father (John 5:30) and Spirit (Matt 12:28), revealing the Godhead's cooperation even in the self-limited sphere of Jesus' own existence as God incarnate. The incarnation boldly asserts that God may remove the impression of an unlimited spatial occupation by replacing it with a direct, personal presence. Deducing that God's general (omni-)presence is experienced through special presence, many would argue that God is *focusing* his everywhere-presence in a more direct or intensified way through the incarnation. On the contrary, what if the exact opposite is true and God's special presences throughout Scripture simply demonstrated a general *local* presence and nothing more than what was literally being manifested in the moment? A special, manifest presence says nothing of omnipresence, but it does undeniably broadcast a local expression. These expressions do not imply omnipresence, only sufficient local presence. The limited sphere of God's presence was finally set free through the incarnation.

Until the incarnation, Yahweh was (self-)limited to the sphere of temporary epiphany or an ethereal presence that throughout history had been far removed from people's experience. Through the incarnation, God was actually shedding the limitation of his heretofore hidden and elusive presence. The incarnation reveals a much less limited God. Not only was he once limited by the hiddenness of his broad presence and the elusiveness of his special, temporary presences, but until the incarnation God was also limited by the absolute inability of people to see or experience him (or they would die)! To a significant degree, the preincarnate limitations had affected God's priority for community and obscured the image of God as relational. It seems that the reasons God would allow this are related to the necessity of epistemic distance but also to the hamartiological distance that was birthed in the garden and experienced in man's hiding. Yet in Christ Jesus, this barrier was removed in a way never before experienced by God or people.

Prior to the incarnation, the Hebrew proverbial tradition described God as transcending our spatial frame of reference: "'Do not I fill heaven and earth?' declares the LORD" (Jer 23:24). Such proverbial traditions instill in us an awe for divine transcendence but propel the immanence of God into a vacuum difficult to escape from, until Jesus. In other words, we never quite understood the deity until the incarnation. In Christ, the elusive and transcendent presence is realized as a personal, immanent presence, and finally we arrive at a frame of reference necessary for understanding God's omnipresence. We learn most about God and his presence through the person, Jesus Christ.

The Son will always be the most reliable indicator of God's presence in the world and the primary source of presence to the world. This truth was especially brought to light at Pentecost when Jesus poured out the Spirit and presence of God.[7] By virtue of Jesus' victory over death, in his tri-fold office of Priest, Prophet, and King, he demonstrated that no one else enjoys the prerogative and privilege of dispensing God's presence into the world. At Pentecost, Peter emphasized the victory of the new resurrection presence of Jesus, declaring, "Exalted to the right hand of God, [Jesus] has received from the Father the promised Holy Spirit and has poured out what you now see and hear" (Acts 2:33). The Father doesn't just release his presence to anyone in any place but has entrusted this ministry to the Son.

Jesus Christ as Controller over the Spirit-Presence

The divine person of the Spirit is the presence of God in the world (cf. Gen 6:3).[8] In common Hebrew parallelism, David petitioned the LORD, "Do not cast me from your presence (*panim*) or take your Holy Spirit (*ruach*) from me" (Ps 51:11; cf. 104:29–30). David beseeched God not to expel him from before his "face" (*panim*), a metonymy representing God's overall presence. Through a synonymous parallel, David equated this to being banned from God's Spirit (*ruach*). This same kind of synonymous parallelism is found

---

7. Regarding the Spirit as God's presence, in his thorough treatment of the Spirit in Paul's writings, pentecostal scholar Gordon Fee says that the Holy Spirit is "the personal presence of God himself" (*God's Empowering Presence*, 6).

8. Moltmann's Trinitarian pneumatology describes the Spirit as "the name given to the experienced presence of God" (*Spirit of Life*, 120). I should clarify, however, that because the Spirit is more than his functions, he is not solely the *experiential* presence of God in the world. He is one person among three who eternally co-exist as the triune Godhead.

in Psalm 139: "Where can I go from your Spirit (*ruach*)? Where can I flee from your presence (*panim*)?" (139:7). Again, the psalmist has no quibble with equating God's Spirit with his presence. Commenting on this verse, one writer says, "In the psalmist's mind the spirit of Yahweh is concomitant with his universal presence throughout all of the created order."[9]

Anthony Thiselton, while describing the Holy Spirit as an agent or extension of God, also concludes that "he is often understood as more than the Agent of God; *he represents God's presence.*"[10] Thiselton points out that after the exile God reassured his people of his presence: "And my Spirit remains among you. Do not fear" (Hag 2:5).[11] Through the words of the prophet Ezekiel, God also anticipated the outpouring of his presence upon a rebellious people: "I will no longer hide my face (*panim*) from them, for I will pour out my Spirit (*ruach*) on the people of Israel, declares the Sovereign LORD" (Ezek 39:29). Yahweh longed for the day his people would experience his Spirit—his presence—in a profoundly personal way. Ultimately, it was the Lord Jesus Christ who fulfilled the promise of drawing God's people into his presence and releasing that presence into our lives (Acts 2:33).

In highly symbolic language, Revelation describes the unique reigning position of Jesus the Lamb as the dispatch center for God's presence through the Spirit: "Then I saw a Lamb, looking as if it had been slain, standing at the center of the throne, encircled by the four living creatures and the elders. The Lamb had seven horns and seven eyes, which are the seven spirits of God sent out (*apostello*) into all the earth" (Rev 5:6; cf. Zech 4:10). The Greek *apostello* emphasizes the sender, drawing attention to the enthroned Lamb as the one from whom the generating Spirit is sent. The hovering Spirit of Gen 1:2 is the same sevenfold Spirit that proceeds from the person of Christ in Revelation. Just as God's Spirit hovered over the face of the dark waters, perhaps the divine presence is much like a roving presence throughout the world.

What would be an adequate illustration to help us understand God's presence in the world? Although no single example will do, let's consider the wind as one possible analogy. Even before God spoke a single word, the Old Testament introduces the divine, creative presence as God's Spirit: "In the beginning God created the heavens and the earth. Now the earth was formless and empty, darkness was over the surface of the deep, and the Spirit (*ruach*) of God was hovering over the waters" (Gen 1:1–2). Seeing that

---

9. Grant, "Spirit and Presence in Psalm 139," 145. Also commenting on Ps 139:7, Christopher Wright states that "Jesus knew that . . . God is everywhere present through his Spirit" (*Knowing the Holy Spirit*, 22).

10. Thiselton, *Holy Spirit*, 4, emphasis original.

11. Ibid., 13.

the Hebrew word *ruach* can be translated breath, wind, or spirit, the context suggests God was manifesting himself like a powerful *wind* hovering over the chaos.[12] Hence, the divine presence throughout the world can easily be likened to wind (Exod 10:13; Num 11:31; Jer 49:36). As the wind blows, its presence is universal, covering the whole earth. But there are some parts of the world that have different intensifications of wind and other areas where wind is totally absent, such as under the dark waters of the sea, under the earth, or in a deep cave or valley at night.

Focusing on this analogy of wind, breath, and presence may help us grasp how God's presence works in the world. While depicting the revival of the nation of Israel after exile, the prophet Ezekiel offers a unique prophetic picture of where the Spirit-presence of God comes from:

> So I prophesied as I was commanded. And as I was prophesying, there was a noise, a rattling sound, and the bones came together, bone to bone. I looked, and tendons and flesh appeared on them and skin covered them, but there was no breath (*ruach*) in them. Then he said to me, "Prophesy to the breath (*ruach*); prophesy, son of man, and say to it, 'This is what the Sovereign LORD says: Come, breath (*ruach*), from the four winds (*ruach*) and breathe (*ruach*) into these slain, that they may live.'" (Ezek 37:7–9)

According to Ezekiel, the spirit/breath blows in from the four winds, a helpful analogy of God's Spirit-presence generally at work in the world (cf. Rev 7:1).

What other analogy might help us to understand God's presence? Per the classical view, one could liken God's general presence (omnipresence) to a valley and his special presence to mountains occasional rising out from it. But in this example the valley would be thought to cover the entire earth. Let's try something else: Rather than a valley, in Christ there is only one Mountain that is the most reliable disclosure of God's presence. Instead of an infinite valley covering the whole earth, the presence of God is more accurately represented by *wind* (Spirit) that surrounds and goes out from that single *Mountain* (Christ): "Now a wind went out from the LORD" (Num 11:31; cf. Gen 8:1). This wind goes out over every valley while being occasionally disrupted by watery places, seas, and oceans. Those seas represent what Scripture has always said they represent, chaos and the enemies of God (e.g., Job 38:8–11). In those watery places, God's windy presence will either be disturbed or in some cases altogether displaced. We

---

12. NRSV translates Gen 1:2b as "a wind from God." For variations on how to interpret *ruach* in Gen 1:2, see Westermann, *Genesis 1–11: A Commentary*, 106–8; and Young, "The Interpretation of Gen. 1:2," 174–78.

can liken those places to godless regions of undisturbed evil, like Sodom and Gomorrah. Like Sodom, those regions of the world are devoid of God's presence because their inhabitants ultimately choose to remain lost at sea. The mountainous presence of Christ confirms the reliability of the more universal presence of God but never guarantees an *exhaustive* presence. Truly, who knows where his winds will blow (cf. John 3:8)?

One of the most ancient decisions of the church, the Niceno-Constantinopolitan Creed, included language that the Holy Spirit proceeded from the Father (cf. John 14:26; 15:26). This pointed to the Father as the source and the Son as the intermediate agency of the Spirit's presence in the world. To this the church later added, *and the Son*, known as the *filioque* clause (which in Latin means, *and the son*). The concern of Eastern theologians has been that this clause haphazardly restricts the activity of the Holy Spirit to where the incarnate Christ is explicitly proclaimed and believed upon.[13] Their concern is legitimate but unwarranted, seeing that Scripture unequivocally points to the Spirit's work beyond the message of Christ in sustaining and being involved in creation throughout history, which the church has wholeheartedly embraced.

Their concern, however, highlights a kernel of doctrine being presented here—namely, that the second person of the Trinity, even the Word incarnate, responsibly and sovereignly bestows God's presence through the Spirit into the world. Just as the roving, investigating "eyes of the LORD move to and fro throughout the earth" (2 Chr 16:9 NASB), so his presence is not limited to the spoken message. Still, the norm for the outbreaking presence continues to be an embodied message delivered directly from the mouths of believers. Their breath brings with it the Sacred Breath.

Is it possible that in a radically open universe the enthroned Christ is at work in the world in some places more than others? Because Jesus pours out the divine presence, naturally he is also responsible for withholding or withdrawing that presence. Hence, the responsibility could have fallen to God the Son to withdraw his presence from Sodom and Gomorrah, resulting in their judgment. This must always be a most painful experience for the Godhead. Whether Lord Jesus dispenses or withdraws the divine presence, his desire remains that all would turn and live: "As surely as I live, declares the Sovereign LORD, I take no pleasure in the death of the wicked, but rather that they turn from their ways and live" (Ezek 33:11). As he observes all that is happening in the world, with tears of passion he longs for all people to come under his loving reign so that he might pour out his Spirit (cf. Matt 23:37).

---

13. Migliore, *Faith Seeking Understanding*, 170.

Incarnation and the Distance of the Cross

So what about our second question: Does the cross event depict God's real distance from sin when the Father *forsakes* his Son? Although we will delve much deeper into Jesus' godforsaken cry in the next chapter, it's important that we take a moment to introduce it here. God cannot separate from God, yet Jesus had radically disturbed the universe when he bellowed out that terrible utterance, "My God, my God, why have you forsaken me?" (Mark 15:34). It would support my argument for divine absence if those words were to convey that God actually turned his back on or distanced himself from Jesus, but that interpretation is highly unlikely.

In what sense, then, was Jesus forsaken by his Father at the cross? Because Jesus recapitulated the life-experience of all humanity from birth through every stage of life into death, Jesus couldn't do otherwise but to identify with human nature in our experience of death, and particularly, death as distance. Jesus' outcry was an expression of empathy characteristic of a shared human nature with all people as they experience the most disturbing distance in life, our *death* due to sin, with emphasis on dying. This truth becomes more apparent when we reduce the difficulty of Jesus' words down to the simple truth that only mortal human nature is capable of uttering words even closely resembling a godforsaken state of abandonment, separation, and distance. These are human words, not divine! These are not words that would befit the experience of an infinite God, yet these are the words God uttered, words reflecting vulnerable humanity. Paul Fiddes comments that "God is not irrelevant to this world marked by death because God shares in the experience of death in sympathy with us. God endures death but is not dead: all that is dead or cancelled out is a certain metaphysical concept of an invulnerable God."[14] Such an outcry could only come from a human nature that was actually "tast[ing] death for everyone" (Heb 2:9). Jesus not only experienced the death of a mortal but also all the turmoil and agony leading up to it, a total cross-death experience.

Jesus' cry reflects two central truths. First, Jesus experienced a mortal's death. By specifically associating with humankind's mortality, in the deepest sense of the word Jesus identified and joined himself in solidarity with humanity's experience of distance from God in all of its animosity, confusion (why God?), and heartbreak. Jesus' words reflect the godforsakenness of the mortal human condition. Fiddes appreciates the solidarity of God with humanity at the cross by drawing our attention to the solidarity of the Father with the man, Christ Jesus. Fiddes says, "In identification with one

---

14. Fiddes, *Participating in God*, 237.

dead man, Jesus Christ, who was most intimately bound up in relationship with God, the being of God goes further into the valley of the shadow of death and yet is not consumed."[15]

Second, Jesus was speaking on behalf of humanity with words that express our reproach toward God for allowing death in the first place. But ironically, because Jesus is God, his words were intended to be reassuring, affirming that God was taking this mission to its ultimate conclusion, namely, death. While Jesus' words conspicuously reflect an open universe (why God?), the repetition "my God, my God" suggests Jesus' apprehension of his Father as *truly my God*. Falling short of patripassianism, the "death of the Father," the Father nonetheless experienced the agony of the cross along with his Son. How could he not, for on that day God died on the cross at Golgotha? The Father remained Jesus' God while maintaining their most intimate relationship beyond the possibility of any real distance or separation. Any separation we might detect in Jesus' words was functional and empathetic, an emotional and spiritual solidarity with mortal humanity.

RELATIONAL OMNIPRESENCE

Jesus Christ and the incarnation have been presented as the most reliable hermeneutic for understanding God's presence and knowledge in the world. We have gleaned much from observing the changeableness of God's essence and presence in the person and life of Jesus Christ, the regulator of divine presence in the world. Although the cross does not depict a Father rejecting his Son, it does demonstrate Christ's ultimate confrontation with death and his solidarity with humankind. Now we will consider what it really means for God to be omnipresent.

Some say, God must be the extreme of everything.[16] He must know everything for the sake of knowing everything. He must be everywhere for the sake of being everywhere. Yet Scripture never defines perfection or almightiness in such terms. Our relational God relates to this world primarily on a relational level, thus the categories of divine omniscience and omnipresence are also relational. Yahweh knows his creation, knows his people, and seeks to know others. He knows in an intrinsically relational

---

15. Ibid., 242.

16. Many classical theologians think in terms of conceivable extremes to describe the omni's of God. For instance, Charles Hodge says, "This simple idea of the omnipotence of God, that He can do without effort, and by a volition, whatever He wills, is the highest conceivable idea of power, and is that which is clearly presented in the Scriptures" (*Systematic Theology*, 1.5.10.B).

manner what is necessary to be known in order to be impeccably faithful in those relationships. He experiences a dynamic, *relational* omniscience and omnipresence.[17]

Karl Barth once said, "God's omnipresence is bound up with the special nature of His presence in His revealing and reconciling work ontologically (in its reality) and not merely noetically (as far as our knowledge of it goes)."[18] Barth identifies special intensifications of God's presence as revelatory reminders of his all-pervading, general presence. In a radically open universe, however, we arrive at a different conclusion. If God's presence is relational and free, he's not required to *limit* himself to being everywhere all the time. God's thoughtful presence and power will be primarily in those areas of the world and the human heart where there is *responsiveness* to divine revelation and reconciliation, to use Barth's categories. When God remains hidden from those who refuse to respond, the divine Spirit is free to depart in much the same way the Spirit departed from King Saul: "Now the Spirit of the LORD had departed from Saul" (1 Sam 16:14).

God is perfect, but his perfection is defined by Scripture in relation to the divine purpose. The purpose of perfect knowledge is not to know everything but to know and relate in the most profoundly personal and beneficial way. This omniscience lacks nothing essential, meeting the perfect standard of a relational God. John Sanders describes the knowledge of God as *dynamic omniscience* because "God, together with creatures, creates the future as history goes along. Hence, God's omniscience is dynamic in nature." Sanders goes on to explain that "God is omnicompetent and endlessly resourceful as he works to bring his creational project to fruition."[19] If God's knowledge of the future is dynamic, and we believe it is, then Sander's terminology is helpful but lacks specificity behind the purpose for such dynamics. The *relational* component takes into account the purpose and function behind divine knowledge. God's knowledge isn't dynamic for the sake of being dynamic, merely because God is free and creative, but because he is relational. Hence, I prefer the designations, relational omniscience and relational omnipresence.

---

17. If relationality is central to God's presence, one wonders what benefit the church derives from the philosophical reflections of the transcendent God described by the classical view. Myk Habets conveys, "In the classical view, . . . God, who is in himself spaceless, can be present only in and to those things that came into being in space and time. God is not 'present' (here and now) to himself, but only to creation" (*Spirit of Truth*, 9). See also van den Brom, *Divine Presence*, 170–230.

18. Barth, *CD* 2/1:476.

19. Sanders, *God Who Risks*, 9.

God knows what is essential and needful to know in relation to his creatures. Together God and his creatures experience the future when it arrives. He has no reason to force the universe into a position where he must know unreal future events before they happen. He knows those events most fully when he and his creatures enter into them, thus his knowledge is very much relational in nature. The same is true of his presence. There is no necessity placed upon Almighty God that he must be everywhere for the sake of being everywhere. Relationships necessarily place restrictions upon him. Relational omnipresence implies contingency; God's presence is largely contingent upon creatures who are in agreement with his purpose, plan, and will. He works primarily with and through those willing creatures to "bring his creational project to fruition," as Sanders put it.

God is described throughout Scripture in spatial terms and is therefore free to be somewhere and not another. This is his freedom, and he has perfect freedom. It would be silly to allege that God is all-powerful and free, yet at the same time, God is unable to *not* be everywhere.[20]

WHY GOD ISN'T OBLIGATED TO BE EVERYWHERE

Relational omnipresence sharply distinguishes open theism from process theism. Process theism holds that God and creation have always been and are therefore dependent upon each other. For freewill theism, Yahweh's creation *ex nihilo* definitively distinguishes him from creation and decisively frees him from bondage to the creation as one who relates and moves freely where he pleases, filling all or even just some space as he sees fit. If God is free not to be everywhere (classical theism) and within everything (pantheism), then Scripture should provide the basis for such a relational omnipresence.

We will look briefly at the relationship between relational omnipresence and the wicked, Torah, the prophets, angels, and the incarnation. These five areas demonstrate why comprehensive omnipresence is not scripturally necessary.

1. *The Rejected Presence by the Wicked*. God does not require an everywhere manner of presence because the wicked have rejected him and therefore want nothing to do with him.[21] This was the issue already addressed in

---

20. Cf. Barth, *CD* 2/1:473.

21. Perhaps the situation for the wicked is reminiscent of a soft deism, though this is not entirely accurate. The divine presence can't entirely abandon the wicked because he's attentive to their victims. His presence in some sense abides and remains open to the cries of all those who suffer at the hands of others, especially the innocent. It was

chapters 1–4. People driven out from the presence of God are left to wander among the nations whom God had previously driven out. In the days of Hosea, the wickedness, sinful deeds, and rebelliousness of the people and their leaders brought on the expression of God's *hate* in driving them out of his house. Yahweh said to the prophet Hosea, "Because of all their wickedness in Gilgal, I hated them there. Because of their sinful deeds, I will drive them out of my house. I will no longer love them; all their leaders are rebellious" (Hos 9:15). Hosea then followed up with an understanding of the consequences of their rebellion: "My God will reject them because they have not obeyed him; they will be wanderers among the nations" (9:17).

Even when Yahweh's own people reject his covenant and force his hand, they become no different than other nations previously displaced. This is a reversal of God's original intent to bring them *into* the Land, because they choose to imitate those who have been driven out: "They worshiped other gods and followed the practices of the nations the Lord had driven out before them, as well as the practices that the kings of Israel had introduced. The Israelites secretly did things against the Lord their God that were not right" (2 Kgs 17:7–9). The wicked, whether in or out of an official covenant with God, have removed authorization of God's presence in their lives. Israel is no exception.

Even when God is most distant, the divine imprint of *general revelation* remains on display before the eyes of the wicked. But because general revelation is insufficient for spiritual deliverance, God is faithful to send *special revelation* in the form of judgment. Ezekiel attests to this variety of special revelation when he speaks against Edom on behalf of Yahweh. This foreign invader naively assumed it could destroy Israel and Judah without giving any thought to their God: "Because you have said, 'These two nations and countries [Israel and Judah] will be ours and we will take possession of them,' even though I the Lord was there, therefore as surely as I live, declares the Sovereign Lord, I will treat you in accordance with the anger and

---

the outcry that drew Yahweh's attention to Sodom and Gomorrah (Gen 18:20; 19:13). When God returns to a people previously abandoned, the reason can be that he refuses to ignore the pleas of the victims of those godless regions: "He punishes them for their wickedness where everyone can see them, because they turned from following him and had no regard for any of his ways. They caused the cry of the poor to come before him, so that he heard the cry of the needy" (Job 34:26–28; cf. Jonah 1:1). The victim is not always an unseen figure but can be the voice of a prophet, such as Jeremiah. Jeremiah beseeched the Lord to intervene with vengeance against his oppressors: "But you, Lord Almighty, who judge righteously and test the heart and mind, let me see your vengeance on them, for to you I have committed my cause" (Jer 11:20; cf. 20:12; Lam 3:60–61). Scripture is clear that the Lord is attentive to the cry of the innocent and suffering.

jealousy you showed in your hatred of them *and I will make myself known among them when I judge you*" (Ezek 35:10–11, emphasis added; cf. 38:16).

2. *The Portable Presence in the Torah.* The Torah consists of the five books of Moses, specifically Genesis, Exodus, Leviticus, Numbers, and Deuteronomy. Of this corpus of literature, Brueggemann joins the majority of scholars in affirming Torah is "received as having the highest scriptural authority in Jewish tradition and, derivatively, in Christian tradition as well." He concludes, "It is impossible to overstate the authoritative force of this literature for Judaism."[22] Boadt acknowledges the same, saying, "For the Jews, [*Torah*] is the most sacred part of the Bible; it is 'the teaching' (*Torah*) par excellence, and the remainder of the canonical writings are really only an enrichment of its message or a commentary on living it out more fully in history."[23] These remarks are fascinating because this collection of God's teaching is thought by many to be the most naive and mythological, yet we receive from it the most authoritative truth. Most telling is that any explicit or suggestive teaching on the omniscience and omnipresence of God is very much lacking in this section of Scripture.

Torah starts human history off in the garden with a woman who is tempted away from Yahweh's presence. Her story never suggests an awareness that God might be "watching" or overseeing her temptation or that she could at once call out for help and God would swoop in to protect her from the serpent. Yahweh had departed from the garden, and when he returned, both man and woman felt they could literally hide from him! Later, Cain is cast out of God's presence. Jacob is surprised to discover God is in Bethel. Moses goes about his business in the wilderness until he finds himself in God's presence before a fiery bush, so he removes his sandals because he discovers he's actually standing on holy ground. At some point Yahweh is alerted to the Israelite's outcry in Egypt because he responds by sending Moses. For the Israelites camped before Mount Sinai, Moses' absence implies God's absence, so they create a golden calf to replace him. Afterward, Yahweh refuses to go with Moses and the children of Israel into the Promised Land but wants instead to send an angel.

The presence of God is unique throughout this corpus. The Spirit is the prominent representation of the presence as far back as Gen 1:2, "hovering over the waters." This ancient presence moved from brooding over waters to brooding over men. At one point,

> The LORD therefore said to Moses, "Gather for Me seventy men from the elders of Israel, whom you know to be the elders of the

---

22. Brueggemann, *Introduction to the Old Testament*, 5, 95.
23. Boadt, *Reading the Old Testament*, 90.

people and their officers and bring them to the tent of meeting, and let them take their stand there with you. Then I will come down and speak with you there, and I will take of the Spirit who is upon you, and will put Him upon them; and they shall bear the burden of the people with you, so that you will not bear it all alone." (Num 11:16–17 NASB)

The Spirit-presence of God had been on Moses as an anointing for leadership over the people. The Hebrew doesn't read that Yahweh will take *the power of* the Spirit from Moses, but it says more simply, *take of the Spirit*. This uniquely changeable presence of God was able to be taken in portion from Moses and transferred, even multiplied, to the 70 elders.

More than the unique presence that rested upon Moses and the 70 elders, the Israelites experienced just how portable and mobile the divine presence was. Yahweh moved along with the camp in a fire by day and a cloud by night, hovering over a golden ark, meeting with Moses in a tent that was repeatedly set up and torn back down. God was a moving God, an elusive and even wandering presence. The Torah doesn't contain a simple category for the presence of Yahweh but recognizes God's dynamic involvement in the events of human history and in the experience of his people.

3. *The Relational Presence in the Prophets.* Yahweh did not manifest himself to the majority but instead chose a spokesman or mediator and cooperated with that person through a dynamic relational partnership. Nehemiah attested to this when he spoke to Yahweh, saying,

> You saw the suffering of our ancestors in Egypt; you heard their cry at the Red Sea.... For many years you were patient with them. *By your Spirit you warned them through your prophets.* Yet they paid no attention, so you [exiled] them into the hands of the neighboring peoples. But in your great mercy you did not put an end to them or abandon them, for you are a gracious and merciful God. Now therefore, our God, the great God, mighty and awesome, who keeps his covenant of love, do not let all this hardship seem trifling in your eyes. (Neh 9:9, 30–32, emphasis added)

It was the prophet who received his words from the Spirit of God's presence, who understood the spiritual condition of the nation, and who recognized Yahweh's right to abandon the people. But the prophet also reminded God of his covenant and stood in awe of Yahweh's unfailing covenant love.

The prophets were privileged to experience firsthand God's relational presence, especially Moses: "The LORD would speak to Moses face to face, as one speaks to a friend" (Exod 33:11). "Since that time no prophet has risen in Israel like Moses, whom the LORD knew face to face" (Deut 34:10 NASB). Yahweh anointed king, priest, and prophet with the "anointing oil" of his presence, but never under old covenant law did he ever anoint the majority of followers. Still, this relational dimension is the most prominent aspect of divine presence and a foundational definition for it. Throughout Israel's history, God's will and guidance became known to the nation through designated individuals and scarcely by other means. Even when Moses' received the law from the LORD, the rest of the people had to keep their distance while Moses fulfilled his mediatory role: "The people remained at a distance, while Moses approached the thick darkness where God was" (Exod 20:21; cf. 24:1–2). The prophets also functioned as special scribes who recorded and maintained the tradition. Under inspiration of God's Spirit, they permanently inscribed their encounters with the manifest presence.

Largely informed by the Priestly tradition and its concern for the holiness of God, the prophets repeatedly identified the reason for death, exile, and distance as Israel's failure to maintain right relationship with Yahweh through covenant loyalty. Covenant outlined the relationship between God and nation, which was the prophet's main concern. In the Hebrew Bible, it was frequently in language that implied a vital relationship, such as Husband and wife (or King and servant), that the nation failed to maintain that relationship (e.g., Jer 2:20; 3:20). But did the Husband, King, and Creator deal with the people directly? Typically not. Instead, it was the prophet, king, or priest who enjoyed the prerogative and privilege of divine fellowship.[24]

4. *The Representative Presence of the Angels.* This is a most interesting category because it is possible that many, if not most, appearances of Yahweh in the Old Testament are actually the mediatory appearance of an angel or other created vehicle, such as a cloud or flaming bush. We are told that it was the angel or "messenger (*malak*) of Yahweh" who appeared to Moses in the fiery bush (Exod 3:2–4) and who interrupted Abraham from sacrificing Isaac (Gen 22:11–15). It is this same *malak* of Yahweh who appeared to Gideon, the judge. Gideon became fearful because he found himself in the very presence of God (Judg 6:11–23)! But some time later in the book of Judges, when the same *malak* appears to Manoah and his wife, the *malak* differentiates himself from God: "The angel of the LORD replied, 'Even though you detain me, I will not eat any of your food. But if you prepare a burnt offering, offer it to the LORD.' (Manoah did not realize that it was the angel of the LORD.)" (13:15–16). And then Manoah expresses great concern that

---

24. The prophet Jonah is an obvious exception. Instead of maintaining a right relationship with God, he pursued distance and actually "fled" from Yahweh's presence (Jonah 1:1–3).

he and his wife are doomed to die because, as he told his wife, "We have seen God!" (13:22).

In Judg 13:9 and other places, this *malak* is also called the "angel of God" (Gen 31:11; Exod 14:19). In the Hebrew Bible, we are told that Moses received the covenant law as "inscribed by the finger of God" (Exod 31:18; Deut 9:10), but in the New Testament, Paul informs us that "the law was given through angels and entrusted to a mediator" (Gal 3:19; cf. Heb 12:2). In the book of Acts, Stephen mentions the "angel who appeared to [Moses] in the bush" and "the angel who spoke to [Moses] on Mount Sinai" (Acts 7:35, 38). Stephen is consistent in crediting angels with activities we'd more naturally ascribe to Yahweh in the Old Testament, and he was quite comfortable doing so. Stephen also reports the Israelites "received the law that was given through angels" (7:53). Both Paul and Stephen understood the representative presence of angels.

The role of angels and particularly the angel of Yahweh is indeed mysterious. It's peculiar that God's prophets describe his appearances in mediatory language, but that is in fact how they tell their stories: "In all their distress he too was distressed, and the angel of his presence saved them" (Isa 63:9). Here in Isaiah, it's quite remarkable that this angel is said to accurately represent the very presence of God. Although we're limited on what we can say about this, angels as agents of God are trustworthy representatives. Because God has reliable representation, it's not necessary for his personal presence to enter situations where his angels have been sent.[25]

5. *The Definitive Presence of the Incarnation.* How can anyone guarantee divine omnipresence when Yahweh himself says, "No one may see me and live" (Exo 33:20)?[26] Surely *seeing* is not the sole concern here but stands as a metonym of presence; more literally, no one may come into contact with my presence and live! The biblical testimony assures us that Hundley's conclusion is correct, that "humanity cannot come into contact with YHWH's true presence."[27] If so, the divine encounters of every king, priest, prophet, and believer have been a secondary encounter at best, until Jesus Christ. If God mediates his presence through the *creation*, then the Father

---

25. See Exod 33:2; Num 20:16; 1 Chr 21:15; 2 Chr 32:21. Holding to the classical view of omnipresence, one may rightfully question the need for *guardian angels*.

26. See Gen 32:30; Judg 6:22–23; John 1:18.

27. Hundley, *Keeping Heaven on Earth*, 51. If humanity (and creation) cannot come into contact with Yahweh's true presence, the classical view of omnipresence could be likened to a soft pantheism. John Miley recognizes this concern when he says, "The doctrine of an infinite essence of being should be carefully guarded in both thought and expression. Otherwise it may become the foundation of pantheism" (*Systematic Theology*, 1:217–18).

uniquely *created* a divine Son to grant us firsthand contact with deity! "No one has ever seen God, but the one and only Son, who is himself God and is in closest relationship with the Father, has made him known" (John 1:18). No one has come into contact with Yahweh, until now.

Regarding the incarnation, Samuel Terrien remarks that "it was the Hebraic theology of presence which dominated all the interpretations of the person of Jesus, from Mark to Revelation."[28] The truth cannot be overstated that Jesus not only defines God's presence in the world but also reveals to us the presence *par excellence*. Through the incarnation, God's presence has been permanently set free from limited expression in the sanctuary, through the prophet, or by angelic agent. The barriers under the old covenant that kept people at a distance were forever destroyed when Jesus split open the way into the Holy of Holies, represented at his death when the temple veil was torn in two (Matt 27:51; cf. 2 Cor 3:15–17). And so "God raised us up with Christ and seated us with him in the heavenly realms in Christ Jesus" (Eph 2:6). Commenting on this verse, Gerald Bray remarks, "This is not mere rhetoric. The symbolic language reflects the fact that the Old Testament experience of Yahweh, whom the people perceived from the 'outside,' has been replaced by a direct experience of God in Jesus Christ."[29] Hallelujah!

As the perfect image of God, Jesus Christ is the final word on the divine presence in the world. Jesus' new covenant ministry of dispensing the Spirit is Scripture's progressive record (in the vein of progressive revelation) of how the incarnation definitively broadcasts God's presence and subsumes any prior knowledge or assumptions. Because Jesus is always at work through his Spirit, believers become bearers of the divine presence in the world, which is our privilege *in Christ Jesus*. Lord Jesus breathes God's Spirit into his people, the Holy Breath (John 20:22). Through this sacred breath of life, believers become the vehicle for the world to experience God's relational presence as we proclaim with anointed breath the gospel of Jesus Christ and his kingdom.

CONCLUSION

In an open universe, Yahweh is relational and free. But in a radically open universe, divine freedom implies God is not *limited* to the classical categories that exhaust his attributes and insist that this is perfection. Must God know everything for the sake of knowing everything, or must he be everywhere just to flex his muscles and be everywhere? Or, can the perfection of divine knowledge and presence be defined in more personal, practical

---

28. Terrien, *Elusive Presence*, 30.
29. Bray, *God is Love*, 180.

ways? Because Jesus Christ is our most reliable hermeneutic, the incarnation demonstrates that God can be localized and limited in what he knows. Jesus' humanity demonstrates the perfect changeableness of God and that God doesn't need to know everything for the sake of exhausting knowledge. *Father, would you take this cup from me? Father, why have you forsaken me?* Furthermore, the eternal nature of the Godhead was forever changed when Jesus was born in a specific time and place and added human nature to the triune essence.

Even though the humanity of Christ doesn't present a complete explanation of God's inner life, he reveals enough to teach us that God's activities in the world prioritize relationship. Jesus depended upon both Father and Spirit throughout the cross event when his Father never once left his side. Prior to the incarnation, throughout the Old Testament Law and Prophets, the elusiveness of divine presence was a formidable opponent to everything relational. Then, in a most dramatic fashion, the incarnation abruptly brought to conclusion the question of divine presence and whether humanity could ever truly experience God. Reigning at the right hand of his Father, Lord Jesus now oversees God's personal presence and sends this Spirit out into the world to revive those who are responsive to his message. The divine presence is and has always been thoughtful and intentional, active in the world with purpose. Although it would be accurate to define God's general presence as dynamic, the term *general* has always been a much too superficial and purposeless description of omnipresence. God's presence is never general but always purposeful and relational. Thus, *relational omnipresence* is preferable and much more descriptive.

The conclusion of chapter 5 is also the conclusion of part one: *In a radically open universe, comprehensive omnipresence is not a biblical necessity.* Is it possible the Bible affirms that comprehensive presence is not essential with regard to the wicked, Torah, the prophets, angels, and the incarnation? The wicked don't have the presence because they've rejected it. The Torah is arguably the most reliable revelation of the Hebrew Bible, but it never once affirms omnipresence, only portable, elusive presence. Furthermore, only prophets, priests, and kings went before God, passing his message on to the nation, bypassing the need for anyone else in Israel to experience a divine encounter. When anyone did encounter Yahweh, it was typically through the presence of angels or another created vehicle, such as fire, cloud, ark, or rock. This fleeting glimpse of divine presence finally came to an end in the incarnation, another local expression of God. But through God incarnate, believers now receive the fullness of divine presence through the abundant outpouring of God's Spirit.

PART II

The Charismatic Presence

The prospects of a radically open universe are intriguing to say the least. I've described this as my theological inquiry to give others the opportunity to consider, question, and dialogue with the material and to ultimately make revisions where necessary. My prayer is that this proposal has been beneficial to those who are embracing or sympathetic to openness theology.

In part one, we reviewed the origin of sin in relation to Satan and the resultant hamartiological distance that sin can create between God and people, an unmitigated absence of divine knowledge, presence, and power. This discussion expanded upon the open theist's perspective of an open future to further include unknowns about the past and present as well. We saw an extensive historical paradigm of sin and death in Israel's exiles. We also developed an abbreviated hermeneutic on the dynamics of a changing God, which was dependent on incarnational revelation and the person of the God-human, Jesus Christ. Throughout our discussion, we moved from the theme of omniscience to a relational interpretation of omnipresence. Our final effort was to outline from Scripture the non-necessity of an exhaustive divine presence in a radically open universe.

Now that we've reached the conclusion of part one, the second half of our inquiry will move away from distance and focus on salvation and the charismatic presence of God. Thus, our inquiry into openness theology continues. Jesus speaks blatantly of the rebellion of his own people when he says, "For if the miracles that were performed in you had been performed in Sodom, it would have remained to this day" (Matt 11:23). This is a profound statement since Jesus seems to be indicating that Sodom's distance from God could have been closed by an overt manifestation of God's charismatic presence. Even if Jesus is using hyperbole to make his point, his message still resonates with the overtones of an open universe. *If* God had decided to miraculously manifest himself to Sodom, *then* Sodom's future could have been different. For Jesus, the purpose of miracles and other *charismata* is to make God's presence known. Some will respond in a positive way, while others will inevitably reject the message altogether. Whatever their response, Jesus was telling his audience how privileged they were to observe God's presence at work. Jesus' point was not that more overt manifestations would inevitably bring salvation and deliverance but that we should consider ourselves privileged when we do experience God's charismatic presence.

If the first five chapters are construed as nothing more than a hypothetical theological universe, the metaphor itself is undeniable: *An unqualified distance can exist between God and the ungodly.* Lying at the heart of divine suffering and a bleak existence for the wicked, such distance creates an exceptional need for evangelism. And the church just happens to be empowered for such a mission. Moving forward, the style and content of part two will look drastically different from our investigation in the first half. I will endeavor to describe the reversal of distance through the salvific presence of God in the church's mission and gifts. The intent is to move into a theological discussion that is more practical and useful to the church. Instead of elaborating on a radically open universe, we'll be asking the question: *What would God's supernatural presence through salvation and Spirit-empowered ministries look like in an open universe?*

6

Salvation
Closing the Distance

We can finally move our discussion away from the gloom of sin's distance and focus on God's more permanent solution for eliminating it. Once sin displayed its power to separate God from his creatures, the heart of God's plan has been to defeat it. Sin always chooses to move away from God's love. Just as love and life are on one side of the freewill spectrum, so death and the rejection of love are on the other. When people refuse God's loving pursuit and validate the wickedness in their hearts through hurtful and unloving acts, divine wrath is all that's left for them. God's final point of contact with sin can be only wrath or forgiveness. The former was the case with Sodom, but the latter is for anyone who repents and turns to God for salvation.

Sin and death have created a nearly impossible problem for people, leaving nowhere else to turn but the cross. Paul declares that the essence of his preaching is Christ and him crucified (1 Cor 2:5). As awful as this message may at first sound—the murder of God's Son—the crucifixion of an imperishable being just happens to be the best news to give the world. As scandalous as the cross was, it is overshadowed *ad infinitum* by the glory of Jesus' resurrection, the testimony of an eternal God conquering death once and for all.

OVERCOMING DEATH AND DISTANCE

Because death and distance are the greatest enemies of humanity (1 Cor 15:26), it is for this that Christ came and died. When people consider their redemption and the array of metaphors and descriptions attached to it (sacrifice, substitute, victor, etc.), ultimately it comes down to this: Jesus Christ died a physical death to deliver humankind from the power of death and the devil. After recapitulating the ongoing experience of every human being in death, Jesus then accomplished what humanity never could when he rose from the grave. Andrew Louth summarizes the hope of every believer: "This belief that Christ did not succumb to death, but overcame death: something manifest in the resurrection, when he demonstrates that death has not taken him, but he has overthrown death—it is this that is the fundamental Christian belief."[1]

Jesus' glorious resurrection was not merely the seal of the Father's approval over what he had done for people, but it stands as the decisive victory over death and distance in a fallen world. Resurrection was the game changer and God's most glorious, sustained display of divine presence! The cross has no merit or meaning apart from resurrection. By rising out from the midst of an historical record of dead mortals, it was Jesus alone who broke that record. Our hope is lost apart from God raising Jesus out from among the dead ones, which is what the cross represents (1 Cor 15:12). Salvation is nothing less than resurrection. Because death rose up in the garden, it is now life that people need most, and that being resurrection life. Truly Jesus is "the resurrection and the life" for all who believe in him (John 11:25).

Resurrection is not alone in its effects for salvation. It empowers such wonderful graces as the forgiveness of sin, removal of guilt, pardon from God's wrath, and justifying righteousness, along with all the other special gifts associated with salvation. That said, it is ultimately resurrection through and with Jesus that remains the essence of our redemption. Hence, resurrection called for Jesus' death. For the One who is both God and human, it's possible that because of his sinlessness, Jesus could have continued to live on the earth without ever experiencing death. He could have continued to enjoy the life he always lived in continual rapport with God because death had no power over him. Because he remained under his Father's authority, distance had no power or claim on him that would lead to death. As with all humanity, the hamartiological distance could have no real influence over Jesus if he never rejected his Father's authority, as Adam had done. Satan's kingdom remained powerless against the second Adam. Jesus

---

1. Louth, *Introducing Eastern Orthodox Theology*, 55.

told his disciples, "The prince of this world is coming. He has no hold over me" (John 14:30; cf. Matt 4:8–10). Perhaps Jesus could have kept on living indefinitely, but instead he freely chose to lay down his life to overcome the distance (John 10:18).

It doesn't fall within the purpose of our study to rehash all the various theological interpretations of atonement (as important and profoundly exciting as they are), but one theory of atonement deserves a brief rebuttal. It's easy to be taken in by the widespread view of the cross as divine punishment, commonly described as penal substitutionary atonement.[2] Quite naturally, this belief results in confusion and an inherent contradiction. Believers seek to emulate and serve a just God, but under this theory we're asked to believe the heavenly Father had literally punished and tortured his own son! Such a contradiction should at least stir a quiet confession that violence is acceptable to God. Worse yet, it may give the world the impression that our heavenly Father would abuse his own child if it would benefit others, so maybe he would abuse me too?

Divorced from any notion of torture from his Father, Jesus suffered at the hands of violent people.[3] But it's one thing to affirm that Jesus *suffered* for sin and quite another to allege that he was *punished* for our sins. Ezekiel teaches that a person cannot be punished and put to death for someone else: "The one who sins is the one who will die. The child will not share the guilt of the parent, nor will the parent share the guilt of the child. The righteousness of the righteous will be credited to them, and the wickedness of the wicked will be charged against them" (Ezek 18:20; cf. Num 35:31; Deut 24:16). The cross rejects every notion of violence and punishment by decisively pointing to the ultimate power of God's love to submit to the hatred of human violence, not divine cruelty, in order to overcome the worst expressions of hatred. The cross is not an expression of divine brutality or retribution, but on the contrary, it remains the most profound display of the longsuffering, vulnerable love of God.

---

2. This theory was developed by the reformers in the 1500s based on Anselm's "satisfaction theory" that was articulated in AD 1098 (*Cur Deus Homo*). The debate over the nature of the atonement includes numerous viewpoints. "To mention just a few spikes in the controversy, we have Abelard's 'moral theory' versus Anselm's 'satisfaction theory' (11th century), the Socinians's attempt to rebuff the Reformers (16th century), John Owen's answer to Hugo Grotius's 'governmental theory' (17th century) and a host of alternatives that arise in the 20th century (most notably Gustaf Aulen's "*Christus Victor*" and René Girard's mimetic theory)" (Jersak, "Nonviolent Identification," 24). For response and rebuttal to the penal theory, see Jersak and Hardin, *Stricken by God?*; and Beilby and Eddy, *Nature of the Atonement*, 99–116.

3. See Matt 20:18–19; 26:2–4; 27:20, 35; Mark 15:24; Luke 22:22; 23:21, 33; 24:20; John 11:53; 19:18; Acts 2:23b, 36.

Hence, the glory of the resurrection is without comparison in all of salvation history. No other religion answers the problem of death because anything short of bodily resurrection capitulates to death. Every human being before Jesus (except Elijah and Enoch, possibly others) ended up in the ground, "for dust you are and to dust you will return" (Gen 3:19). Resurrection reverses that death sentence through Jesus Christ, guaranteeing that those who stand with Jesus will share in the same resurrection. According to James Payton, "Christ became the guarantee of the fulfillment of God's original creative purpose for all of creation—namely, life with God forever."[4] Because Jesus stands as victor in the face of our greatest enemy, he becomes victor over all our enemies and can be trusted with our very lives. Louth says it another way: "Because it is death that Christ has overthrown—death that reduces all our efforts to nothing—Christ is shown to be beyond the reach of any power that could threaten us."[5] Because Jesus is well beyond the reach of Satan, sin, and death, and saves us from each one, one of his most appropriate titles is that of Savior.

ATONEMENT BY DEATH OR DISTANCE?

Returning to a topic introduced in chapter 5, while the Mediator of salvation hung suspended between heaven and earth, he cried out, "My God, my God, why have you forsaken me?" (Mark 15:34; Matt 27:46; cf. Ps 22:1). Those words sent shockwaves throughout the creation! Spoken from the lips of the one who is truly God and truly human, this was an extremely strange utterance for deity. At first glance, Jesus' question seems to imply distance, broken relationship, and even separation. Spoken by God himself, what could this question possibly mean?

In chapter 5 we concluded that the cross does not depict a Father rejecting his Son, but it does demonstrate Christ's ultimate confrontation with death and his solidarity with humankind. So we can build on those thoughts as we further develop this doctrine of non-rejection.

Could the Father Abandon His Son?

Historically, some have understood Jesus' outcry as a total abandonment by the Father, an ontological separation. The logic is that because the Father is

---

4. Payton, *Light from the Christian East*, 125.

5. Louth, *Introducing Eastern Orthodox Theology*, 55. See Rom 8:38–39. Louth adds that "Christ's love for human kind is able to overcome death, for it does not succumb to death, but seeks it out" (ibid.).

both holy and perfect in every regard, without any blemish or possibility of fault or flaw, he cannot have contact of any kind with the stain of sin. True enough! They would argue, then, that when Jesus was made "to be sin on our behalf," the Father separated himself from the Son, just as sin has separated people from God. Moreover, the Father punished the Son for humanity's sin, an idea I objected to earlier in this chapter. Dean Harvey remarks on what is arguably the most common understanding of this event: "*[Jesus] was now sinful*, and since God cannot look upon sin, God had to turn his back on Jesus . . . for a moment in eternity, never to be repeated again, the Father *withdrew His presence and turned His back*; He couldn't look any more."[6] You heard him right; according to Harvey, Jesus was now sinful!

Representative of the popular view, one wonders what could possibly be involved in the Father withdrawing his presence? If Harvey is suggesting God merely withdrew from *fellowship* with the Son, what could that conceivably entail? Rather than in pretense only, do they believe the Father's actions resulted in the total dismissal of his presence? If so, wouldn't the end result resemble the hamartiological distance, a true removal of divine presence? Otherwise, in what manner could the Father have withdrawn to result in a truly broken fellowship? I'm lost for an explanation, other than to conclude that some who hold to this separation are alleging that an ontological distance, even absence, had occurred at the cross. Although this supports what I've been arguing all along regarding the separation that's caused by sin (and death, for that matter), and though my position could benefit from such an interpretation, I find this explanation highly unlikely, if not impossible.

Regardless of the degree of distance that's thought to have occurred on the cross when the Father *turned his back*, we're asked to believe that the eternal fellowship of the triune deity was in some sense disrupted for a time. Doesn't basic theology inform us that God is truly one, not many, and without division or distinction in essential nature? Along with the Spirit, the Father and Son are coexistent, coequal, and coeternal, one in essence, and therefore indivisible in their shared nature. The Trinity cannot cease to be the Trinity or God would cease to be God. Truth that applies to the Father must equally apply to the Son. Thus, if it was said of the Father, it must also be said of the Son. Because God the Son is also holy and perfect in every regard, without any blemish or possibility of fault or flaw, he too cannot possibly have any contact with the stain of sin, before, during, or after the cross! Indeed, Jesus was *not* now sinful, as Harvey would have us believe.

---

6. Harvey, *Ransom: High Cost of Sin*, 93, 99, emphasis added.

"Him Who Knew No Sin"

Paul tells us that God "made Him who knew (*gnonta*) no sin to be sin on our behalf, so that we might become the righteousness of God in Him" (2 Cor 5:21 NASB). Jesus' total lack of experience with sin is the shared reality for his Father as well.[7] If the Father could not in any true sense experience sin at the cross, the same remains true of the second person of the Trinity. The Father did not turn his back on Jesus because Jesus did not in any metaphysical sense become sin for us. He only *became sin* in the sense that Isa 53:10 asserts, that his life was made an "offering for sin." Because Jesus did not literally become sin in any metaphysical experience, he qualified as the perfect, stainless Lamb of God who takes away the sin of the world.

From *ginosko*, the participle *gnonta* basically means to know or to have knowledge. In the participle form, *gnonta* indicates Jesus simply had no knowledge of sin. Because Jesus had no personal knowledge of sin, he never experienced it. Because God's knowledge is relational, sin becomes an issue for the experiential nature of divine knowledge. Because God cannot familiarize himself with iniquity as he does with the rest of creation, we might say he can only be a secondhand observer. But for God to truly know someone, there must be firsthand experience, an ontological solidarity. Since sin is not merely isolated acts but intrudes upon every area of mortal existence, the God *who knew no sin* cannot truly know the person who lives in sin apart from his salvific presence.

At the cross, Jesus dealt the death blow to sin's claim on humanity. Remarkably, he accomplished this great feat without ever coming into contact with sin. Jesus can truthfully declare to sin, *I never knew you*. He was never informed by sin and has remained unacquainted with it in every possible self-experience. God is not limited because Jesus lacks knowledge of sin; on the contrary, this "deficit" was vital to qualify him as the perfect, sinless sacrifice. Because Jesus had never known sin, he remained free from its dominion, consequently stripping sin of all its power and leaving it without any authority to take his life. Even though Jesus experienced death *because of* sin, he did not and could not experience sin *unto* death as fallen humanity is doomed to. The sin of the world undoubtedly led to Christ's death on the cross, but he freely surrendered his life and died because of the sins of others. In order to free us from sin's deathful distance, Jesus undeservedly experienced the consequences of sin in death.

---

7. Jesus has always been entirely free from sin in nature, thought, temptation, and deed; see Matt 7:11; 11:29; John 4:34; 8:29, 46; 15:10; Acts 3:14; 2 Cor 5:21; Heb 4:15; 7:26; 1 Pet 1:19; 2:22; 1 John 2:1; 3:5.

Helplessness: A Rhetorical Idiom

How should we interpret Jesus' rather unusual utterance, *Why have you forsaken me?* Let's start with God himself. Whatever interpretation we arrive at cannot violate God's essential nature; thus, whatever the final meaning of those words may be, separation of divine persons was not involved. Jesus' declaration must be interpreted within the entire scope of his experience with death, being face-to-face with the evil and wicked hatred of people. In that moment of personally experiencing humanity's violent hatred, Jesus questioned the Father but knew full well why he hung in anticipation of death. In one sense, his question must be rhetorical because he was well aware of the necessity of forsakenness, having directly questioned the Father in Gethsemane on that very subject just hours before the cross. It was there at Gethsemane that Jesus resolved to surrender himself to the Father's plan, determining, "Father, if you are willing, take this cup from me; yet not my will, but yours be done" (Luke 22:42). Despite Jesus' emotional, agonizing outburst on the cross, we know that he could have sounded the trumpet call for legions of angels to rescue him (Matt 26:53). But thank God that didn't happen!

On the topic of rhetoric, one plausible explanation is found in interpreting Jesus' words idiomatically of the state of helplessness he found himself in. Although it's not immediately apparent in the lexicons, a nuance of the term *egkataleipo* ("forsake") in the New Testament and other early literature means *to remain or leave helpless*, not merely to forsake and cause separation.[8] Jesus was asking the Father why he had left his Son helpless in the midst of this deadly experience. When such an interpretation is not only possible but even likely, it eliminates the need to posit such a challenge to a doctrine as essential as the perichoretic penetration of Father and Son.[9] Jesus was expressing the pain and humiliation of the cross experience yet remained helpless to do anything about it, because that was the plan both he and the Father agreed to. The vulnerability of the Son became fully expressed in his succumbing to this oddly wise and surprising plan. Jesus

---

8. BDAG, "ἐγκαταλείπω," 909. BDAG provides only two definitions. The first is to cause something to remain in a positive sense, *leave behind progeny*. The second is to separate connection with, *forsake, abandon, desert*. An undetected nuance is a third definition, which involves leaving alone but not necessarily separating connection; i.e., *to leave helpless or uncared for*. For instance, Heb 13:5 says, "Never will I leave you; never will I forsake (*egkataleipo*) you." The first term means to separate connection ("leave"), hence the latter term would likely contain a different nuance, such as to leave someone uncared for, *helpless*. Also cf. Matt 27:46; Mark 15:34; Acts 2:27, 31; 2 Cor 4:9.

9. *Perichoresis* is a theological term used to describe inner Trinitarian life. It refers to the interpenetration of all three persons into and throughout each other.

who is truly God would allow his eternal nature to painfully suffer in order to bring life and freedom to the world. God refuses to put himself above the pain of this risky world he brought people into.

Even if the full force of *egkataleipo* is accepted here as abandonment in separation, these definitions are by no means cold, mechanical molds to force uncomplicated ideas into. Language is often open to idiomatic expression and even overlap with the less frequent meanings of the same term, especially when the language used is a quotation of poetry, which we find here (see Ps 22:1).[10] In light of the overall context of the cross and what led up to it, the idiomatic nature of Jesus' words should be maintained. This is evidenced by the fact that within a few breaths, Jesus uttered words reminiscent of familiarity and utmost trust. Luke tells us that "Jesus called out with a loud voice, 'Father, into your hands I commit my spirit.' When he had said this, he breathed his last" (Luke 23:46). Even moments before death, the Father remained close enough to take hold of his Son.

Special attention should be given to the fact that it was not until the moment Jesus breathed his last breath that he experienced the full brunt and consequence of sin. This truth could not be more evident throughout the New Testament: "Christ died for our sins, just as the Scriptures said" (1 Cor 15:3 NLT; cf. 1 Pet 3:18; Heb 9:28). At that moment, Jesus confronted the most ruthless enemy of humanity, death itself (1 Cor 15:26). Truly it was in death that Almighty God's judgment against sin was fulfilled at the cross, the *tetelestai* moment. Just prior to death, in John 19:30 Jesus cried out *tetelestai*—it's finished!—in *anticipation* of ultimate victory over sin and death. If we can identify a moment in time that God would abandon Jesus because of sin, it would be that moment of physical death, "for the wages of sin is death" (Rom 6:23).[11] Yet it is in that very moment that Jesus cried out in dependence and utter confidence in his relationship to the Father, committing himself to his God and Father, saying "into your hands"—into your care and personal presence—"I commit my spirit."

---

10. In the context of Psalm 22 (*why have you forsaken me?*), the conclusion and divine response is one of presence and not distance: "For he has not despised or scorned the suffering of the afflicted one; he has not hidden his face from him but has listened to his cry for help" (22:24).

11. Sin is not *quantitative* as "satisfaction" and "penal substitution" theories have suggested, as if sin can be counted up and quantified so that a restitution or punishment equal to or greater than the offense is required. Scripture never teaches that all humanity's individual sins were somehow imputed to Jesus on the cross, so that he could pay for, be punished for, or make restitution for trillions of sins. At the cross, the "imputation" of sin was rather the *qualitative* reality of death itself. When Christ suffered physical death, the judgment of God was final and sin was overcome.

The extreme emotional toll Jesus experienced was expressed in a desperate plea. That plea, however, did not signal distance but was rather a heart ultimately seeking comfort. His groping was a last ditch effort to experience relationship in the midst of a nightmare. Far from being a cry of abandonment at the cross, perhaps Jesus' outburst expressed the exact opposite and even represented the closest of rapport between him and his Father. To quote Fiddes again, "It is a cry of protest, . . . but even in that cry he is beginning to relate his experience of death to God."[12] Although he remained helpless to change what was happening to him, Jesus knew that if everyone else abandoned him entirely, on another level altogether he could still look to his Father and share his grief with his God in the midst of extreme agony. Jesus cried out to the only one he could look to for comfort in that dreadful hour. The sense would be something akin to, "Oh my God, my Father, the only one who can help and comfort me, why do you leave me helpless in this deathly experience?"

Regarding the Father's abandonment, Moltmann remarks, "It was a deep division in God himself, in so far as God abandoned God and contradicted himself, and at the same time a unity in God, in so far as God was at one with God and corresponded to himself."[13] Theologians often make reference to God's inability to accomplish contradictory things, such as creating a circular square. If the contradiction for Moltmann exists in the area of God abandoning God, the only honest conclusion can be that in the godforsaken death of Jesus Christ, he was not in any real sense abandoned. Hence, the contradiction is removed. Instead, Jesus *felt* helpless and remained helpless to remove the necessity of the cross from his Father's plan. But the emphasis necessarily falls on an ongoing "unity in God" at the cross, which was indeed the case. Derek Flood understands this point well, stating, "This image of the suffering God revealed in the weakness of the cross means that no matter how helpless and alone we may feel, God is with us."[14] Truly God is with us, just as he remained with Jesus.

Facing Death: A Real Fear

Jesus' godforsaken cry was far more involved than just idiom and figure of speech. Death is so significant because it is the absolute end to life, when all living ceases. This truth adds a heightened significance to the death of Christ. Paradoxically, the Eternal Life arrived at the metaphysical end of

12. Fiddes, *Participating in God*, 158.
13. Moltmann, *Crucified God*, 244.
14. Flood, "A Relational Understanding of Atonement," 42.

life, experiencing the horrors and "agony of death" (Acts 2:24). The most important aspect of Jesus' outcry is derived from the context of death from which it was uttered. A literal translation would be akin to, "Oh my God, why have you left me for dead?" Yet this interpretation is incomplete. Is it possible that what Jesus thought he had prepared for in Gethsemane was proving to be more than he could bear?

In the form of a question from the divine, *Why is this happening?*, this query makes little sense. It would make more sense had Jesus said matter-of-factly, you've forsaken me, *you've left me for dead!* But he didn't; he posed a question, as if to say, *I don't understand what's happening!* With a frame of reference that includes both an understanding of death as truly dead and the backdrop of an open universe, we're equipped to move forward with a more satisfying explanation.

For the first time, death becomes plain to Jesus. Prior to this horrific experience, death was a future hypothetical, unreal to his eternal experience of life. Now Jesus is face-to-face with death for the first and last time. Death was staring him in the face in all of its raw and brutal glory. In a most profound revelation of death, Jesus now sees *only* death and, most significantly, loses all prospects for life beyond the grave—death is final! Fiddes offers a similar thought when he says, "God is now confronted by a nothingness and a death which is experienced as alienating and strange. Otherwise the pain of God would be simply all God's own work, God's making God's self suffer, which . . . would be no suffering at all. Nor would God's experience of death be anything like ours, and divine empathy with us would be a charade."[15]

The finality of death for the Eternal Life is the essence of Jesus' question, which makes sense of his confusion and misunderstanding: "Oh my God, why have you left me for dead *with no prospects beyond the grave?*" In a radically open universe, Jesus was facing a black hole and no longer had a hopeful vision beyond the grave. Death was now inevitable and so he expressed this new reality in terms of forsakenness. The true nature of death is forsakenness from the life of God, which was the guarantee of death in the garden. Jesus screamed out in horror because he couldn't see beyond death! Death had blinded his sights, just as sin, death, and distance can blind Almighty God to godless regions of death in hamartiological distance.

It wasn't that his Father had left him alone, but that his Father had allowed him to lose sight of life beyond the grave, an utter helplessness. This is what death does; in fact, this is what death is. In the truest possible sense, Jesus was experiencing death *and the fear of death* (Heb 2:15). Nevertheless, the Father remained by Jesus' side to reassure him so that he could

---

15. Fiddes, *Participating in God*, 236.

ultimately declare, "Father, I entrust my spirit into your hands!" (Luke 23:46 NLT). There was much more to his cry than merely a sense of helplessness to avoid the grave but also helplessness beyond the grave.[16]

Then Jesus, the Son of God, died. He spent one . . . two . . . three days in the tomb wrapped in burial cloths and expensive spices, demonstrating to the Roman and religious worlds that Jesus' death meant dead.

Distance: A Functional Equivalent

Ultimately, Jesus' godforsakenness pointed to the Father's refusal to intervene in his Son's death, leaving him helpless and without rescue, though only temporarily. This experience was cut short by resurrection as the Father's conclusive answer to Jesus' helplessness. With resurrection looming on the horizon, Jesus was able to finally express thoughts of safety and assurance, saying, *Father, I commit my spirit into the care of your strong hands.* Jesus' godforsaken cry had expressed a *functional* distance rather than the ontological, hamartiological distance that people can experience apart from God's life. Yet that functional distance was real in the sense that God experienced physical, human death.

Naturally, Jesus was never isolated from the Father's knowledge, presence, or power because he remained without sin, the very thing that made his sacrifice acceptable to God. Jesus was never cut off from the blessed presence of his Father, nor was he secluded from his "ever-present help" (Ps 46:1). It had to be a functional rather than ontological equivalent because, in the face of real death, humanity never cries out to God as Jesus did. If anything, mortal nature groans for its idols while crying out *against* God. Jesus' experience of the functional equivalent of godforsakenness does not diminish the reality of it, nor does it remove the sting of death that he endured for all people. Jesus literally died, for all of us. He suffered in order to save us. Fiddes sums it up this way:

> It is not that God abandons God, that one person of the Trinity expels another. Rather, God is willing to experience God's own relationships in a new way in the face of death. God is willing to allow otherness to become alienation, to take a journey into the unknown, into "no man's land." This is a risk for God, sharing

---

16. Jesus' solidarity with mortal nature was complete once death eclipsed any hope beyond the grave. Job summed up this perspective of mortality when he said, "What strength do I have, that I should still hope? What prospects, that I should be patient? Do I have the strength of stone? Is my flesh bronze? Do I have any power to help myself, now that success has been driven from me?" (6:11–13).

the risk of creation. What it might mean for the divine life cannot be predicted ahead of its happening, any more than can any journey of forgiving love. God is open to the strangeness of a new, dark movement in the dance of love. God encounters death, and uses it to define deity, in victory over death as the living God.[17]

There should be no doubt Jesus experienced a "judgment" of God at the cross (Mark 14:27; cf. Zech. 13:7), but the metaphor of judgment coincides with and should be equated with his physical death. This is why the New Testament authors so often refer to the "blood" of Christ to summarize the significance of the cross.[18] At Golgotha, there was no punishment or separation between the triune identities but only the closest connection and union, as was the case for all eternity. The victory of the Godhead over the powers of darkness—the defeat of sin, death, and the devil—became a reality through the precision of triune teamwork in flawless cooperation of tri-unity. Far from being driven apart, the Trinity accomplished their assault on the kingdom of darkness as a united, organized cohort. On the cross at Calvary, it was "*Christ*, who through the eternal *Spirit* offered himself unblemished to *God*" (Heb 9:14, emphasis added).

Believers can now rejoice because they are free from sin and death, not because Jesus hung on a tree, but because Jesus underwent the full experience of death on their behalf (Heb 2:9). In selfless love, Jesus surrendered to a world full of hate. Hate wrapped its ugly arms around him, tortured him, and the world abandoned him, while the Father would not, and in fact could not, neglect his Son. Jesus experienced the torment and agony of the cross and finally died a physical death in the arms of his heavenly Father. This death was the consequence of sin. There have been two sides to this coin since the very beginning, something Paul describes as a definite "law of sin and death" (Rom 8:2).[19] For Jesus to die and conquer death by rising out from the grave meant that he was victorious over sin and can deliver those in bondage to it. Jesus overcame death and the Demon who holds the power of death (Heb 2:14). Jesus overcame a competing kingdom of sin and death established under Satan's rule all the way back in the garden.

---

17. Fiddes, *Participating in God*, 244.

18. See Matt 26:27–28; Mark 14:23–24; Luke 22:20; John 6:53–57; 19:33–34; Acts 20:28; Rom 3:25; 1 Cor 10:16; 11:25–27; Eph 1:7; 2:13; Col 1:19–20; Heb 9:12–14; 10:3–14, 19–22, 28–31; 12:24; 13:11–12, 20; 1 Pet 1:1–2; 1 John 1:6–9; 5:6; Rev 1:5–6; 5:9–10; 7:14–17; 12:10–11.

19. See also Gen 2:16–17; Deut 24:16; Prov 10:16; Rom 5:12, 14, 21; 6:16, 23; 7:13; 8:2; 1 Cor 15:56; Jas 1:15.

All believers now attest that the blood of Jesus Christ has cleansed us from all sin and has bridged the distance that kept us from God. The church can now proclaim that "in Christ Jesus you who once were far away have been brought near by the blood of Christ" (Eph 2:13). Through the precious blood of Jesus, every believer stands righteous before God, reconciled, redeemed, ransomed, and fully rinsed with a washing that makes us white as snow (Isa 1:18).

FORGIVENESS IS COMPLETE IN CHRIST

God's extravagant love has always offered forgiveness in unexpected ways. Even without a sacrifice, God can still forgive sin! He forgives when someone repents, but he has also forgiven rebels who didn't deserve it (Mic 7:18), and he's forgiven still others because someone interceded (Num 14:20; Luke 23:34). The basis for such forgiveness has always been the merciful love of God (Ps 51:1). God never once fails to love his enemies, the ungodly, sinners, and every other human being deceived by Satan and the tormenting dread of death. The cross boldly displays God's radical love for all the world to see, so the cross solves the sin problem once and for all. Scripture declares that at just the right time, in deepest compassion, God sent his one and only Son to die a gory, bloody death on a tree (Rom 5:6–8). The essence of that cross-death was to manifest perfect love in the face of human evil and to confront and conquer Satan's kingdom of sin and death once and for all. The powerful, loving influence of the cross is designed to draw all humankind to salvation. When people respond to God's message of grace through Jesus Christ, their sins are washed away.

Jesus forgave sin before and after the cross, demonstrating that God chooses forgiveness whenever possible: "But I want you to know that the Son of Man has authority on earth to forgive sins" (Mark 2:10). Today, the believer stands as one who is *totally* forgiven, thoroughly washed white as snow. The psalmist pleads, "Hide your face from my sins and blot out all my iniquity" (Ps 51:9). He's begging God not to look on his sin any longer but to forgive and blot it out forever. The Lord responds in another place, "I, even I, am he who blots out your transgressions, for my own sake, and remembers your sins no more" (Isa 43:25). *This is for God's own sake!* The Lord suffers terribly from every broken relationship and thus is infinitely eager to forgive and eradicate all sin from his memory. Once a person enters a saving relationship with God through Jesus, sin has no standing whatever between them and God.

The psalmist also says, "Because of your great compassion, blot out the stain of my sins" (Ps 51:1 NLT). With a forgiveness full of compassion, God does that very thing. Even though no believer can become sinless, we all remain in God's total forgiveness and can never be any less than pardoned. God holds nothing against us but draws us near to himself in newness of life. The psalmist experiences the potential rooted in this forgiveness because God keeps his feet from slipping. He sees salvation as a rescue from death into a walk of newness in God's presence—no distance whatsoever! "For you have rescued me from death; you have kept my feet from slipping. So now I can walk in your presence, O God, in your life-giving light" (56:13 NLT; cf. 1 John 1:7). Only a new life in the divine presence can keep his feet from slipping. When sin and death no longer darken the believer's path to God's presence, she can be confident it was a divinely compassionate forgiveness that sealed her victory.

Even after salvation, confession and the Christian's struggle with sin never change that person's status as forgiven. The first Johannine epistle is largely misunderstood as teaching that believers must continually "confess" sin in order to remain in fellowship with God, which some equate with a post-salvation need for forgiveness: "If we confess our sins, he is faithful and just and will forgive us our sins" (1 John 1:9). However, the author is writing about salvation from a rather strict perspective. Either you abide with Jesus in the light of salvation or you abide in darkness among the unsaved; i.e., you're in or you're out! Thus, the following is true of *every* believer: "But if we are living in the light, as God is in the light, then we have fellowship with each other, and the blood of Jesus, his Son, cleanses us from all sin" (1:7 NLT). The fact that this purification is an ongoing reality is reflected by the Greek present tense: The blood of Jesus *keeps on continually purifying us* from all sin. This deepest, abiding cleansing belongs to every believer because we all share the same perspective, that we must "confess our sins, [just as] he is faithful and just and will forgive us our sins and purify us from all unrighteousness" (1:9). Claiming that one is sinless before God is the position of the unbeliever (1:8, 10), but acknowledging that my own sin has kept me from God's presence is the confession of every true saint. Confession is the attitude of a new life that remains in God's forgiveness because that person is now "living in the light, as God is in the light."

When believers confess any sin that becomes known to them, they don't become any more forgiven. Rather, confession and repentance are as much an emotional exercise as a spiritual one, designed to open up the confessing heart to God. Confession makes the heart and conscience transparent to God's presence in a manner that welcomes divine healing, deliverance, and holiness to replace the deceitfulness of sin. Even though confession can't

SALVATION

add a crumb of forgiveness to my life, it does apply the gentle, cleansing ointment of God's renewing presence: "Cleanse me with hyssop, and I will be clean; wash me, and I will be whiter than snow.... Create in me a pure heart, O God, and renew a steadfast spirit within me" (Ps 51:7, 10).

Although forgiveness is the enduring possession of every believer, it is within the realm of possibility to return to death's trajectory. The warnings of Scripture are numerous, that any believer can potentially lose their salvation.[20] This is probably one of the rarest occurrences in history but a possibility nonetheless. We'd do well to share the attitude of the writer of Hebrews, who says, "Even though we speak like this, dear friends, we are convinced of better things in your case—the things that have to do with salvation" (Heb 6:9). In fact, we should be confident that the majority of humanity will be saved.[21] Indeed, Jesus died for all! Jesus has confronted and overcome death in all its multifaceted complexity. When anyone expresses even a mustard seed of faith toward the provisions of their Creator, they can be saved through Jesus Christ.[22]

Because this chapter addresses matters of salvation in an open universe, we will turn our attention to the two sacraments of the church, water baptism and the Lord's Supper. Through these sacraments, believers receive forgiveness and partake in the divine presence.

RITUAL OF ENTRANCE: WATER BAPTISM

Entrance into the community of faith has always been open to everyone, even under the old covenant (e.g., Isa 51:4–5; 66:18–19). However, the call to follow and serve God was not always connected to water baptism as it is today under the new covenant. Since the moment John the Baptist announced the arrival of "the Lamb of God who takes away the sin of the world" (John 1:29), the church's message has been uniquely tied to repentance and water immersion, a public rite of passage. Nearly in every case, the earliest records of the call to repent in the book of Acts include instruction

---

20. See Matt 10:22; John 15:6; 1 Cor 15:2; 2 Tim 2:12; Heb 6:4–6; 10:26; 2 Pet 2:20–21.

21. For a defense of biblical inclusivism, see Sanders, *No Other Name*; and Pinnock, *Wideness in God's Mercy*.

22. The solid assurance of such a glorious salvation rests on the overt testimony of a person's faith in Christ. But, believers should also cling to the hopeful expectation that God's love is far more extravagant than any one of us could ever conceive. This curious hope throws itself at the mercy of the sacrificial love of God through Jesus Christ to save anyone who gropes for help in a world ravaged by death and distance.

to be *immediately* submerged in water:²³ "Repent and be baptized, every one of you" (Acts 2:38).²⁴ Based on the Acts passages alone, we can deduce that the first-century church knew nothing of an acceptance of salvation in Christ that did not include being baptized, usually on the same day.

There should be no doubt that any person who believed in Jesus was baptized without delay. Regarding the Philippian jailer, Scripture attests that "immediately (*parachrema*) he and all his household were baptized," *parachrema* meaning at once or without delay (Acts 16:33). This passage is by no means exceptional, as even a cursory review of Acts demonstrates that this urgency was the norm.²⁵ When Paul encounters a group of John's disciples who had only received John's baptism of repentance, Paul informs them, "'John's baptism was a baptism of repentance. He told the people to believe in the one coming after him, that is, in Jesus.' On hearing this, they were baptized in the name of the Lord Jesus" (19:4–5). Based on this episode, Robert Stein concludes, "It should be noted in this account the need of repentance (whether preached by John the Baptist or the Christian church) along with Christian baptism is assumed as necessary and inseparable in the experience of conversion to the Christian faith."²⁶

When someone today expresses faith in Jesus, we should be asking the same question posed by the Ethiopian eunuch, "What can stand in the way of my being baptized?" (Acts 8:36). Nothing at all! By all means, you should be baptized! This was exactly Philip's response, to baptize without delay. This echoes Ananias's urgency toward Paul's baptism: "And now what are you waiting for? Get up, be baptized and wash your sins away" (22:16). Moreover, on the occasion of the Gentile Pentecost, the Apostle Peter "ordered (*prostasso*) that they be baptized in the name of Jesus Christ" (10:48). The term *prostasso* is emphatic, used even of the "appointed times" marked out by God (17:26). Thus, baptism should regularly accompany faith.

---

23. See Acts 2:41; 8:12–13, 16, 36, 38; 9:18; 10:47–48; 16:15, 33; 18:8; 19:3–5; 22:16.

24. Some object to Peter commanding people to be *baptized* in this passage, arguing that only the imperative to *repent* holds the force of a command. Robert Stein responds, stating, "No great weight should be put on the fact that the dual command in 2:38 involves a second person plural imperative ('you repent') and a third person singular imperative ('each one of you be baptized'). The latter simply seeks to underscore emphatically the command to each one addressed. Examples of the use of a second person plural imperative and a third person singular imperative side by side can be found in Exod 16:29; Josh 6:10; 2 Kgs 10:19; Zech 7:10; 1 Macc 10:63 in the LXX and in *Did.* 15:3" ("Baptism in Luke-Acts," 37 n. 10).

25. Where faith and baptism are closely linked, see Acts 8:12–13, 35–39; 10:43–48; 16:14–15, 31–34; 18:8; 19:4–5.

26. Stein, "Baptism in Luke-Acts," 38.

Baptism is scripturally and apostolically designated as a necessary component in a person's overall response to the gospel invitation. As an act of obedience, baptism is essential to repentance. Though there are obvious exceptions, like the thief on the cross who died without baptism (Luke 23:42), Christian baptism is important because it saves in a *temporal* sense (cf. 1 Pet 3:21). Salvation is both visible and hidden, both people-oriented and God-oriented, both temporal and eternal. The believer's *temporal* salvation is experienced in history and displayed to the community by confessing Jesus Christ as Lord (Rom 10:9) and submitting to the waters of baptism. The community recognizes the public rite of baptism as a priority of obedience and therefore a sign that one has yielded to Christ's authority. Eternal salvation is not hindered when baptism is impossible or neglected, but temporal salvation is hindered when the community doesn't observe that person's rite of passage into the kingdom of God's saints. In a temporal application, baptism saves by bringing the person out of the world and associating her with the community of the faithful. Baptism belongs as much to the community as it does to me.

The immediate, faith-accompanying act of water baptism is important because of what it represents. Though a passage like Rom 6:3–4 interprets Christian baptism as being "baptized into [Jesus'] death," which is clearly the case, the book of Acts opens up the dimension of baptism that relates to the Spirit's presence. In Acts, Christian baptism is the initiatory ceremony, the rite of passage, into the new covenant promise of the Spirit. This is the promise that God's presence abides with his people through the Spirit. Whereas Paul highlights the negative side, that a death has taken place, Acts focuses on the positive side, which illustrates submersion into a new experience of God's presence. The waters of baptism anticipate the flood of the Spirit's presence.

"For John baptized with water, but in a few days you will be baptized with the Holy Spirit" (Acts 1:5). Here Jesus contrasts John's baptism of repentance with the newness of an outpouring of the Spirit, which finds its first complete fulfillment during Peter's sermon. Boldly confronting a distant generation, Peter declares, "Repent and be baptized, every one of you, in the name of Jesus Christ for the forgiveness of your sins. And you will receive the gift of the Holy Spirit. The promise is for you and your children and for all who are far off" (2:38–39). Notice Peter's invitation is open to all who are *far off*, anyone distant from God and his people. Also note that the Spirit's reception immediately follows water baptism. Throughout Acts, baptism is closely connected to a believer's initial reception of the divine presence and entrance into the new life of the Spirit.[27]

This unity of both water and Spirit Baptism becomes evident in Paul, "one Spirit, . . . one baptism" (Eph 4:4–5; cf. 1 Cor. 12:13), and through Jesus' words to Nicodemus. Jesus says, "Very truly I tell you, no one can enter the kingdom of God unless they are born of (*ek*) water and the Spirit" (John 3:5). Regarding Jesus' statement, Frederick Bruner comments that "Jesus is describing *one* event, signaled by the *single* preposition *ek* (literally, 'up out of') connecting the two nouns, 'water and spirit.'"[28] Furthermore, the use of the Greek preposition *ek* ("out from") rather than *en* ("in") suggests immersion into and up out of the waters of baptism.[29] Anyone who wants to enter God's kingdom must be birthed out from the baptism that is *both water and Spirit*, again indicating the close connection between baptism and God's holy presence.

The waters of baptism serve to illustrate entrance into the visible and hidden kingdom of God. Baptism is the public rite of passage accepted by the community and thus an acknowledgment of the Spirit's preparatory work. Baptismal waters accompany the sovereign work of the Spirit, apart from whom no one would approach God to begin with (John 3:8). The climax of this prevenient work of grace is experienced in salvation as the waters wash over me and guarantee my new position in a spiritual family, the visible kingdom of God. Those same waters provide entrance into God's hidden kingdom through the all-consuming presence of God's Spirit. Initial reception of the Spirit is likened to total submersion into waters that fully cover and encompass. Believers are thus introduced to God's kingdom through immersion into the fullness of God's presence, a baptism of water and Spirit.

Water baptism is portrayed another way in Peter's writings. The apostle writes that "God waited patiently in the days of Noah while the ark was being built. In it only a few people, eight in all, were saved through water, and this water symbolizes baptism that now saves you also—not the removal of dirt from the body but the pledge of a clear conscience toward God" (1 Pet 3:20–21). Rather than a guilt-ridden heart that bears an overwhelming sense of distance from God, the flood waters of baptism represent God's presence via a cleansing that produces a "clear conscience" untainted by distance.

---

27. There are a few passages, however, that mention baptism without any explicit event of the Spirit; see Acts 8:36–39; 16:14–15, 31–34; 18:8.

28. Bruner, *Gospel of John*, 175, emphasis original.

29. Ibid., 176.

According to Peter, the waters of baptism function as an antitype to the flood waters, making the flood of water baptism reminiscent of that ancient deluge. The flood waters didn't save, they destroyed; it was the ark that Noah built that brought salvation. Hence, the early floodwaters represent God's remorseful heart in his attempt to correct what had gone terribly wrong, a distance of wickedness that grew totally out of control (Gen 6:5–7; 7:4). The wicked of that world met their final distance from God under the waters of just judgment. The baptismal floodwaters are therefore the *reversal* of the waters of judgment and distance, so humanity can now experience the waters of blessing, forgiveness, and the divine presence.

Peter goes on to say, "[Baptism] saves you by the resurrection of Jesus Christ, who has gone into heaven and is at God's right hand—with angels, authorities and powers in submission to him" (1 Pet 3:21–22). Peter reminds us that baptism is based on the resurrection life of Jesus, which forever stands opposed to death and distance. Jesus' victory over death means he stands victorious over every power, most notably over Satan and the demonic powers who wielded the power of death to keep people in bondage to guilt and fear (Heb 2:14). The reversal of the flood's condemnation and the deliverance wrought by God's flooding presence is dramatically portrayed in Christian baptism.[30]

CEREMONY OF PRESENCE: THE EUCHARIST

The Lord's Supper, Eucharist, Communion, the Table is by its very nature a dynamic ritual of presence involving both word and action, while the gathered community observes the eating of broken "flesh" and the drinking of spilt "blood." Believers see Christ's sacrifice in front of them and personally appropriate the elements by faith while receiving Christ to themselves with all the benefits of his salvation: "Is not the cup of thanksgiving for which we give thanks a participation (*koinonia*) in the blood of Christ? And is not the bread that we break a participation (*koinonia*) in the body of Christ?" (1

---

30. Who may administer Christian baptism, and how should one be baptized? Baptizing new Christians is open to any believer who is willing to do so; Scripture never restricts this open aspect to ordained clergy, deacons, or anyone else. Scripture, however, does restrict those who may be baptized. Those who are baptized must readily and consciously express the decision to accept God's way as revealed in the person of Christ. This is therefore a denial of infant baptism, which has been adequately addressed elsewhere; see Aland, *Did the Early Church Baptize Infants?* For very early sources, see Lewis, "Baptismal Practices," 1–17. Finally, full bodily immersion is the ideal means for baptism. A full dunk best illustrates both burial with Christ and complete immersion in the Spirit.

Cor 10:16). We experience the "fellowship" (from *koinonia*) of his body and blood by mysteriously *participating* in his loving sacrifice. This participation points to our own transformation when we vividly encounter the truth behind the elements and grasp that we too must lay down our lives following Jesus' example.

Besides the fellowship of Jesus' body and blood, believers also enjoy the *koinonia* of the church as body of Christ, one loaf rather than many: "Because there is one loaf, we, who are many, are one body, for we all share the one loaf" (1 Cor 10:17). As one body, the church is brought to terms with the reality that new covenant election and participation includes every believer who has placed trust in Jesus Christ for salvation. Through this celebration, we therefore renew the terms of the covenant, which include both our part and God's part. On our part, we're expected to renew our obligations of faith and obedience. On God's part, his obligation is to make the benefits of his presence fully known in order to lead us into the fullness of salvation. Finally, as we feast together with God's community, we look forward to the eschatological day that we will be reunited with our King in a restored paradise (Matt 26:29; Mark 14:25). Only then will we experience God in an even greater way than the Edenic presence of Yahweh that was experienced by our ancestors.

The Reformers believed it was fundamental to the experience of salvation for the gathered church to locate the presence of Christ in the sacrament in one manner or another. Seeing that the resurrected humanity of Christ is spatially located, the Reformers differed on their opinions of how that presence is revealed in the Supper. For the Reformers, the elements were not transformed into Christ's physical body as was the case in Roman Catholicism's doctrine of transubstantiation.[31] For Martin Luther and the Lutherans, Jesus' physical presence was invisible but nonetheless real and intermingled with the elements; it was somehow located "in, under, or beside" the bread and wine. Calvin and the Reformed tradition held the doctrine of virtualism, which teaches that "although Christ's body ascended to heaven, the Supper of the Lord, when received with true faith, conveys a unique spiritual power [virtue]."[32] Calvin reasoned that it was necessary for the Holy Spirit to unite our souls with Christ in heaven because the second person of the Trinity now exists as both God *and human,* thus limiting his

---

31. Transubstantiation teaches that the physical elements of bread and wine are changed, though not in appearance, into the physical, *substantial* body and blood of Jesus Christ. This is historically what Roman Catholicism has intended by real presence.

32. Campbell, *Methodist Doctrine,* 75. John Wesley and the Methodists also held to a form of virtualism.

physical presence to his current seat at the right hand of God.³³ Others maintained that the Lord's Supper presents Christ purely in terms of a memorial or reminder. This view was held primarily by Ulrich Zwingli and his followers, as well as the Anabaptists. Even though Christ is present, it is not due to any unique connection to the elements.

While the debate still rages over the nature of Christ's presence in the Eucharist, believers can unite over the truth that they are indeed partakers of divine presence through the Communion. The church is the body of Christ because we have all equally entered God's presence through repentance and Christian baptism. Whether that presence is somehow real and invisible or a symbolic reminder that Jesus is always with us, the presence of the one who died and rose again is received in an exceptional way through partaking of the elements of bread and wine in the context of the community of faith.

Not only are believers saved men and women who have spiritually entered into the King's presence through faith and water baptism, but we also enjoy the privilege of experientially feasting upon that presence in a most spiritually profound way. By the experience of both word and deed, we receive the body and blood of Christ. We feast beside brothers and sisters in Christ, observing in the words and actions of the community a truth that is lived out before our very eyes. Not only is separation and distance from God overcome and done away with, but so is the distance between one another as Christians unite to celebrate the elements as *one body* in unity of *one faith*.³⁴

---

33. Calvin, *Institutes*, 104–7. The idea behind Calvin's virtualism is that Jesus' humanity now consists of a resurrected human body that can only be in one place at any given time. His physical body remains at the right hand of the Father in heaven, making it impossible for him to be physically united with the elements while the Eucharist is being observed in many places throughout the world.

34. Who may *administer* the Lord's Supper, and who may *participate*? Once again, any willing believer is able to administer the Supper. As with baptism, Scripture nowhere restricts this open aspect. There is strong evidence that the earliest practices of the Lord's Supper took place in the context of an actual meal, the *agape* feast (Acts 2:42, 46; Jude 12; 2 Pet 2:13). Whether it was Christian families or other believers partaking of a meal that included the elements, the New Testament church never requires ordained clergy to reside over it. Though an actual meal is the best context for the Eucharist, in most cases throughout Christian history the church has deviated from this, serving only a minimal amount of wine (or juice) and a morsel of bread. Partaking from a single cup and a single loaf is ideal but not required.

The other question of who may *partake* of the Meal is even more open. With full knowledge that Judas would betray him, Jesus still permitted Judas's presence at the institution of the Eucharist on the night Jesus was betrayed. Though certainly not ideal, the participation of unbelievers is ultimately left open by Jesus' acceptance of Judas at the Last Supper. John Wesley apparently permitted unbelievers to the Table if they came with *trust* ("faith") that God would act. Wesley's thought on this may resemble the Puritans who believed that committed, church-going "unbelievers" were not justified

CONCLUSION: CLOSING THE DISTANCE

A climactic tone was set forth in this chapter in the dramatic reversal and defeat of death and distance through God's most glorious display of presence in resurrection. But before enjoying such a victory, Christ Jesus experienced true mortality. In a radically open universe, the raw honesty of Jesus' outcry reveals the shock and dread of the mortal nature in the face of death: *Oh my God, why have you left me for dead? Why have you left me without hope beyond the grave?* This cry reflects the backlash of mortality and Jesus' solidarity with every human being. God's experience with death was real but was strikingly disappointed by its reversal in resurrection.

Jesus' physical suffering and sacrifice point to salvation being secured through a physical death on the cross, as blood was spilt. Redemption has nothing whatsoever to do with any distance between Jesus and his Father. Rather, the veracity of the cross depends on the sinless perfection of the One who knew no sin and on his resolute love in the face of hatred and grotesque violence. God the Father did not punish his Son on the cross but stood by him while the world rejected him. Jesus voluntarily surrendered his life in order to defeat death as the greatest expression of cruel evil. Because the Father never turned his back on or abandoned his Son to any real distance, Jesus could confidently commit his spirit into the care of his Father's hands at his death. It was there from the Father's care that the greatest victory of all human history came in the event of the resurrection of Jesus out from among death and the dead ones. Jesus overcame death once and for all, having experienced death for everyone.

Once anyone enters salvation, their cleansing is thorough and complete, never requiring any more or any less forgiveness. Confession of sin is important because it keeps us "real" with God, but it never changes our status as totally forgiven. Even so, the remote possibility exists to lose one's salvation if God is ultimately rejected. This should not deter our confidence, however, that God will protect our relationship with him and even save the majority of humanity. This hope rests on the extravagant, sacrificial love of God to always do abundantly above all that we could ask or think.

The church now preaches the gospel of knowing God through resurrection life: "Now this is eternal life: that they know you, the only true God, and Jesus Christ, whom you have sent" (John 17:3). When people embrace

---

until they had a special experience. That said, one could come to "saving faith" through partaking of the Eucharist. It was ordained by the Lord as "a means of conveying to men either preventing, or justifying, or sanctifying grace, according to their several necessities" (Outler, *Works of John Wesley*, 1:381). See also Curnock, *Journal of Rev. John Wesley*, 2:361.

this profoundly simple message, they submit to the waters of baptism and thereby become immersed into God's presence for the first time. This new life in the divine presence is then celebrated through the Eucharist meal, a celebration of closeness with God and all believers.

7

Pentecost
Open Expansion

In an open universe, the revelation and impact of divine presence far outweighs the distress of distance. In the last chapter, we introduced the defeat of distance through the cross of salvation, so we can now review the impact that the resurrection has on the church, a sustained encounter with divine presence. Through resurrection, Jesus was crowned Victor and exalted to the right hand of the throne of God where he now reigns over sin and death. The cataclysm of the cross was followed by the world-changing event of the resurrection, which ushered in the glory of Pentecost, God's most splendid and sustained expression of divine presence.

When Jesus introduced resurrection into a world of mortality, the whole program changed. From his throne in the heavenlies, divine life could now touch a dead world—the portal was opened! In Scripture, God's throne in the heavens is largely symbolic of the (untouchable immortality of the) fullness of divine presence. But the heavens were rent! Jesus' death tore a hole in the fabric of a mortal universe to make room for immortality and the presence of God. The division between mortality and immortality was forever broken, creating a free flowing channel between the two. Mortals can now be touched with the gift of eternal life, and these are the children of God! The re-creation of the universe in the divine presence begins with God's people, a new community for a new era under the newness of God's Spirit.

We're going to look closely at Jesus' spiritual reign and the initial impact of resurrection on the kingdom of saints, the arrival of the pentecostal presence of God. We'll see how Christ is Lord over an open kingdom in a spiritual reign that is both relational and dynamic. Once delivered from the distance of an enemy kingdom, believers can experience the endless possibilities of kingdom life through the presence of a King most actively involved in the life and mission of his people.

INTRODUCING AN OPEN, COVENANTAL KINGDOM

When God approached Abraham to covenant with him, he promised to bless the whole world through Abraham and his descendants. This promise was partially carried out through each covenant to follow, the Mosaic and Davidic covenants. Even still, the prophets anticipated more. Thomas Schreiner summarizes many features of their expectations: "The prophets looked forward to a day when God's saving promises would be fulfilled, his kingdom would come, the New Covenant would be inaugurated, a new exodus from Babylon would be realized, the Spirit would be poured out on Israel, and Israel would keep God's law. The prophets promised a new creation, a new temple, a new covenant, and a new king."[1]

Throughout Acts we see these expectations being fulfilled under the new covenant, which provides the architectural design of a new spiritual kingdom in the dawning of a new age under God's rule. The reality of covenant joins the people of God to the presence of God, while the kingdom is the sphere for living out life in his presence. This new covenant kingdom is God's way of comprehensively satisfying the expectations of Israel and her prophets, those who were looking forward to the forgiveness of sin, the arrival of an ultimate deliverer, and a special relationship to God's Spirit, the very presence of God.[2] This doesn't at all imply that the Hebrews had never experienced forgiveness, or a work of the Spirit, or even divine deliverance under the old covenant. But the sense behind the promise of newness was something permanent and decisively victorious for Israel. This was a final acceptance of God's people to himself, the final closure of past distance, and a final rebuke to the dark forces at work against them.

The new covenant would satisfy these and other hopes, bringing victory over sin, victory by a new activity of God's Spirit-presence, and an anointed Deliverer who would bring the decisive victory blow to God's

---

1. Schreiner, *New Testament Theology*, 44.

2. Regarding a unique deliverer's anointing with the Spirit, see Isa 11:2; *1 En.* 49:3; 62:2; *Pss. Sol.* 17:37; 18:7; *T. Levi* 18:6–8; *T. Jud.* 24:2. On the forgiveness and cleansing from sin that are wrought by the Spirit, see Ezek 36:25–26; 1QS 4:20–21; 1QH 16:11–12.

enemies. This new Deliverer would be the messianic finale to trump all of Israel's previous deliverers, a Savior *par excellence*.

From Covenant to Kingdom

Before the cross, both believing and unbelieving Israelites were called out from the world to live under Moses' law, the distinguishing legislation of a people privileged to live under theocracy and God's rule. Among believing and unbelieving Israel, some abided in the spiritual sphere of God's kingdom while others intentionally or unwittingly dwelt in the kingdom of Satan. The former lived close to God, the latter at a distance. Nonetheless, Israel was the experiment of world history intended to eliminate God's absence and keep him close to the world through a chosen race of mediators, interceding between God and the kingdoms of this world. Moses' law functioned as a tutor to point both believer and unbeliever to God (Gal 3:24). Sadly, the warnings (including death) of that law were often met with resistance, resulting in increased distance (Rom 7:5).

The law defined sin, which produces death, the ultimate distance (Rom 7:7–13). Yet those who lived so long under Moses' law, or what we think of as the old covenant or the Old Testament, were expecting a revision. What they did not comprehend was that the change would mean a radical move away from a national law to an international, otherworldly, spiritual law, falling under the designation of a *new* covenant (Jer 31:31).[3] There were hints of Gentile inclusion, but the deliverance always belonged primarily to Israel (Matt 10:6; 15:24). Under the old law, God's chosen people continued to fail miserably, on an individual as well as national level. Even this pointed to the need for something better, something intrinsic and dynamic, a new covenant.

The new covenant would mean the law of God written on people's hearts by the Spirit (2 Cor 3:3)—God's Holy Presence—who fills *and frees* the believer (3:17; cf. Rom 8:21). This covenant would reach so deep as to cleanse the conscience (Heb 9:14) and would extend so far as to bring about a new community of followers indwelt with the God-presence (2 Cor 3:6), a new community in a new era designed to highlight a unique fellowship with the triune God. The new covenant marks an era when the former distance is mocked by the uniquely close fellowship believers now experience in union with Israel's Messiah, a King from the lineage of David, who possesses and gives away "the Spirit without measure" (John 3:34 ESV).

---

3. See Jer 32:40; 50:5; Isa 24:5; 55:3; 61:8; Ezek 16:60; 37:26.

Under the old covenant, God poured the Spirit's presence into a few individuals for important service, such as priests, prophets, and kings. But with Jesus' own blood as the basis for the new covenant, by the removal of sin's distance through forgiveness and the removal of death's distance through resurrection, God brings every member of the church into a true unity for ministry through a living source of unity, the gracious gift of God's Spirit. Once a person's eyes are opened by the light of the glory of the gospel of Christ and she realizes that her entire life has been lived enslaved in Satan's kingdom, she can surrender to God's reign. By placing faith in the God of a new covenant made up of many members, believers enjoy entrance into the present spiritual kingdom of God and of his Christ (Col 1:13).

In this spiritual kingdom, God's presence within his people has made true unity and a united mission possible, creating a new movement characterized by "one body and one Spirit, . . . one Lord, one faith, one baptism" (Eph 4:4, 5). This new spiritual sphere of existence, entered into by faith and surrender to Jesus Christ, is designed to display the kingdom of Christ on earth. Yet for the remainder of this age it exists primarily as a spiritual rather than physical kingdom. The church is not the kingdom, but believers are royal citizens of that kingdom who manifest the presence and reign of King Jesus on earth.

Manifesting a Spiritual Kingdom

Through Jesus' life and ministry of signs and wonders—signs of God's presence and wonder toward his worth—he introduced to the world an in-breaking of the kingdom of God and manifested the power of that kingdom reign through his own person. The kingdom of God was present in and through Jesus' personal presence (Luke 11:20; 17:21).[4] That same Jesus now reigns at the right hand of the throne of God! In highest position of power and authority, his presence extends to his church through the medium of the third person of the Trinity. The reign of Christ's kingdom is currently made known through the experience of the Spirit in his church. The book of Acts and the event of Pentecost present the climax of the kingdom of Christ in this age.

It is regarding this invisible, spiritual kingdom that Jesus alludes to at the opening of Acts when the disciples ask him if Messiah would now restore the socio-political, Davidic kingdom to Israel. They expected this manifest kingdom to conquer the Roman world! In response, Jesus contrasts the visible, conquering theocratic kingdom that they want with the present invisible,

---

4. In Luke 17:21, "the kingdom of God *is in your midst*" can also be translated, *is within you* (KJV).

spiritual kingdom: "[Jesus] said to them: 'It is not for you to know the times or dates the Father has set (*etheto*) by his own authority. But you will receive power when the Holy Spirit comes on you; and you will be my witnesses in Jerusalem, and in all Judea and Samaria, and to the ends of the earth'" (Acts 1:7–8). Notice that the kingdom the disciples have in mind remains open-ended for the time being. The Greek term *etheto* indicates that the kingdom they were anticipating is "set" or fixed for a future time that God the Father alone has the prerogative over. At least for now, the permanent establishment of the kingdom of Christ over the entire world remains open and *not yet*.

Though inaugurated, Jesus' kingdom will not be fully established until the end of the age (1 Cor 15:24–27), but this eschatological kingdom is not the only thing left open. In a different way, so is the expansion of Christ's spiritual kingdom as it exists today within the sphere of power from God's Spirit. Leading up to Pentecost, Jesus assured his disciples that the presence of the Spirit would cause an open, relational kingdom to expand out from Jerusalem all the way to the ends of the earth.[5] Jesus' summary of the kingdom's advance was used by Luke to outline the book of Acts, allowing us the readers to experience the journey of this encroaching kingdom mission from Jerusalem to the Roman world in chapters 1–28.

At Pentecost, Christ's spiritual kingdom became an invisible reality for the church, though a reality nonetheless (Luke 17:20–21). Invisible only in the sense that we do not yet see all enemies subdued under the Lord Jesus (Acts 2:35). Yet we do see his kingdom very much manifest through the presence of the Spirit, through signs and wonders, and through a kingdom of priests and the prophethood of all believers who obey their Lord's marching orders.[6]

LAUNCHING AN OPEN KINGDOM: SPIRIT BAPTISM

While speaking about the kingdom of God in Acts 1, Jesus informs his disciples to wait for *the promise of the Father*, which we immediately learn is the Holy Spirit (1:4–5). This prediction would have been significant not only to the disciples but to all Israel. We might simplify the matter of first-century Jewish expectation by the three fundamental ways in which the Israelites viewed God's Spirit: an eschatological outpouring, a special empowerment of God for prophetic utterance, and characteristically resting upon the Messiah who was to come.[7]

---

5. Amos Yong uses the designation, "God's relational kingdom," in his article "Relational Theology and the Holy Spirit," 20.

6. On the church as a kingdom of priests, see Rev 1:6; 5:10; Exod 19:6.

7. Menzies, *Empowered for Witness*, 102.

Within this matrix of hope, Jesus announced the Spirit's in-breaking ministry. Regarding this impending promise of the Father, both John and Jesus used the same language of Spirit Baptism (Luke 3:16). Being the last of the Old Testament prophets, John cryptically began to announce what the Old Testament prophets were indicating, namely, that Messiah himself would be their link to the Spirit-presence of God. Despite Messiah and Spirit coming together in John's proclamation, even he misunderstood Jesus' role as Messiah (Matt 11:2–3), not unlike other Jews who still anticipated messianic deliverance from Rome.

The Anticipated Spirit

Initially, anyone with a heart to repent would go out into the desert to be submerged in water by John, the forerunner to Israel's Deliverer (Luke 3:3). Those people had lived all their lives under the old covenant and under all the many laws given to them by Moses. In the context of life under Moses' law, even John's isolated desert ministry of baptism was rather unusual. It was peculiar to the times of silence, having not heard the voice of a prophet for the past 400 years! Then came John, presenting himself like other Old Testament prophets who dressed and ate similarly.[8] For the most part, Yahweh was silent since the era of the last prophet Malachi, but now the voice of God had come to speak uniquely through John and then through the man, Jesus of Nazareth.

Taking up John's message, Jesus began to unfold new truth to his disciples. He succinctly expressed the transition from the old to the new, which was a movement away from John, the last great prophet under the old covenant, to Jesus who is the new Prophet like Moses. Throughout Jesus' earthly ministry, the Jewish people believed their expected Messiah would have something to do with a new work of God. But the Old Testament scrolls remained somewhat vague, except for an occasional ambiguous promise, such as what we read from the prophet Isaiah: "The Spirit of the Sovereign LORD is on me, because the LORD has anointed me to proclaim good news to the poor" (Isa 61:1). The first-century Jews had no idea when or how God's kingdom plan was going to come together, so they forcefully sought to make Jesus their king (John 6:15). It was not until the kingdom story began to play out in Acts that anyone could begin to see a clearer image of God's kingdom in this age. It would not be an abrupt and dominating kingdom but an open-ended reign that slowly progresses through the kingdom message.[9]

---

8. See 1 Kgs 19:19; 2 Kgs 1:8; 2:13–14; Zech 13:4; Matt 3:4; Mark 1:6.
9. See Matt 13:31–32; Mark 4:30–32; Luke 3:18–19.

Because the new covenant is characterized by a new experience of God's Spirit-presence, which is also characteristic of the coming Messiah, Jesus stepped into his role as the new Prophet of God and succinctly brought these many thoughts together when he announced his own ministry of Spirit Baptism: "Do not leave Jerusalem, but wait for the gift my Father promised, which you have heard me speak about. For John baptized with water, but in a few days you will be baptized with the Holy Spirit" (Acts 1:4–5). Indeed, this baptism of the Spirit is the promise of the Father, a promise stated and restated throughout the Old Testament prophets for centuries beforehand.[10] Finally, God's presence would be sustained among his people.

In connection with the promises and images of newness expressed in the Old Testament, this *promise of the Father* would satisfy the expectations of inspired men like Ezekiel, Jeremiah, and Joel. They merely gazed indistinctly upon these truths, longing to understand what was mostly hidden prior to Jesus' uttering these words (cf. 1 Pet 1:10–11; Luke 10:24). But now the language of Spirit-outpouring was being adapted for a new community in a different age and time from when those prophetic announcements were made. Although quite misunderstood, God's presence was coming in a new and comprehensive way.

At the outset of Acts, Jesus announced the ushering in of God's current kingdom activity as directly tied to the presence of God's Spirit. This would be a new era for the people of God, even a new direction, one in which all God's people would soon be Spirit-directed under a united kingdom surrendered to the rule of Jesus Christ. So Jesus told his followers to wait together and remain united until they received his promise. In the midst of a united body of Spirit-indwelt believers, Jesus would further establish his kingdom on earth, an open and ever expanding kingdom presence.

The Spirit as Baptism

The baptism of God's Spirit is mentioned in only six places in the Gospels and Acts. In each occurrence, it follows immediately after mention of John's water baptism.[11] In two of those places it is called the baptism of "the Holy Spirit and fire" (Matt 3:11; Luke 3:16). In one instance Luke says that Messiah "will baptize you with the Holy Spirit and fire. His winnowing fork is in his hand, to clear his threshing floor and to gather the wheat into his barn, but the chaff he will burn with unquenchable fire" (Luke 3:16–17 ESV). Here in Luke, John

---

10. See Jer 32:39; Isa 42:6; 49:8; 59:21; 54:10; Ezek 11:19; 18:31; 34:25; 36:26; 37:26; Hos 2:18–20.

11. Matt 3:11; Mark 1:8; Luke 3:16; John 1:33; Acts 1:4–5; 11:16.

declares that the Messiah would indeed mediate the Spirit, paralleling predictions of the old covenant prophets (e.g., Isa 44:3).

Moreover, this language of Spirit and fire speaks both of blessing and judgment. Centuries before John, the prophet Isaiah expected a divine Deliverer to one day operate "by a spirit of judgment and a spirit of fire," an end-time outpouring of both judgment and blessing (Isa 4:4). Numerous Old Testament prophecies point to a future outpouring of God's Spirit, a ministry consisting of both purification and punishment, depending on whether the message was accepted or rejected.[12] Such an outpouring was long anticipated throughout the prophets of old. Among others, Ezekiel writes, "I will no longer hide my face from them, for I will pour out my Spirit on the people of Israel, declares the Sovereign LORD" (Ezek 39:29). In poetic, parallel fashion the *presence* of God's "face" is revealed through the *Spirit*.

Similar to Isaiah's promise of a Spirit-and-fire baptism, when John spoke of Jesus' ministry he also used language reminiscent of the end of the age: "His winnowing fork is in his hand, and he will clear his threshing floor, gathering his wheat into the barn and burning up the chaff with unquenchable fire" (Matt 3:12; cf. Luke 3:17). This language resonates with images of Jesus' final judgment when he returns at the end of the age to resurrect the just and the unjust and finally establish his eternal kingdom. According to charismatic theologian Larry Hart, in comprehensive language John the Baptist is summarizing the total impact of Jesus' saving mission, one of both judgment and blessing, Spirit and fire. This Spirit-and-fire phase of God's kingdom mission was initiated when Jesus came on the scene and will conclude at his second and final appearance, when "his winnowing fork is in his hand" to subdue every last power beneath his supreme reign. Hart remarks, "John is speaking in the broadest terms of how Jesus both inaugurates and consummates the kingdom," through a baptism of Spirit and fire.[13]

Because the prophets before John spoke of an outpouring, John could naturally adapt this fluid metaphor to his own ministry by contrasting his water baptism with Jesus' spiritual one. Similar liquid metaphors would become the standard way of describing the Spirit's activity; e.g., outpouring, filling, being full of the Spirit.[14] Each metaphor illustrates the dynamic

---

12. Larry Hart conveys these thoughts in "Spirit Baptism," 111. See Joel 2:28–32; Ezek 36:25–27; Mal 3:2–3.

13. Hart, "Spirit Baptism," 111.

14. Throughout Acts, the Spirit's activity on the day of Pentecost is described in seven ways by seven different metaphors: the promise of the Father (Acts 1:4; 2:33, 39), a baptism (1:5; 11:16), coming or falling on (2:3; 8:16; 10:44; 11:15; 19:6), a pouring out (2:17–18, 33; 10:45), a gift (2:38; 10:45), received (2:38; 8:15), and a filling. As a common thread throughout Acts, believers are described as being *filled* with the Spirit.

movement and flexibility of God's presence in the lives and ministries of his people, a perfect changeableness. Thus, it is best to interpret the baptism of the Spirit as a flexible and open metaphor, recognizing that the Spirit's ministry cannot be restricted to one designation or another. The language of the Spirit's ministry is rather inconsequential. What matters is the dynamic, relational, ever-continual provision and empowerment of the Spirit-presence.

The metaphor of Spirit Baptism is intended to illustrate the believer's immersion into the interpenetrating presence of God *and into the rule of Christ*.[15] Because John was tying Spirit Baptism into a summary of how Jesus both establishes and consummates his eternal kingdom, the baptism of the Spirit is not a *single* pentecostal event in history but includes Jesus' overall ministry of blessing and judgment throughout this age. Jesus' ministry under the new covenant is to continually pour out God's Spirit into people's lives for the duration of his kingdom program. The age of the open kingdom of God depends on it!

The church has now been commissioned to unleash the presence of God into the world through the expansion of the kingdom message. One might even say that the divine presence has been restored to the church for the express purpose of empowerment for this mission.

LEADING AN OPEN KINGDOM: MESSIAH'S PRESENCE

After Jesus conquered sin and death by experiencing the cruel reality of the cross, he rose victorious from the grave and ascended to the right hand of his Father's throne. His first act as reigning King of the universe is visibly manifested and experienced in Acts 2 when the Spirit is climactically poured out: "When the day of Pentecost came, they were all together in one place.... All of them were filled with the Holy Spirit and began to speak in other tongues as the Spirit enabled them" (Acts 2:1, 4). In fulfillment of the Father's promise, not some but *all* are filled with God's pervading Spirit. Jesus' promise that they would soon be baptized with the Holy Spirit is realized in this all-inclusive, communal *filling* of God's presence, adding another liquid metaphor to the Spirit's end-of-the-age activity.

The book of Acts contains a total of six references to believers being filled with the Spirit (πίμπλημι: 2:4; 4:8, 31; 9:17; 13:9; πληρόω: 13:52).

15. Because the kingly rule of the Lord Jesus is such a primary feature of Spirit Baptism, which entails a continual yielding to Christ as King and Master, the charismatic/pentecostal injunction to surrender for *fresh* baptisms remains intact as an important doctrine for the church today, even in a decisive, crisis-moment experience.

Shortly after this dramatic event, under unction of this Spirit of prophecy, Peter proclaims that what the people see and hear is the *outpouring of the Spirit on all people* as prophesied by the prophet Joel (Acts 2:16–17; Joel 2:28).[16]

Messiah Sits on His Throne

This infilling, empowering, enabling life of the Spirit-presence did not originate in a vacuum. When Pentecost arrived, Peter spoke up and made emphatic the connection between the Spirit's outpouring and Christ's enthronement: "Exalted to the right hand of God, [Jesus] has received from the Father the promised Holy Spirit and has poured out what you now see and hear" (Acts 2:33). Through Trinitarian outreach, the last days promises of God were meted out as Jesus took his throne in the heavenlies. The baptism of the Spirit, the very outpouring anticipated by the prophets and now infusing every believer, resulted from and forever remains the reigning provision of the final Davidic King.

The promised Deliverer had come through the line of David (Acts 13:22–32), ratified the new covenant, and inaugurated David's kingdom; he is now forever seated on David's throne (15:16). After Yahweh sought to dramatically reduce the distance between him and the world through the Abrahamic covenant by extending blessing to every person throughout the world, God's covenant with David ensured that God's presence would eventually be experienced in the context of kingdom life. In fulfillment of those covenants of old, it is from David's throne that our King releases an outpouring of God's presence. Those who repent and are baptized come to know not only the presence of God but the realized promise of complete forgiveness, which is a distinguishing mark of the new covenant message (2:38–39).[17] Forgiveness removes rebellion and frees the world to receive the reign of God's presence!

The Lord Jesus is the long-awaited Messiah of Israel and the Deliverer of the world. He has taken his seat on the Davidic throne in fulfillment of the Davidic covenant. He has also received from the Father a commission related to the presence. Although numerous metaphors are attached to the Spirit's work in Acts, he has only one unique new covenant ministry. In

---

16. That the outpouring of the Spirit upon the church in Acts is one of a prophetic nature, even a Spirit of prophecy, is confirmed by the consistency of inspired (or prompted) utterance accompanying the Spirit's filling activity in both Luke (1:41–42, 67) and Acts (2:4; 4:8, 31; 13:9). When believers were filled with the Spirit, they immediately spoke.

17. The new covenant is tied to the forgiveness of sin throughout the New Testament; see Matt 26:28; Mark 14:24; Luke 22:20; 1 Cor 11:25; Heb 9:15; 12:24.

Trinitarian sophistication, Messiah is continually pouring out the Spirit-presence on every believer in order to enable, empower, and embolden us to declare his victory reign. Among other things, Jesus fulfilled the role of another Prophet like Moses (Acts 3:22–26; Deut 18:15), the ultimate Prophet, Priest, and now reigning King. Jesus' ministry brings believing men and women everywhere into the actual presence of God.

For the rule of Christ to become complete on earth, it must first become full in the lives of God's people. The church experiences that kingly rule under a new covenant relationship as the Spirit is continually poured out upon us. The initial outpouring and the manner in which people receive the Spirit is open-ended. In the book of Acts, the Spirit was initially received by 120 believers who waited in an upper room, having given themselves to prayer. At other times the Spirit came through the laying on of hands after belief and baptism (Acts 19:5–6), or through the laying on of hands *accompanied with prayer* after belief and baptism (8:15–17). Still at other times the Spirit was given at the moment of faith before being baptized (9:17–18). In another place, the filling of the Spirit followed after belief and baptism (2:38). On another occasion water baptism followed after receiving an evidentiary filling of the Spirit (10:44–48). The Spirit's openly dynamic activity is reminiscent of Jesus' earlier description of the Spirit's initial work in salvation: "The wind blows wherever it pleases. You hear its sound, but you cannot tell where it comes from or where it is going. So it is with everyone born of the Spirit" (John 3:8).

The new covenant ministry of the resurrected King is initiated the same way for everyone who believes, a Spirit Baptism into a new kingdom life that's characterized by God's presence and power. In contrast to a few individuals who were "filled" with the Spirit in Luke's gospel, the precursor to Acts (Luke 1:14, 41, 67; 4:1), it was said that after Jesus ascension "all of them were filled with the Holy Spirit" (Acts 2:2). But that was just the beginning. Another openness aspect of Christ's kingdom is the limitless potential for every believer to be *freshly* baptized in the Spirit, being frequently and even daily "filled" with God's Spirit and the fruit of his presence: "And the disciples were continually filled with joy and with the Holy Spirit" (13:52 NASB; cf. Gal 5:22–23).[18] Being *filled* means there is an active agent performing this filling, none other than Jesus himself. Under the new covenant, the risen King remains dynamically involved in the daily life of his church by being the ongoing source of the Spirit.

---

18. In Acts 13:52, the Greek imperfect tense emphasizes the continual nature of the filling that occurred.

This open-ended, all-inclusive outpouring was the divine response to Moses' wish expressed so many years before: "I wish that all the LORD's people were prophets and that the LORD would put his Spirit on them!" (Num 11:29). Now all believers have an inseparable link to the King of kings and Lord of lords; they have been immersed into the kingdom reign of God's presence! Believers experience this on an individual, personal basis. Throughout the book of Acts we see disciples repeatedly filled with the Spirit, including Peter (Acts 2:4; 4:8, 31) and Paul (9:17; 13:9). They are both repeatedly filled and should be understood as representative of the larger following of disciples. Thus, we see examples of ongoing, continual filling with the divine presence as Jesus remains actively involved in the life of his church.

Messiah Reigns through the Spirit

The kingly rule of Christ has begun in a demonstrative way under the new covenant. Jesus announced this covenant at the Last Supper (1 Cor 11:25) and ratified it at Pentecost when key features of that covenant were experienced by his followers, such as the forgiveness of sin and the Spirit's outpouring. Jesus' primary message had always been the kingdom of God, which would continue to be the message of his church, not only in word but also in action and experience. The Spirit's power was evidence of the kingdom even in Jesus' earthly ministry before Pentecost: "But if it is by the Spirit of God that I drive out demons, then the kingdom of God has come upon you" (Matt 12:28). It's fitting then that Jesus' first official act as reigning King, Priest, and Prophet was to pour out, not merely a gift of divine Spirit, but the equivalent of a visible manifestation of the King's own presence. This was displayed initially in the miracle of tongues and then in every kind of sign and wonder in the book of Acts.

In Acts 2, the prophetic expression of unlearned tongues and other more general prophetic unction were the immediate evidence that Messiah had initiated fulfillment of new covenant hope (2:4, 14). As Peter preached fulfillment, his inspired preaching of Old Testament Scripture exemplified the profound truth that all Scripture points to Jesus (2:16–39). Thus, the first example in Acts of inspired exposition was intended to direct our attention to this realized truth about Messiah. When Jesus unleashed this Spirit of prophetic unction, he fulfilled Scripture not by providing just any divine gift but the gift *par excellence* of restoring God's presence to believing humanity. This was the gift of all gifts! The presence of God was immediately experienced as a felt fellowship of the spoken word. The evidence couldn't have been clearer in Peter's bold declaration of kingdom truth and by the supernatural utterance of tongues as people were declaring "the wonders of God" as revealed in Jesus Christ (2:11).

The presence of God has come to his people in a dynamic, relational fashion. Even though we see believers throughout Acts intermittently filled with the Spirit, Luke's emphasis is certainly not that the nature of the Spirit's interpenetrational activity is temporary or fleeting. On the contrary, such regular fillings demonstrate that the reigning Christ has ordered his kingdom in such a way that he remains active and available to the life of his church; he's always present to pour out this fresh, renewing empowerment. The dynamic of an open kingdom requires an open, ongoing dynamic of Spirit-provision to accomplish the kingdom mission. Christ our King truly is "with [us] always, to the very end of the age" (Matt 28:20).

In Acts, every aspect of the Spirit's work that pertains to the believer fits into this single scenario: Jesus is always dynamically involved through the Spirit. The Holy Spirit is inseparably related to the Lord (Yahweh) Jesus and to his reign. Because the Spirit's work is decisively Christ-centered, the Spirit is called both the *Spirit of Yahweh* and the *Spirit of Jesus* (Acts 8:39; 16:7; cf. Rom 8:9; Gal 4:6). Messiah's ministry is the continual, dynamic provision of Spirit-motivated mission and Spirit-driven unction for the new community.

For Jesus to remain involved in believers' lives and in his reigning ministry through us, he continually pours out his Spirit directly from God's throne. Such a ministry has a ubiquitous effect, bringing believers directly into the eternal throne of the royal, divine presence. Now the church lives in the presence of the King! Because Jesus has delivered the promised Spirit to the sacred assembly, he has opened the door for a relationship with his creatures that resembles the relationship that exists within the triune Godhead. That relationship is one of unity and peace with God, and by the mystery of divine indwelling, there now exists an interpenetration of his life into the believer. Now with God in us, believers share the perfect mixture and beautiful blending of divine life with human nature, such that God and his people are filled with each other in an astonishing dance of united, loving life. This life is experienced on the level of a hidden, spiritual kingdom presence but remains true nonetheless. Through Spirit-infilling, believers are forever in God and God in them. The church is united in fellowship for the sake of intimacy and for the practical purpose of fulfilling its moment-by-moment kingdom mission.

The Acts narrative demonstrates that the provision of the Spirit is not just a onetime event at Pentecost, which was only the beginning, or that God's Spirit permanently lives within us, which is also true, but that Christ is dynamically and vigorously involved in our daily Christian mission. The permanent indwelling of the Spirit that every believer receives at the moment of salvation guarantees that Christ is reigning *in* us, while the ongoing ministry of fresh Spirit Baptism ("filling") guarantees that Jesus will reign *through* us. Christ the King remains dynamically engaged with his people through continual baptism with the Holy Spirit. Praise God for restoring his presence to the people of this world!

MANIFESTING AN OPEN KINGDOM: WORD, SIGNS, AND WONDERS

The church has been anointed to manifest Christ's kingdom both in word and deed (Acts 8:12; 19:8; 20:25; 28:23), made possible through the prophetic Spirit who is still being poured out on everyone who believes. Hence, our Spirit-empowered ministry is for the purpose of mission and to manifest and witness to the kingdom of Christ. The *word* of the kingdom is the emboldened declaration of the good news of the King. The supreme Conqueror over sin, death, and the devil overcame all opposition by one decisive victory blow at the cross, being raised in power because death could not possibly hold him in its clutches (2:24). The *deeds* of the kingdom include every act of love and forgiveness and every manifestation of the King's presence and power. Early on in Acts, Jesus promised the disciples that they would receive "power" when the Spirit came upon them (1:8). That power belongs to and flows from the only true Sovereign.

Regarding that power, Craig Keener asks, "What does Luke mean by power? Although not all references involve healing and exorcism, these constitute the most common expressions of that power in Luke's narrative."[19] Stephen is one example of a person who was not among the apostles but who, being "full of God's grace *and power*, performed great wonders and signs among the people" (Acts 6:8, emphasis added). Power is clearly connected here to the miracles that accompanied Stephen's ministry. Jesus Christ's own anointing with the Spirit and power is later summarized by Peter as manifested both in *doing good* and in miraculous *healing*. Peter says, "You know what has happened throughout the province of Judea, ... how God anointed Jesus of Nazareth with the Holy Spirit and power, and how he went around doing good and healing all who were under the power of the devil, because God was with him" (10:37–38).

These passages point to an anointed ministry in the presence and power of God, available not just to Jesus or Stephen but to every believer to empower

---

19. Keener, "Power of Pentecost," 49. See Luke 4:26; 5:17; 6:19; 8:46; 9:1; Acts 3:12; 4:7. For Paul's perspective on power and the Spirit, see Fee, *God's Empowering Presence*, 35–36.

the overthrow of Satan's kingdom through word and action.[20] What the Spirit accomplished in Acts both in power and mission is intended not for a select number but for all believers for all time: "God says, I will pour out my Spirit on all people. Your sons and daughters . . . your young men . . . your old men . . . Even on my servants, both men and women" (Acts 2:17–18).

This talk of power should not detract from the truth that Christ's kingdom reign is one of humility and meekness. In fact, it is a reign of power through weakness! This humility was demonstrated in Christ's obedience to the Father all the way to the cross (Phil 2:8). The weakness of the cross was devoured by the power of the resurrection (2:9)! Jesus succumbed to the hate and violence of men who exacted the power of evil hatred against him at the cross so that these worldly powers would be shown in the end to be powerless. Jesus was powerfully raised from the grave of humanity's destructive hatred.

Now from the highest position of humble authority, Jesus graciously seeks to restore the vice-regency that he initially entrusted to humanity in the garden (Gen 1:26–30). Through vice-regency God shares his authority over the created world. That responsibility is restored through the church when believers manifest Jesus' kingdom authority in the same ways he did, through healing, casting out demons, prophesying, and boldly declaring the kingdom of God. Believers truly are kingdom representatives! This was the case when Paul cast out a demon "in the name of Jesus Christ" (Acts 16:16–19); Paul was acting as Jesus' representative. We are Christ's ambassadors ministering in his stead (2 Cor 5:20). In the garden, a demonized serpent stole that God-given authority, but in the new paradise of God's kingdom on earth, believers take authority over the demonized and in this way manifest the reign of Christ and the restoration of their vice-regency.

Just as the King has made room for the church within the community of the triune identity, he does not hoard the Spirit but graciously anoints his followers with his dynamic presence. Through the Spirit, Jesus remains involved in the world through the community of faith. In addition to the intimacy of fellowship this affords to the church, there are two primary reasons for this anointing. First, for empowerment to accomplish what we *cannot* do ourselves, and second, for enablement to carry out what we *would* not do in our own strength. The church's anointed mission remains the same since the day of Pentecost: to extend the kingdom of God through the

---

20. Throughout Acts, the ministry of the Spirit is characterized by amazing works accomplished by Christ's followers in numerous expressions of signs, wonders, and miracles of every kind. Reading Acts, one never gets the sense that God intended such manifestations merely for a transition from the old to the new but as bindingly characteristic of the new age.

gospel of Jesus Christ. While this kingdom advances, the enemy's kingdom is subdued, thus the need for an empowered anointing also implies conflict with the opposition.

On our own, humanity cannot participate in God's war against the forces of darkness because the ensuing battle occurs in the spiritual, supernatural sphere and then overflows into the seen world (Eph 6:12). Until salvation, people remain in Satan's kingdom of lost souls under the authority of the prince of darkness. Through the Spirit, believers are at once freed and given supernatural weaponry to wage war against supernatural forces of darkness. Paul tells us, "The weapons we fight with are not the weapons of the world. On the contrary, they have divine power to demolish strongholds" (2 Cor 10:4). The kingdom of Satan is confronted by and overcome by the kingdom of Christ manifest through the church. As the weapons of God, every believer becomes a spiritual conduit through which Christ's reign temporally faces off with the kingdom of Satan. Christians manifest the kingdom and reign of Jesus Christ by boldly confronting the dark powers with a gospel far more powerful, "because the Spirit who lives in you is greater than the spirit who lives in the world" (1 John 4:4 NLT).

The gospel message is a claim to reality over and against the kingdom of Satan. Every supernatural act of God that defies the laws of nature functions as an assault against that demonic kingdom. Satan has usurped God's rightful authority over the created order. Therefore, even aspects of nature will experience the wonders of God anew when Jesus reminds nature of his reign. This was evidenced in Jesus' encounters with both people and nature. When confronted by a demoniac, Scripture attests, "Jesus rebuked (*epetimesen*) him, saying, 'Be quiet and come out of him!'" (Luke 4:35 NASB; cf. 4:41). Using the same language, Mark describes Jesus approaching nature with similar nerve when he "rebuked (*epetimesen*) the wind and said to the waves, 'Quiet! Be still!'" (Mark 4:39; cf. Matt 8:26). Jesus approached both people and nature as forces opposing the Creator and needing to be subdued, and he accepted it as his mission to confront those powers. In the same missional spirit, the anointed disciples went out into the world with the same exorcising, miracle working power. This provides the church with a faithful model for taking the same evidentiary message to the world (Luke 9:1–2).[21]

Before concluding this chapter, a few comments on prophecy and tongues are in order.[22] The individual and communal infusion of the prophetic Spirit inspires both natural and supernatural utterances but also

---

21. On signs and wonders accompanying evangelism in the early church and today, see Wimber and Springer, *Power Evangelism*.

22. For further elaboration on tongues and prophecy, see chapter 8.

manifests the supernatural power of the kingdom. That otherworldly power cannot help but break through into the natural realm. In Acts 2, the initial evidence of Christ's reigning presence was an observable shaking with fire from heaven and the supernatural gift of tongues.

On the day of Pentecost, tongues were an *expression* of prophecy spoken in fulfillment of Joel 2. Whereas Paul distinguishes between tongues and prophecy (1 Cor 12:8–10; 28–30), Luke presents tongues as an expression of prophecy. Tongues are the only result cited in Acts 2 as fulfilling Joel's words regarding the Spirit's connection to the prophetic. Immediately after they *began to speak in tongues as the Spirit enabled them* (Acts 2:4), the Apostle Peter explains this phenomenon. Peter favorably quotes Joel as the prediction of what is taking place, where Yahweh declares, "I will pour out my Spirit in those days, and they will prophesy" (2:18; cf. Joel 2:29). The expression of prophecy in the second half of this verse ("and they will prophesy") does not appear in the Hebrew text of Joel 2, highlighting Luke's emphasis and the intentional connection between the prophetic and Spirit-evidenced tongues.[23] This indicates that prophecy is open to more than one expression.

Tongues are mentioned on only three different occasions in Acts, and on the last occasion prophecy appears with it (Acts 2:4; 10:36; 19:6). Tongues and prophecy are a common evidence of the Spirit, illustrating that the presence of the kingdom enters human history with credible manifestations of a supernatural nature. That is not to say tongues are always the evidence of the anointing, however. Due to the descriptive rather than prescriptive quality of Acts, we can affirm that tongues are indeed *an* evidence of both salvation and ongoing empowerment, but we cannot affirm that tongues are the *sole* or primary evidence of such empowerment.

CONCLUSION: CLOSING THE DISTANCE

Jesus announced the presence of an encroaching kingdom in his very own person. In seedling form, Yahweh announced that kingdom to Abraham and fleshed it out with King David. When Jesus conquered the grave and was seated on the Davidic throne in the heavenlies, his kingdom was inaugurated but not fully established. The new covenant lays out the kingdom's spiritual architecture, bringing together the promise of forgiveness and a new ministry of God's presence through Messiah, even a Spirit Baptism. In Jesus' role as Messiah and resurrected "Prince and Savior" (Acts 5:31), he

---

23. For an introduction to the prophetic in the early church, see Aune, *Prophecy in Early Christianity*; Burgess, *Holy Spirit: Ancient Christian Traditions*; Hill, *New Testament Prophecy*; and Kydd, *Charismatic Gifts in the Early Church*.

announced the Spirit's presence as characteristic of the new covenant age. Jesus' baptism of Spirit and fire summarizes his role throughout the age—a special divine agent who brings blessing and judgement, depending on a person's response. Under the new covenant, the risen King remains dynamically involved in the daily life of his church by being the ongoing source of God's Spirit, the divine presence.

Christ's spiritual kingdom manifests throughout this age as a relational, open-ended kingdom. Every day this kingdom is adding new kingdom-priests—a prophethood of believers—who are ever expanding God's kingdom reign through Christ in them. There remains incalculable, untapped potential for God's glorious kingdom presence to be revealed through the church's faithful message and miraculous exploits. The furtherance of such a mission depends on the believer's faithfulness, obedience, and surrender to her King. It is yet to be decided who will ultimately constitute the eternal kingdom, but it remains open to Jew and Gentile, slave and free, male and female alike (Acts 10:34–35; Gal 3:8). The dynamic of an open kingdom requires an open, ongoing dynamic of Spirit-provision to accomplish the kingdom mission.

Through the Spirit's empowering ministry, the bold declaration of this kingdom is advancing, according to the book of Acts, from Jerusalem all the way to the Roman world. But this is only the beginning! Keener encourages us that "Acts does not conclude with the completion of the mission but offers a model for its continuance and completion: the good news to the ends of the earth, including parts of the world that Luke's audience could not have known about."[24] As the kingdom continued to advance in Acts, the story was left open for believers today to continue the mission.[25] The church now shares the responsibility and privilege of fulfilling our new covenant kingdom mission under the rule of Christ, who remains dynamically involved through the indwelling Spirit, actively leading his church from one day to the next.

Jesus' resurrection ushered in the glory of Pentecost, God's most sustained expression of divine presence. The baptism of the Spirit, an outpouring anticipated by the prophets, forever remains the reigning provision of the final Davidic King. For the rule of Christ to become complete on earth, it must first become full in the lives of God's people. Hence, the church has been commissioned to unleash God's presence to the world through the expansion of the kingdom message in its demonstration of mercy and miracles.

---

24. Keener, "Power of Pentecost," 54.

25. On the open-endedness of Acts, see Dunn, *Acts of the Apostles*, 278; and Marguerat, *First Christian Historian*, 152–54, 230.

8

Worship
Open Freedom

In chapter 7, we developed the idea that God closes distance through the new covenant ministry of the Lord Jesus who continually pours out his Spirit. In our final three chapters, we set forth that God's concerted presence among believers finds expression through individual Spiritual gifts (chapter 8), through a fivefold ministry (chapter 9), and through prayer and the unique experience of revival awakening (chapter 10). Each chapter emphasizes the openness and potential of Spirit-gifted ministries as well as the available and limitless expressions of grace given to every believer to exploit those ministries.

Because this chapter is entitled "Worship" and our focus is on charismatic gifts, it's important to note that life's worship and the worship of the local church involve true worship when believers are *ministering* to one another. Worship is service to God and ministry to people. God is worshipped as we compassionately minister to the needs of those around us and allow the divine presence to release the liberating power of the cross through the church. In Paul's first letter to the Corinthians, the chapters addressing Spiritual gifts and ministries also describe the gathering of believers for worship, which should be read as a single unit (1 Corinthians 10–14). The Bible nowhere describes a "church service" but rather a gathering of gifted believers where every member ministers. In other words, worship is ministry.

In the following pages, the openness of the *charismata* refers primarily to the freedom and potential for fulfilling ministry, but that's not all. Charismatic openness also means that God is fundamentally relational and closely involved with his church, so he remains open-minded in the many creative and resourceful ways that he uses the *charismata* to reach the world through the gospel of his presence. If God desires to make the divine presence known throughout the world, in a free and open universe, much of that mission will depend on believers fulfilling their ministry. The greatest expression of ministry is found in the virtues of faith, hope, and love, but those virtues are most effectively expressed through the full range of *charismata*. Paul says, "Now you have every spiritual gift you need as you eagerly wait for the return of our Lord Jesus Christ" (1 Cor 1:7 NLT).

Although there are many different aspects to worship, such as singing, giving thanks and adoration to God, etc., our focus will remain on the mutual ministry that's intended to occur when God's people come together.

INTRODUCING CHARISMATA IN AN OPEN UNIVERSE

We now turn our attention to the charismatic element of God's presence, the *charismata*. *Charismata* is the plural form of the Greek noun *charisma*, which means gift.[1] Every ministry and gifting in the church is charismatic service, i.e., the gracious gift of God.[2] Paul tells us that "there are different kinds of gifts (*charismata*), but the same Spirit distributes them" (1 Cor 12:4). Under the unction of the Spirit, God graciously gifts his church for service. The key word here is *gift*. In every place that the Greek *charismata* or the singular *charisma* is used, "gift(s)" is an appropriate translation.[3] These gifts are intended to be understood in connection with God's gracious presence.

We've already been introduced to God's changeability and the changeability of the divine presence under the care of the Lord Jesus Christ. Because God's presence can change, it can occupy and partner with human vessels, thus making the charismatic mission possible. The ultimate consequence of a closed relationship with God is absence and the tragic permanency

---

1. *Charismata* is the transliteration of the Greek noun χαρίσματα, the plural form of χάρισμα.

2. Throughout the next two chapters, I'll be using the language of *gifts* and *ministries* interchangeably. Kenneth Berding argues that the "gifts" of the church are not primarily special abilities but rather functions of *ministry*. Thus, believers should not be overly preoccupied with discovering Spiritual abilities but should rather step into edifying service. Berding finds the language of "ministry" most appropriate to the Scriptural portrayal of gifts rather than the language of gifts or offices. He also helps us to see just how open the ministries are, encouraging believers to simply live out the new birth incarnationally through ministry service. Berding doesn't deny special abilities, especially when stepping out in the miraculous, but feels they are not the starting point for *charismata*. See *What Are Spiritual Gifts?*

3. See Baumert, "'Charism' and 'Spirit-Baptism,'" 149.

that follows at the end of the age. But the ultimate blessing in an open and abounding relationship with God is sharing the vitalizing dynamic of his presence through the *charismata*. This divine presence is poignantly expressed through the worship and service of ministry gifts that liberate both church and world as the people of God function as his hands and feet. With love as the primary motivation, we can become most useful in our service.

Every ministry and gifting in the church is charismatic and carried out under the unction of God's Spirit. The triune God is actively at work distributing ministries as he sees fit while taking into account our input, our passions, our availability, and our potential under his power: "There are different kinds of gifts (*charismaton*), but the same Spirit distributes them. There are different kinds of service (*diakonion*), but the same Lord. There are different kinds of working (*energematon*), but in all of them and in everyone it is the same God at work" (1 Cor 12:4–6). There are so many "different" expressions of the Spirit's work, different in kind and quality (gifts, services, workings), but also different in number and endless application. Paul goes on to say, "It is the one and only Spirit who distributes all these gifts. He alone decides which gift each person should have" (12:11 NLT). Harley Schmitt in his book on Spiritual gifts acknowledges that every aspect of their distribution remains open under the Spirit's direction: "The Spirit decides where, when, and at what moment to dispense the gifts."[4]

In the New Testament, no single ministry is ever clearly defined, which is evident with the various lists of Spiritual gifts that never really describe their actual function.[5] Most ministries are mentioned only in passing. Even when the function of a gift is described, it's quite brief and never fully explained. The fact that every listing of *charismata* is different implies these lists are not exhaustive but open and flexible. God is not restricted in the number or types of gifts he can distribute at any given moment. The Spirit, who graciously and often spontaneously gifts the church, is open to meeting any ministry need and filling any void with whatever manifestation he decides is appropriate. In the Spirit's infinite resourcefulness and wisdom, he will provide for the needs of the church in the moment, distributing at times even gifts or ministries we have never seen before. Fiddes suggests that "it is not the *charismata* themselves that display the work of the Holy Spirit, but the dimension *within* them that is always opening situations up to new possibilities."[6]

---

4. Schmitt, *Many Gifts One Lord*, 97.

5. The primary Pauline lists of gifts are found in Rom 12:6–8; 1 Cor 12:8–10; 28; Eph 4:11. Gifts are also mentioned in 1 Pet 4:11.

6. Fiddes, *Participating in God*, 271, emphasis original.

The *charismata* function simultaneously to equip and to edify believers while extending sacrificial service through the church. But this is not the most important reason for God to so graciously gift us. We are meant to understand the very heart of God by them. The dynamic inner life of God resembles the beautiful organism of the diversely gifted body of Christ working in unison, the universal as well as local expressions of the church. *Charismata* are therefore revelatory of God's inner life but are also incarnational, revealing the inner social and sacrificial life of God while at the same time manifesting characteristics of God's own personality and presence through incarnational ministry. We see God when grace-gifts are at work. We experience God when grace-gifts are at work. We receive grace when grace-gifts are at work. Thus, we can only fully experience the gracious presence and love of God when we are using our God-given gifts and living out our God-given ministries.

Kathleen Cahalan remarks that "charisms are incarnational gifts, a graced presence that becomes enfleshed in our lives."[7] Because these gifts are incarnational, we find that the ministry of Jesus Christ as well as the liveliness of the divine presence are mediated through these grace-gifts. In fact, God's presence is our gift. His universal presence can and does concentrate locally to find expression through us as charismatic vessels: "[Charisms] are to be embodied actions, lived out and expressed in word and deed."[8] Our bodies, actions, and words become the transforming channel through which the divine presence and the ministry life of Jesus impact the world for the greatest good. Jesus is Emanuel, God with us, not only through the indwelling of the Godhead by virtue of salvation but also through the radical testimony of *charismata*, the divine life through the believer.

DYNAMIC MINISTRY IN CORINTH

When first-century believers gathered together for fellowship and worship, it was not a formal service but an organic, mutual ministry one to another. They naturally came together as a spiritual family, whether in the temple, individual homes, the synagogue, or other public places of prayer. We are quite limited on descriptions of worship in the early church. Other than a summary of the daily worship that the churches enjoyed in Acts 2:42–47, the only other glimpse we're privileged to is found in the Corinthian church and only because Paul was writing to correct errors.

---

7. Cahalan, *Introducing the Practice of Ministry*, 35.
8. Ibid., 33.

The Corinthian believers were facing abuses related to worship, especially with regard to Spiritual ministries. To correct these, Paul provides extensive instruction on the proper use of Spiritual gifts in the context of the gathering of believers. He describes a rather dynamic interaction of believers who are each responsible to use their gifts to build up God's people at any given meeting: "What then shall we say, brothers and sisters? When you come together, each of you has a hymn, or a word of instruction, a revelation, a tongue or an interpretation. Everything must be done so that the church may be built up" (1 Cor 14:26). Paul leaves his readers with the impression that it would be foreign to this congregation to merely sit by as spectators while one or two others lead in teaching and worship, as is often the case today. Rather, every member is expected to be involved in the mutual exercise of gifts, one to another.

In an open universe, the relational aspect of the *charismata* is highlighted. First Corinthians 14:26 assumes that an individual can't have every gift, but everyone is dependent on the gifts of others, so everyone should be willing to operate in any gift God has given them. In an open universe, every believer retains tremendous freedom, a libertarian freedom in fact. As the Spirit of God is working in the congregation, he remains dependent upon the willingness and faithfulness of believers to operate in the gifts he has so graciously distributed. The *potential* for operating in a gift is not the same as freely choosing to use that gift. If the future is open and flexible, believers may opt out of utilizing their gifting for the benefit of the body.

When believers step out by faith and begin to walk in the Spirit's power, they bring aspects of the open future into the present. Even though the consummation of God's kingdom remains open, an eschatological experience of that kingdom is brought into our experience through the *charismata*. Stephen Barton echoes this thought when he says that "the charismata make possible what would not be possible otherwise in the time prior to the coming of the kingdom of God: anticipatory, partial sharing in the life of heaven."[9] In the future consummation, all the temporary, partial gifts will be done away with because the fullness of what they anticipate will finally belong to the believer (1 Cor 13:8–12). For the time being, however, the future kingdom overflows and spills backward into the present age, giving the church waves of God's glorious power to ride in on. We can ride the waves of the *charismata* all the way into the kingdom of heaven! Hence, it would benefit God's church to acquaint herself with the Spirit's glorious gifts.

As mentioned earlier, the absence of an exhaustive list of Spiritual gifts in the New Testament implies the *charismata* remain open for the duration

---

9. Barton, "1 Corinthians," 1343.

of this age. They are spontaneously invented and distributed at the Spirit's sovereign prerogative wherever ministry needs arise. Since this is the case, it is not necessary for us to review every so-called gift or ministry named or described in the New Testament because by their very nature they remain open and flexible. We'll spend most of this chapter looking at the charismatic gifts in relation to God's *unilateral* presence. They are the more extraordinary or "supernatural" gifts that noticeably, even unilaterally, depend on the divine presence. Those gifts cannot be manufactured or reduced to natural talent. Specifically, we will look at the gifts of prophecy, tongues, healings, miracles, the discerning of spirits, and faith (1 Cor 12:9–10). Through these unilateral gifts, the believer becomes a channel for theophany (or epiphanic presence) and the manifest display of God's sovereign presence. Paul says, "If an unbeliever or an inquirer comes in while everyone is prophesying, . . . they will fall down and worship God, exclaiming, 'God is really among you!'" (14:24–25). For Paul, one dimension of the *charismata* is to reveal more poignantly that God's presence truly is among us, functioning as a channel for manifesting himself.

In contrast, the *bilateral* gifts include serving, teaching, encouraging, giving, administration, and showing mercy, which are comparable to a more practical incarnation (Rom 12:6–8). These gifts do not overtly manifest the divine presence, but they do authorize believers as incarnational representatives of God. Fiddes comments that "the *charismata* should be seen as the taking up of natural faculties into the perichoretic life of God, into interweaving movements of love and justice."[10] All gifts from God, whether perceived as supernatural or natural, are useful and important in the accomplishment of our kingdom mission because God is sharing his perichoretic life-presence through us.

In the course of investigating these unilateral and bilateral gifts, we will emphasize two things: *the openness of God and the divine presence*. The dynamic impact of the *charismata* upon the world is made possible by the openness of the universe, the freedom of creatures to receive and exploit grace, the freedom of God to creatively impart fresh gifting, and the direct involvement of God's Spirit. In addition to the theme of openness, these gifts are only possible because distance is overcome by divine presence. The church is now privileged to enjoy and share God's presence as we become partakers of the mighty powers inherent in the age to come.

Just as Paul gives prophecy and tongues the majority of space in his instruction on the *charismata*, they will receive the majority of our attention.

---

10. Fiddes, *Participating in God*, 271, emphasis original.

CHARISMATA'S UNILATERAL PRESENCE: OPEN PROPHECY

For those who walk in step with the Spirit, there exists a stream of supernatural intuition made possible by the God who speaks to his church with a bold vulnerability. Paul called this gift prophecy (1 Cor 12:10). Even though we accept a written canon consisting of 66 inspired books, it's intuitive to a living relationship with God that his word is not altogether closed.[11] Blessed with the indwelling presence of the Living Word, Jesus Christ, the church enjoys an immediate and even spontaneous voice from heaven to meet us in current situations. We intuitively get the sense that divine guidance can be fresh and frequent. In the gift of prophecy and other gifts like it, God has dynamically gifted his people with such specific and direct guidance.[12]

Prophecy was among the most prominent gifts in the Corinthian church (1 Cor 14:1–5), which should also be highly regarded in light of an open universe. Without a divine blueprint outlining the details of the church's spiritual battles and victories or accomplishments and failures in ministry and mission, the church may be even more dependent upon God's immediate guidance. Such ongoing dependence certainly doesn't downplay the relevance of the written word but adds an aspect of dynamic application that would otherwise be lacking. In general, divine guidance always requires a certain sensitivity to God's inner voice, that "still small voice," as he seeks to use his people to apply divine ingenuity to otherwise impossible situations (1 Kgs 19:12 KJV).

Prophecy: The Gift of an Open Universe

We might classify the gift of prophecy as a gift of an open universe. The gift itself is dependent on God's dynamic knowledge of the past, present, and future as it is applied to the church's current situation. Prophecy as it was practiced in the New Testament church involved a spontaneous revelation from God to the individual, which was then spoken to the congregation (1

---

11. The Protestant Canon consists of 39 Old Testament and 27 New Testament books. The Catholic Bible consists of 73 books, which include seven deuterocanonical books.

12. Rather than addressing the "word of knowledge" and "word of wisdom" (1 Cor 12:8 KJV), these are being considered variations of prophecy, which has historically been characteristic of charismatic and pentecostal practice. Readers can review thorough descriptions of these two gifts in Williams, *Renewal Theology*, 2:349–58; and Grudem, *Systematic Theology*, 1080–82.

Cor 14:30–31).[13] Prophecy is the dynamic process of receiving revelation and releasing it to the community. Prophecy can be either forth-telling or foretelling. Forth-telling focuses on the past and present, while foretelling includes predictions and warnings related to the future. Specific to foretelling, the gift of prophecy is God's word for the church as it relates to what is possible, what is probable, or what is certain to take place.

Beyond God's mere knowledge, predictive prophecy often depends on God's *intentions* to bring something about. If God purposes to bring about an expected future, it moves from the possible to the probable or certain. Take, for example, Isa 46:10–11. The LORD says, "I make known the end from the beginning, from ancient times, what is still to come. I say, '*My purpose will stand, and I will do all that I please.*' From the east I summon a bird of prey; from a far-off land, a man to fulfill my purpose. *What I have said, that I will bring about; what I have planned, that I will do*" (emphasis added). Just a few verses earlier, the LORD distinguishes himself from the weakness and ignorance of human-made idols (46:5–7). In contrast to the inability of those lifeless, inanimate statues, Yahweh declares that "everything I plan will come to pass" (46:10 NLT).

The LORD's powerful declaration, however, is nowhere said to be based on exhaustive foreknowledge of future events. In v. 11, Yahweh announces that his foresight is based specifically on what he has "planned" and what he will "bring about." The LORD brings about what he has planned by persuading and influencing people ("a man to fulfill my purpose") and circumstances through the wisdom of his power, all the while working with free creatures. Yahweh also says in this context, "I have made you and I will carry you; I will sustain you and I will rescue you" (Isa 46:4). When believers realize that God has been sustaining them and helping them along the path of life, they can increasingly open their hearts to work with him for the consummation of his plans.

The fulfillment of prophetic promises also frequently depends on the believer's faithfulness. For a practical example, consider a situation in which God grants a revelation to an individual in your congregation. He impresses heavily upon that person that he will add 100 people to the church by this time next year (I use this example because something similar occurred in our local church, and God is in the process of fulfilling that very thing!). Assuming this person has rightly heard the Lord's voice, it may not be enough

---

13. The following passage may also hint at revelation being the content of prophecy, based on word order: "How will I benefit you unless I bring you some *revelation* or knowledge or *prophecy* or teaching?" (1 Cor 14:6 ESV, emphasis added). The revelation mentioned here could be the content of prophecy, just as knowledge is the content of teaching.

that God has good intentions toward that congregation and desires to bring this about. This prophecy could potentially fail if the church does not follow through with its responsibilities in evangelism, prayer, and outreach toward the real needs around them. Our God is one of influence and persuasion who respects the freewill that he's given his people, and he honors that freedom by stepping back enough to allow for our obedience.

In an open universe, prophecy is never cut 'n dried. It's not a black and white prediction of the future. Its fulfillment could depend on God's knowledge of future possibilities, his promise or intention to bring about a future course, or it could largely depend upon our response and faithfulness. Now that we understand a little better what prophecy is, we'll look at Paul's instructions to the Corinthians on the use of prophecy in local gatherings.

Prophecy: A Potential for Error

The disorder in Corinth required special instruction regarding the order of the prophetic. Even though such abuses don't occur in every congregation, Paul's instructions hold equal authority for churches today. Paul instructed the Corinthian believers that "two or three prophets should speak, and the others should weigh carefully what is said" (1 Cor 14:29). No two prophets are to speak at the same time, and each needs to be considerate of the others. The "others" who carefully evaluate what is said are likely the rest of the congregation. Because these prophecies are thoughtfully evaluated, it's evident the revelation comes through a dynamic impression rather than a definite dictation.

We're told earlier in the book of Corinthians that some have a gift of "distinguishing between spirits" (1 Cor 12:10), which would be particularly helpful in evaluating the prophetic. In Paul's list of gifts, the *discerning of spirits* follows immediately after prophecy. This may be significant because the interpretation of tongues also follows immediately after tongues-speaking in the same list: "And to another prophecy, and to another the distinguishing of spirits, to another various kinds of tongues, and to another the interpretation of tongues" (12:10 NASB). Hence, the discerning of spirits could be an *interpretive* gift intended to accompany and validate prophecy.

Because such evaluation and critique is commendable and even required in new covenant churches, a strong distinction exists between prophecies today and prophecies under Moses' law. Today, evaluation is not only permitted but required, which implies there may be flaws or inaccuracies in the content of the prophetic utterance. Under Moses' law, the general understanding was that a false prophecy would result in the prophet's execution as an imposter (Deut 18:20; cf. Jer 14:15), which is clearly not the consequence today. Those false prophets were excluded from God's presence, just as Yahweh warned them, "I will banish you and you will perish" (Jer 27:15). We are never told why this contrast exists between the Old and New Testaments, but it does imply that even the accuracy of prophecy remains open today.[14]

Paul encourages the Romans to prophecy "in accordance with your faith," or better, in proportion to or by the measure of your faith (Rom 12:6). If the faith Paul refers to here can exist in one measure or another, then this faith is not the content of prophecy (i.e., the body of faith or the gospel) but rather the vehicle through which it is spoken. In other words, prophecy is only as reliable as the subjective degree of one's faith. As Witherington notes, "Paul has already suggested that some have more faith and some less, and he will go on to say that some have strong faith and some weak (chs. 14–15). The point here is that, if one prophesies beyond the measure of one's faith, the prophecy will be five-parts inspiration to perhaps three-parts perspiration or mere wishful thinking."[15] Because there is always the potential for error with prophecy today, the church must carefully evaluate what's spoken.

Prophecy: The Future and God's Interrupted Knowledge

Paul told the Corinthians, "But if someone is prophesying and another person receives a revelation from the Lord, the one who is speaking must stop. In this way, all who prophesy will have a turn to speak, one after the other, so that everyone will learn and be encouraged" (1 Cor 14:30–31 NLT).[16] Paul's instruction is somewhat peculiar. Those who prophesy are sitting by in the congregation when God suddenly, even spontaneously, reveals a word to

---

14. The distinction may be due in part to different audiences under the old and new covenants. Prophetic speech is different when it's directed to a nation versus speaking to a congregation. When the prophets of old spoke to the nations, God was speaking to entire people groups, often declaring either warning or blessing on a national level. Hence, the prophet's responsibility to speak for God had national ramifications. Some passages suggest that prophets were trained in schools of prophets, as in the case of Samuel and Elisha (1 Sam 10:5; 2 Kgs 2:3, 15). For the most part, we do not have the benefit of such schools today. And rather than speaking to nations, we speak to one another.

15. Witherington and Hyatt, *Paul's Letter to the Romans*, 289. Cf. Chrysostom, *Hom. Rom.* 21: "[Prophecy] does not flow forth freely at random but is given only in proportion to our faith."

16. Or, "the person speaking should conclude" (NET). The present imperative of σιγάω means to become silent or stop speaking. Despite the wording of the NET translation, the idea is that the speaker is not able to conclude because he is interrupted.

one of them. That prophet stands up and utters the revealed message. Then all of the sudden that person is forced to stop speaking if someone else receives a revelation. Why would God speak a word to one prophet, only to interrupt him by giving a word to another? There are many possible reasons for this, which we will briefly consider.

First, the first prophet would prophesy and then elaborate on the revelation he received, providing his own commentary or clarification on what God had impressed upon him.[17] While doing so, he would also apply the content of the prophecy to the current situation in the church. If interrupted, the prophet would conclude his personal commentary to allow another prophet to speak. In this way, the content of the inspired revelation would not be interrupted, only the prophet's elaboration and application of it. Such commentary would not be unheard of for either Old or New Testament prophets (e.g., Isa 20).

A second possibility is that the prophet would enter into discussion with the congregation, perhaps the "others" who are evaluating what was said. This would involve the prophet in the evaluation process as he responds to questions or comments. The prophet would then conclude this conversation if another prophet receives a revelation.

A third option is that the prophet is indeed in the middle of declaring exactly what the Spirit had revealed to him. Before arriving at the conclusion, the content of his revelation is interrupted by another prophet. Hence, the first prophet is unable to finish his edifying speech. It's possible the revelation received by the second prophet is itself a continuation or clarifying revelation that piggybacks on the first prophecy. Since God is not a God of disorder or confusion, it would be rather unusual for him to bring a dissimilar word that might detract from the first. Both prophets' revelations would be in sync with each other.

Rather than speculating *ad nauseam*, a fourth option is that the future is open and the dynamics of prophecy are such that God keeps his church attentive to the most needful revelation. This option takes the passage most literally, that an important revelation has been interrupted. Also, in light of an open future, it's much easier to posit the benefit of an interruption. Notice that the text does not say that another prophet sitting by *will* in fact receive an interrupting revelation. Instead, it states that another prophet *may* ("if") receive an interrupting revelation, i.e., it is within the realm of possibility and could be a rare exception. If God chooses to interrupt the first, then take heed, church! Take heed and be attentive to the next revelation because

---

17. Speaking of "he," there were also female prophets; see Acts 2:17–18; 21:9; 1 Cor 11:5. Cf. Luke 2:36.

of orderliness but also due to the importance and high priority of an urgent revelation.

In an open universe, the nature of revelation itself makes the prophetic gift of utmost importance. If a prophecy is uttered, God is confident about that future and the part we play in that future to reveal this important truth.[18] God's knowledgeable planning for the future is often conditioned on the freedom and obedience of his creatures. His knowledge of the future changes as choices are made for right or wrong, for or against his love. If the future is open and therefore changeable, God is still able to effortlessly reveal the most needful truth to his people in the moment. The prophecy then sheds light on the role he expects us to play in bringing it about. This should impress upon us the high value of prophecy.

Consider the value of this gift in light of an open future that is constantly changing. The future is constantly changing due to the free agency of creatures, due to God's own constant influence upon circumstances and people, and even due to angelic beings entrenched in warfare. Because of all these dramatically changing factors, once God reveals something about the future, we should take special note of it. After all, it has held up through the rigors of a dynamically changing future! Even so, the future is not so volatile and so drastically changing that God cannot keep up with it or is forced to frantically work to keep the church aware. It rather impresses upon us the sense that God is *relationally omniscient* and fully in tune with anything helpful to the church's mission at any given moment. It reveals that God is aware of the flexibility of the future, so by revealing such truth in the moment, he demonstrates that he is in control and not caught off guard by it.

God purposely chooses to inspire interrupting revelation. This gives us a clue to the nature of God's own dynamic knowledge of an open and ever changing future. Whether the future is open or not, God could certainly wait for the first prophet to conclude before revealing something to another, or he could have instructed the church to have the second prophet wait to speak until the first concludes, but this isn't the case. Instead, God chooses to act in such a way that subtly points to the flexibility of an open future, all the while maintaining control over it. God's own knowledge of what would or might occur is interrupted by a flexible future.

---

18. As mentioned before, not all prophecies relate to the future. Prophecy can pertain to the past or present, though this is much rarer. Throughout Scripture, prophecy tends to be predictive, particularly in the New Testament (e.g., Acts 11:28; 21:10–11).

Prophecy: God Speaks in the Present

We've already said that prophecy can be either foretelling of the future or forth-telling of a past or current truth, yet all prophecy always "speaks to people for their strengthening, encouraging and comfort" (1 Cor 14:3). This does not mean, however, that the message will always be a positive one. It may be a word of warning or potential doom if repentance or obedience is not taken seriously. Although prophecy is generally for the benefit of God's people, it can at times be directed elsewhere. One such example is worthy of our attention.

In the following case, prophecy is not predictive but forth-telling and directed to the unbeliever. Paul says, "But if an unbeliever or an inquirer comes in while everyone is prophesying, they are convicted of sin and are brought under judgment by all, as the secrets of their hearts are laid bare. So they will fall down and worship God, exclaiming, 'God is really among you!'" (1 Cor 14:24-25). At times an inquirer comes into the assembly who doesn't know God or understand that the church worships in his literal presence. When the *charismata* are exercised one to another, God occasionally reveals the secret content of the inquirer's heart.

A literal translation of 1 Cor 14:24 says of the inquirer, "he is convicted by all, he is examined (*anakrino*) by all." The two phrases make the situation emphatic in that they are nearly synonymous; the unbeliever is being both convicted and examined by all. The emphasis points to the inspired *and inspiring* content of the prophecy. The prophetic message inspires the inquirer to such a degree that he is overwhelmed by the word in a very personal way. He is at once struck with the reality that the divine presence itself is behind this human utterance, inspiring what was spoken.

The term *anakrino* is related to the same root word used to describe the careful evaluation of prophetic utterances: "Let two or three people prophesy, and let the others evaluate (*diakrino*) what is said" (1 Cor 14:29 NLT). Being "examined by all" who prophesy, the inquirer is examined by the *content* of the prophetic word. The inquirer has no background to evaluate the word of God, but he is instead evaluated by it. This revelatory gift discloses what only God himself could possibly know. The point is not that the person's sins are publicly exposed; they are rather "laid bare" to the individual, which could simply entail an internal conviction rather than a public exposure. At the same time, he is struck by the truth that God knows him more personally than anyone else could. Most profoundly his inquiry has led him to become aware of God's presence! All former distance is exposed and laid bare.

As we have already addressed, this passage demonstrates that God knows the thoughts of even the unbeliever, though to what extent remains open. He also knows the likelihood for repentance if a certain prophetic word is uttered. With confidence, God reveals the "secrets of their hearts" to his prophet. If the prophet steps out in faithfulness to the revelation, the prophet can share God's confidence that the unbeliever will say yes to God and "will fall down and worship" (1 Cor 14:25). Obviously there are times the unbeliever refuses to obey God's convicting truth. In such cases the prophet's responsibility remains the same, speaking God's heart as he has revealed it. This is a warfare aspect of the gift of prophecy, that Satan and the dark powers are relentlessly at work to maintain the blackout of the unbelieving heart even after God's word reaches it with conviction (Matt 13:19; 2 Cor 4:4). God graciously waits in anticipation for people to make that final decision to repent and turn to him. In the meantime, the prophet remains the instrument of divine presence for making war against the distance (cf. 1 Tim 1:18).

CHARISMATA'S UNILATERAL PRESENCE: OPEN TONGUES AND INTERPRETATION

The other most prominent and notorious gift in the Corinthian church is the gift of tongues or languages (1 Cor 12:10, 28). Even though Acts portrays tongues as a subset of prophecy, as we saw earlier, Paul distinguishes between this and prophecy: "For anyone who speaks in a tongue does not speak to people but to God.... But the one who prophesies speaks to people" (14:2–3).

Long held by Pentecostals to be the qualifying evidence of Spirit-baptized empowerment, this gift remains among the most controversial topics regarding Pentecostalism today. Yet Paul implies that believers can practice tongues without even practicing love (1 Cor 13:1)! Rather than the determinative evidence, tongues is only one of many possible signs that someone is filled with the power of divine presence (Acts 19:6; 1 Cor 12:30). Among the most reliable indicators is the fruit of the Spirit (Gal 5:22–23) and the bold, active declaration of the gospel (Acts 14:31). Paul reflects on the superior quality and duration of the fruit of the Spirit, particularly love, as evidencing the true Christian life for this age and the age to come: "Prophecy and speaking in unknown languages and special knowledge will become useless. But love will last forever" (1 Cor 13:8 NLT). Indeed, tongues are temporary but love is forever.

Tongues: Open to Everyone?

The question of who can and will speak in tongues within the Christian community is a matter of openness. The open aspect of the *charismata* depends largely on ministry needs and God's sovereign prerogative to distribute gifts and to respond to our prayers for effectiveness in ministry. That said, the question of the openness of tongues is important because Paul wishes that "all" the Corinthian believers could speak in tongues: "Now I wish that you all spoke in tongues" (1 Cor 14:5 NASB).[19] But this can't be the case! Paul was not saying that he expected all to speak in tongues; rather, he was emphasizing that tongues are not limited to an elite few. Tongues are open to any believer! Regarding Paul's desire, David Garland comments, "This wish that 'all' speak basically democratizes the gift. It need not belong to an 'elitist monopoly.'"[20] There is never a monopoly on gifts by a few "super spiritual" believers, but the gifts remain open for every believer to pursue and apply in love.

Often times theological inquiry is an echo in the halls of ambiguity because we find that the biblical writers typically weren't asking the same questions we are, so they also don't give us straightforward answers. Fortunately, due to problems caused by the *charismata* in Corinth, Paul anticipated at least the question of whether all believers would have the ability to function in all the various gifts. He advises his readers rhetorically, saying, "Are all apostles? Are all prophets? Are all teachers? Do all work miracles? Do all have gifts of healing? Do all speak in tongues? Do all interpret?" (1 Cor 12:29–30). The construction in the Greek text implies a negative answer. The obvious answer to Paul's rhetoric is included in the New Living Translation at the end of v. 30, which succinctly states, "Of course not!" There should be no question about it: *Do all speak in tongues?* No way! According to Paul, all gifts are open and available to the church, but no single believer can possess every available gift.

A common teaching in pentecostal circles has been that one category of tongues is a "prayer language" for those baptized in the Holy Spirit, something every empowered believer should possess. They would add that an altogether different gift is an evangelistic use of tongues. To arrive at these two different aspects, they pick and choose from the description of tongues found in 1 Corinthians 14 and the book of Acts, mixing and matching what suits these two distinct gifts.[21] In response, when Paul refers to tongues

---

19. This wish is no less serious than those Paul expresses in 1 Cor 7:7, 32; 10:1, 20; 11:3; 12:1; 14:19; 16:7.

20. Garland, *1 Corinthians*, 634.

21. This was my personal experience when I attended Mount Zion School of

in his epistle to the Corinthians, he speaks generically, referring only to "tongues" without any further qualification.[22] He never distinguishes one brand of tongues from another. He was addressing the Corinthians on a well-known expression of the Spirit that only required further instruction when used in the context of the local assembly. Paul was addressing an issue of *context* rather than the purpose or content of the gift. Rather than two separate tongues-gifts in the church, the gift is open to various expressions in a variety of contexts (1 Cor 14:15–17).

Tongues: Open Expressions

The openness of tongues comes across in its many dynamic expressions. God has placed in the church the plurality of "different kinds of tongues" (1 Cor 12:10, 28) rather than any single expression. Throughout history, God's voice has creatively spoken *in one way or another* (Job 33:14). It shouldn't surprise us then that the speaking gift he empowers in the church also includes multiple faces. The gift is truly a supernatural expression of the divine voice through people. It's difficult to determine whether Paul was speaking hypothetically, but he offers the possibility that tongues may involve more than human languages: "If I speak in the tongues of men or of angels, . . . " (1 Cor 13:1). Regardless, the true benefit of this gift is that men and women can only speak in the tongues of men (or of angels) as "the Spirit enable[s] them" (Acts 2:4).

In the context of the assembly, the gift is directed to God in the hearing of others (1 Cor 14:2). But out in the community, this same praise crosses language barriers and can function evangelistically (Acts 2:4, 7–11). The context and surroundings will determine how the gift is used. If tongues are spoken in public outside the local congregation, as in Acts when an international audience was present, there's no need for interpretation: "When they heard this sound, a crowd came together in bewilderment, because

---

Ministry in the late 1990s. This school was founded by Pastor David Wilkerson, former senior pastor of Times Square Church and author of *The Cross and the Switchblade*. At the time, the school's president described two different gifts of tongues, mixing and matching seemingly random portions of Acts and Corinthians to support the claim. Despite this unfortunate handling of the text, Mount Zion (now Summit International School of Ministry) remains a school of excellence in preparing students for ministry.

22. 1 Cor 12:28, 30; 13:8; 14:2, 4, 5, 6, 13, 14, 18, 19, 22, 23, 27, 39. Paul distinguishes between interpreted and uninterpreted tongues, but never once does he suggest there are two distinct gifts of tongues. Throughout 1 Corinthians 14, the KJV translates uninterpreted tongues as "unknown tongues," though the term *unknown* is not found in the Greek text. Paul also mentions "the languages of earth and of angels" (13:1 NLT), which are two different expressions of tongues rather than two separate gifts.

each one heard their own language being spoken" (2:6). No one needed an interpreter! God will use the gift in the public context differently than he uses it in the local church gathering. When the gift is used in private there is no need for interpretation because the believer who prays in tongues will "speak to himself and to God" (1 Cor 14:28; cf. 14:18–19).

When the gift is directed toward others in the context of the assembly, the gift must be interpreted so that the entire congregation can be edified. Besides, if unbelievers or those uninformed on the Christian way are present and they hear believers speaking in uninterpreted tongues, they will conclude that you are "out of your mind" (1 Cor 14:23). There's just no benefit to it! If the believer speaks in tongues but can't interpret, Paul says, "the one who speaks in a tongue should pray that they may interpret what they say" (14:13). It's remarkable here that the believer is encouraged to ask God for a gift that is lacking. In other words, not all gifts are imparted at the moment of salvation. Instead, if this gift is any indication, the *charismata* are open to believers to "eagerly desire" and request from God (14:1).

A gift for believers, tongues can also have an impact on the nonbeliever, and not in a positive way. Scripture enunciates a negative purpose for tongues in the assembly: "Tongues, then, are a sign, not for believers but for unbelievers" (1 Cor 14:22). When tongues are spoken without interpretation, they become a *sign* to nonbelievers, that is, a sign of judgment. Regarding this negative sign, Paul quotes Isa 28:11, saying, "In the Law it is written, 'By people of strange tongues and by the lips of foreigners will I speak to this people, and even then they will not listen to me, says the Lord'" (1 Cor 14:21 ESV). Paul's logic is that nonbelievers would find themselves in like company with Old Testament Israel when they were invaded by foreign peoples with an unfamiliar, unintelligible language. Uninterpreted tongues leave a very wrong impression! Tongues must therefore be interpreted; otherwise, there's room for serious misunderstanding.

Paul's overall concern is that the congregation won't benefit from what they can't understand and neither will the nonbeliever. But if tongues are interpreted, everyone can benefit. Paul concludes,

> I will *pray* [in tongues] with my spirit, but I will also pray with my understanding [by interpreting the prayer]; I will *sing* [in tongues] with my spirit, but I will also sing with my understanding [by interpreting the song]. Otherwise when you are *praising* God in the Spirit, how can someone else, who is now put in the position of an inquirer, say "Amen" to your *thanksgiving*, since they do not know what you are saying? You are giving thanks well enough, but no one else is edified. (1 Cor 14:15–17, emphasis added)

Paul's logic is straightforward—he wants the congregation to benefit from tongues by understanding what is voiced, so the tongue must be followed by an interpretation. Notice from these verses all the various examples for expressing tongues: *praying, singing, praising, and thanksgiving.* Tongues are open to many different expressions.[23]

Could there be a more dynamic voice than to speak in a Spirit-charged tongue? The Spirit commands the church throughout this age to be open to this divine voice: "Therefore, my brothers and sisters, . . . do not forbid speaking in tongues" (1 Cor 14:39).

CHARISMATA'S UNILATERAL PRESENCE: OPEN MIRACLES

The gift of miracles or "miraculous powers" is essentially a creative action of God *ex nihilo*, out of nothing (1 Cor 12:10)![24] Miracles are the dynamic interchange between the divine presence and the natural order, interrupting the common place with kingdom power. God's fully realized kingdom may be postponed during this age, but that doesn't stop the church from experiencing the "powers of the age to come" (Heb 6:5 ESV). Because the future of God's kingdom is open-ended, God can pull powers of the future kingdom into our present experience. These powers are available to the church to whatever degree Almighty God is open to exercise his prerogative to act, creatively and spontaneously, through his people. It remains his sovereign prerogative when, where, and how to accomplish the humanly impossible and demonstrate purely supernatural displays of divine presence. God's almightiness is on display!

However, there is a human side to the gift. The human side remains the same for us as it was for Jesus, namely, that even miracles at times depend on human faith and acceptance. The Gospel of Mark reveals a significant limitation in the miracle ministry of Jesus the Nazarene. When Jesus was ministering in a certain place, Scripture says, "He could not do any miracles there, except lay his hands on a few sick people and heal them. He was amazed at

23. It's possible there are even more expressions of tongues than what we've touched on. Paul said, "Now, brothers, if I come to you speaking in tongues, how will I benefit you unless I bring you some revelation or knowledge or prophecy or teaching?" (1 Cor 14:6 ESV). Paul could have meant one of two things. Either, along with tongues, he must *also* bring a revelation, knowledge, prophecy, or teaching in order to benefit the church. Or, the tongue itself could express one of these four things, so the congregation would benefit once the tongue is interpreted.

24. Ludwig Feuerbach describes Jesus' miracle of turning water into wine as a miracle that is "a pure *creatio ex nihilo*" (*Essence of Christianity*, 131).

their lack of faith" (Mark 6:5–6). Mark emphasizes a powerful hindrance to Christ's ministry, highlighting the fact that Jesus quite literally *could not do* the miracles he may have wanted to. Speaking of the same incident, Matt 13:58 makes the connection with faith even more explicit, adding that Jesus didn't do many miracles there "because of their lack of faith." It was not due to the *weakness* of the faith of believers but rather to the *nonexistent* faith of those Jesus encountered who were unwilling to believe. I'm focusing here on Jesus' ministry of the miraculous because it is in fact that ministry that believers inherit in the gift of miraculous powers, just as with healings. This gift is open to an unlimited number of manifestations, yet even when God desires to impact the world with impressive displays of divine presence and power, he may not be able to when people refuse to believe.

At one significant point during Jesus' miraculous ministry, he made a clear declaration on human freewill and its connection to miraculous signs: "And you, Capernaum, will you be lifted to the heavens? No, you will go down to Hades. For if the miracles that were performed in you had been performed in Sodom, it would have remained to this day" (Matt 11:23). Jesus emphasizes that in their freedom to choose, the "people's response to him . . . would determine their standing at the coming judgment."[25] Although we may detect some level of hyperbole, the implications are tragic and reminiscent of other passages that suggest a dark side to an open universe: If someone would have been in Sodom to minister faithfully in the power of God, to stand in the gap as we might say, things may have been different (cf. Ezek 22:30). The dark side of an open universe is the potency of freewill and the possibility that some will refuse to heed the call to repent *or take the message to the lost*, even in the face of the miraculous presence of God.

After Jesus performed wondrous miracles, he released the same displays of divine presence through the apostles *and his church*. This truth is represented by a non-apostle, Stephen, who performed miracles in the book of Acts (Acts 8:6–7). In another place, John had made known to Jesus that they encountered "someone" casting out demons and told the person to stop (Mark 9:38). Jesus then rebuked John: "'Do not stop him,' Jesus said. 'For no one who does a miracle in my name can in the next moment say anything bad about me'" (9:39). This unnamed disciple, this "someone," should encourage believers to expect God to use anyone he chooses for his miraculous ministry. Jesus knew nothing about this person's faith and doctrine other than his or her success at casting out demons, yet Jesus still gives

---

25. Keener, *Gospel of Matthew*, 344.

his seal of approval over the believer's ministry. Hence, Jesus leaves open the possibility for God to use any true believer in the ministry of miracles.

We'll also mention here that the casting out of demons most likely falls under the umbrella of miracles, which might explain why it isn't included in any New Testament list of Spiritual gifts. The demon possessed person represents a body that God's presence has departed from altogether. The Gerasene demoniac sitting with broken chains in the cemetery is a vivid, localized portrayal of a godless region of undisturbed evil: "This man lived in the tombs, and no one could bind him anymore, not even with a chain. For he had often been chained hand and foot, but he tore the chains apart and broke the irons on his feet. No one was strong enough to subdue him. Night and day among the tombs and in the hills he would cry out and cut himself with stones" (Mark 5:3–5). This man was isolated from Jesus and the rest of society, but Jesus chose to enter into this area of hamartiological distance to bring freedom: "When he saw Jesus *from a distance*, he ran and fell on his knees in front of him" (5:6, emphasis added).

The gift of miracles is open to various displays of divine presence and power in this age. In an open universe, believers should be open-minded and believe along with Jeremiah that "perhaps the LORD will be gracious and do a mighty miracle as he has done in the past" (Jer 21:2 NLT).

CHARISMATA'S UNILATERAL PRESENCE: OPEN HEALING

Healing is the dynamic of divine presence imbuing human flesh (1 Cor 12:9, 28), another *ex nihilo* gift of God's presence. This ministry is important today because the church lives under the new covenant, a covenant of healing.[26] It is because of the new covenant that "by his wounds you have been healed," a reference to every child of God (1 Pet 2:24). Through Jesus' victory over sin and death, believers are not only made spiritually whole but also physically. Although our wholeness won't be complete until the future resurrection, healing temporarily reverses sickness and disease as encroachments of death and decay. In these last days, the church is privileged to experience supernatural healings in differing displays of divine power. That power is manifested under the new covenant as God is in the process of gradually healing humanity and all of his creation because of the magnitude

---

26. Prior to Jesus' ministry, healing was involved in every covenant that God made with people (e.g., Ps 105:37; Exod 15:26). For instance, in God's covenant with David, he promised to heal all their diseases (Ps 103:2–4).

of Christ's resurrection (cf. Rom 8:19–21). Anyone who turns to Christ is one more body made whole for the kingdom of Christ.

In an open universe, the gifts of healings have a variety of applications. In Jesus' earthly ministry, he used a variety of methods and means for healing. At one moment, he would ask someone to perform an act such as stretching out a limb, and it was instantly made whole (Matt 12:13). On other occasions, he might simply touch the body (Luke 22:51), or spit on the eyes (Mark 8:23), or spit in the dirt (John 9:6), or even put his fingers into someone's ears and spit on their tongue (Mark 7:33). Jesus had the power to merely speak the word from a distance to effect the cure (Matt 8:8, 13)! After commenting on the literal rendering of *gifts of healings* in 1 Cor 12:9, a double plural in the Greek, Harley Schmitt makes a significant observation about the open and relational nature of this gift. He remarks that what this passage "means to say is God the healer keeps his options open. There is no specific way that God heals. God heals in various ways. . . . He may choose to heal in ways that are completely foreign to us. The Lord needs to be the focus, not the healing or the way the healing is accomplished."[27]

Jesus Christ is still the Healer who creatively distributes and utilizes a plurality of "gifts" of various manifestations of "healings" through his church. Schmitt goes on to say that "God is a God of variety and the true working of the Spirit never is limited to one specific method through which people are healed."[28] If healing can be as simple as the laying on of hands, anointing with oil, or speaking a prayer of faith over someone, we should follow the advice of Naaman's servant. When the prophet Elisha told Naaman to dip seven times in the Jordan river for his healing, he stubbornly refused: "But Naaman went away angry and said, 'I thought that he would surely come out to me and stand and call on the name of the Lord his God, wave his hand over the spot and cure me of my leprosy'" (2 Kgs 5:11). Naaman had his own preconceived notions on the dynamics of healing rather than being open to God's direction. Fortunately he had a wise servant, and his servant's logic is just as applicable today as it was then: "Sir, if the prophet had told you to do something very difficult, wouldn't you have done it? So you should certainly obey him when he says simply, 'Go and wash and be cured!'" (5:13 NLT).

Because of God's creativity and open-mindedness, it would be a practice in futility to develop a "handbook" on healing. Instead, the church should step out in bold faith while seeking God to heal in the midst of even the most casual circumstances of life.

---

27. Schmitt, *Many Gifts One Lord*, 105.
28. Ibid.

CHARISMATA'S UNILATERAL PRESENCE: OPEN DISCERNMENT

The distinguishing or discerning of spirits has been considered a "companion gift to prophecy," as we introduced earlier (1 Cor 12:10).[29] As a companion gift, the discerning of spirits requires the same spontaneous revelation as prophecy, thus this gift could be mistaken for prophecy. The difference between this gift and the prophetic is in the content of the revelation. Whereas the content of prophetic revelation is a message of *edification* for the church (14:3), the content to discern spirits is a message of *origins* (Acts 16:16–18). The discerning of spirits is a dynamic of wisdom to thoughtfully receive the Spirit's critique. It grants supernatural knowledge as to the origins of a message, whether that message arose from the source of God's Spirit, the individual, or a demonic spirit. Hence, this is the gift of discerning the *source* spirit. In the immediate context of Paul's letter to the Corinthians, the most direct use of the gift may have been to assist in the assessment of prophecy (1 Cor 14:29), much like the gift of interpreting tongues is useful and even necessary to understand tongues (14:27–28). When prophecy is spoken and evaluated by the congregation, however, its assessment is open to the entire congregation and not limited to those with the gift to discern spirits. Paul simply says to "let the others evaluate what is said" (14:29 NLT).

One possible example of this gift is found with the Apostle Paul himself. When Paul encounters a demon-possessed servant girl in Acts, he is attentive to receiving divine discernment in his ministry. It's important for believers to remain open to the Spirit's spontaneous ignition of any gift. As in Paul's ministry, he was not immediately aware that the source of this girl's profound message was actually a powerful demonic spirit. Luke relates the story this way:

> Once when we were going to the place of prayer, we were met by a female slave who had a spirit by which she predicted the future.... She followed Paul and the rest of us, shouting, "These men are servants of the Most High God, who are telling you the way to be saved." She kept this up for many days. Finally Paul became so annoyed (*diaponetheis*) that he turned around and said to the spirit, "In the name of Jesus Christ I command you to come out of her!" At that moment the spirit left her. (Acts 16:16–18)

The content of Paul's rebuke demonstrates the powerful gift of the Spirit's presence to discern the true source. Interestingly, the prompting for

---

29. Thomas, *Understanding Spiritual Gifts*, 178.

it was an annoyance or, better yet, a physically exhausting irritation. The participle *diaponetheis* indicates that an inner struggle was taking place. Based on the context, this internal, spiritual struggle abruptly came to an end by Paul's precise, even inspired, assessment of the situation. When Paul was finally grieved and well beyond any human resources to accurately assess and confront the matter, the Spirit opened his heart to what was happening. This dynamic process led to a confident rebuke. In a dramatic way, Paul's discerning of spirits reveals that *charismata* are open, dynamic, and contingent upon the Spirit's sovereign prerogative in terms of when, how, and to what degree gifts are effectuated. Gifts may be given and removed, lasting for a moment, a day, a mission, or a lifetime. This appears to be a momentary gift, at least in Paul's situation.

Just as tongues illustrate a reversal of the judgment at Babel, so the gift to discern the source spirit functions as a reversal of the deception of the serpent in the garden (and the subsequent disturbance of good and evil after eating from the tree). Despite having Yahweh's immediate presence to warn against the enemy's schemes, Adam and his wife had failed to discern the source of their temptation. Today, the supernatural discerning of spirits exposes Satan's work. It is yet another means to fulfill God's abiding presence with his people as it was intended to be experienced in Eden.

CHARISMATA'S UNILATERAL PRESENCE: OPEN FAITH

Faith is always the gift of God (Eph 2:8). For every believer, faith is the gift that works together with grace and our free acceptance of the gospel to initiate us into the community of faith. Faith belongs to every saint, yet there is something unique to the gift of faith (1 Cor 12:9). Faith just might be the most open gift of all among those considered *charismata's* unilateral presence. Faith is the broadest category because it is the "unifying aspect" of all other gifts, all of which require some degree of faith to perform.[30] For instance, miracles fall under the umbrella of faith, while healings fall under miracles, but both depend on faith. Healing is just one example of a miracle, and miracles are just one consequence of a faith that believes and accepts. The gift of faith is the supernatural dynamic of *acceptance*. When my life is so filled with God's Spirit, I can accept any dynamic move of the divine presence.

One illustration of the gift of faith is Paul's description of a hypothetical function of the gift. In the course of emphasizing the need and importance of godly faith, hope, and love, particularly love, Paul maintains that "if

---

30. Ibid., 30.

I have a faith that can move mountains, but do not have love, I am nothing" (1 Cor 13:2). The primary feature of this kind of faith is the momentous occasion of the soul where one's trust in God becomes so intensified that the greatest of obstacles can be overcome, even mountains! God does not abandon the believer to be overcome but provides a means for defeating the enemy in the worst of storms, something he does at times through the gift of faith.

Surely this gift is required to some degree in the use of any supernatural gift, believing God to the point of stepping out in word and deed to effect what God has prompted by the Spirit. By faith Paul discerned the demonic spirit that gave voice to that slave girl, and by faith Paul cast out that demon. The believer is often called upon to step out in faith, accepting with confidence that God will perform what he has impressed upon the heart. This is the case for miracles, tongues, healings, prophecy, etc. (e.g., Rom 12:6; Acts 27:25).

Perhaps another nuance of the openness of faith is imparting confidence that God will employ the *charismata* in the moment they're needed—the right gifts, at the right time, in the right way.

CHARISMATA'S BILATERAL PRESENCE: A SUMMARY

Having looked at the gifts of unilateral presence that depend on a more dynamic, supernatural intervention of God, we will look briefly at the *charismata* that function in combination with our own natural gifts and talents. These gifts also require the presence and power of God to fulfill Jesus' ministry in the world, albeit in a bilateral fashion, hinging on the believer's natural abilities and input in a more apparent way than the unilateral gifts. We have already looked at Paul's list of gifts in 1 Cor 12:9–10, so we will now briefly address a less formal list in Paul's letter to the Romans. This list includes serving, teaching, encouraging, giving, leading, and showing mercy.

Paul introduces the list of ministries in Romans 12 with this positive assertion: "We have different gifts (*charismata*), according to the grace given to each of us" (12:6). In other words, God has poured out grace in the form of ministry so that believers will excel in what we do:[31] "If your gift is prophesying, then prophesy in accordance with your faith; if it is serving, then serve; if it is teaching, then teach; if it is to encourage, then give encouragement; if it is giving, then give generously; if it is to lead, do it diligently; if it is to show mercy, do it cheerfully" (12:6–8).

---

31. The NLT reads, "God has given us different gifts for doing certain things well."

Because we've already looked at prophecy as a unilateral gift, we'll start with the second item in the list, serving. The Greek word *diakonia* literally means to wait on tables and is interpreted as serving or general ministry. Just as faith is the principle unifying aspect of all *charismata*, serving is the functional unifying aspect. Those who minister always do so at some cost to themselves, following the example of the suffering God: "For even the Son of Man came not to be served but to serve, and to give his life as a ransom for many" (Mark 10:45 ESV). God opens many different doors for service, which the church is responsible to walk through. But servers don't wait for needs to arrive at their door, they seek out opportunities to serve regardless of personal cost or any attention or praise they might receive. Although the heart of a servant should permeate all other *charismata*, some believers will be especially gifted to serve.

Teaching and encouraging are also special graces that God gives to some (Rom 12:7, 8). Those who teach impart knowledge and those who encourage impart optimism. Paul's reason for this list is not to exhaust every possible ministry but to prompt every believer to perform wholeheartedly in their area of ministry, reaching full potential by "grace" and through the divine presence. In the way he qualifies the gifts that are mentioned next, Paul makes it evident that he wants the church to excel: "If it is giving, then give *generously*; if it is to lead, do it *diligently*; if it is to show mercy, do it *cheerfully*" (12:8, emphasis added). The grace-empowered opportunity to excel is open to every believer, and Paul is telling us to take advantage of it!

One final word of warning: Although the gifts are open and available for every believer to pursue and excel in, Paul warns that Christians must not breach areas of ministry intended for others. Instead, we should accept the grace and measure of faith apportioned to each one of us individually, and we must choose to excel in those areas: "For by the grace given to me I say to everyone among you not to think of himself more highly than he ought to think, but to think with sober judgment, each according to the measure of faith that God has assigned" (Rom 12:3 ESV; cf. 15:20; 2 Cor 10:13–15). Some are tempted to think too highly of their own gifting, while others can be tempted to think too little and even neglect it. Though we can be tempted to give more weight to certain gifts over others and to certain gifted individuals, those gifts that seem less extraordinary are essential to the successful function of all the rest (1 Cor 12:14–26).

Ministry requires that each of us freely and openly choose to serve in the areas of our gifting. The open-ended potential to possess and not lack any Spiritual gift (1 Cor 1:7) is not the same as fully exploiting those gifts through the grace we've received. Kathleen Cahalan comments on the believer's freedom to use their God-given gifts: "Charisms are a gift to be received, recognized, and acted upon, which means they can be ignored, rejected, and diminished, by either individuals or the community. . . . Because freedom too is a gift, some persons are free to use and accept charisms or not."[32] Although I am free to minimize my gifting, that does not negate my responsibility to fulfill the "heavenly calling" (Heb 3:1). Ministry is the outworking of this heavenly call, beckoning us to live out the united witness of the one body of Christ, finding our best fit and serving one another toward the full maturity of God's people.

CONCLUSION: CLOSING THE DISTANCE

We spent this chapter looking at the charismatic element of God's presence, the *charismata*, which refer to God's gracious gifts. First, we looked at the gifts of prophecy, tongues, miracles, healing, the discerning of spirits, and faith, gifts associated with God's *unilateral* presence. These ministries depend uniquely on God's presence and cannot be manufactured or reduced to natural talent. Through these gifts the believer becomes a channel for theophany.

We focused the majority of our time on prophecy and tongues. In each case, we emphasized the dynamic process of divine and human interaction. Prophecy is the dynamic process of receiving revelation and sharing it with the community. We classified prophecy as a gift of an open universe because it is dependent on God's dynamic knowledge of the past, present, and future as it is applied to the church's current situation. The *charisma* of languages is the dynamic voice of a Spirit-charged tongue; believers speak as the Spirit enables them. The openness of tongues comes across quite poignantly in its various expressions: praying, singing, praising, thanksgiving, and perhaps even the tongues of angels. These tongues are one of many possible evidences of Spirit-empowerment, the most reliable being the fruit of the Spirit and particularly love. Believers are encouraged to pray to God and ask for a gift to interpret tongues if they don't already have it, which implies other gifts are open to being received by prayer.

Among the other gifts, miracles are the dynamic interchange between the divine presence and the natural order, interrupting the common place with kingdom power. Miracles also include the casting out of demons, which brings wholeness to people who represent godless regions of undisturbed evil. Healing is the dynamic of divine presence imbuing human flesh and the temporary reversal of sickness and disease as encroachments of death and decay. The gift of discerning spirits is a dynamic of wisdom

---

32. Cahalan, *Introducing the Practice of Ministry*, 33, 37.

to thoughtfully receive the Spirit's critique on whether a message has come from the individual, God's Spirit, or a demonic spirit. This gift represents a reversal of the demonic deception that occurred in the garden of Eden when Adam and his wife failed to discern the source of their temptation. Finally, the gift of faith is the supernatural dynamic of acceptance and the principle unifying aspect of all *charismata*.

We then summarized the *bilateral* gifts, with special emphasis on service, which we described as the functional unifying aspect of all other gifts. The bilateral gifts include serving, teaching, encouraging, giving, leading, and helping. These are not associated with God's overt, manifest presence, but they do authorize believers as incarnational representatives. This is by no means an exhaustive list of the ministries available to the church, but they tell enough of the story to illustrate God's special, ongoing involvement with his people.

Looking at each of these gifts, we emphasized the divine presence and the openness of God. The impact of both bilateral and unilateral *charismata* is most profoundly felt in an open universe where their impact is real and their potential rests in people's freewill and God's personal involvement. The divine presence is dynamically manifest through his church as free creatures choose to pursue and excel in ministry. There are different kinds of gifts, different kinds of service, and different kinds of working, indicating that the church is free to receive, discover, explore, and act out a multiplicity of Spiritual empowerment.

God in his creative genius is not threatened by the diversity of personalities who are the vehicles for a variety of gifts, but rather he excels in his role of mixing and matching our gifting to the needs around us, resulting in church unity and growth. God has granted an incredible degree of freedom, ingenuity, and imagination to believers in their pursuit of fulfilling kingdom ministry while exploiting the *charismata* of God's grace.

9

Ministry
Open Involvement

In the last chapter, we looked at numerous gifts that are birthed and delivered through the divine presence, what we described as *charismata's* bilateral and unilateral presence. This chapter will focus more on the openness of various leadership and ministry roles as we look at the flexible dynamics of our Christ-dependent ministries. Because Jesus is Shepherd over his people, personally and actively involved in our daily lives, he has arranged ministries within the church in a manner that exalts his leading role. Every ministry is ultimately a responsibility of thoughtful, dynamic dependence on the Chief Shepherd as every local church learns to surrender to God's word and the movement of his presence.

For our benefit, Jesus is the premier Leader over our daily service: "Now these are the gifts Christ gave to the church" (Eph 4:11 NLT). As Chief Shepherd, he takes responsibility for the flock. He personally sets ministries in place while delegating shepherding responsibilities and other ministry roles to men and women who become qualified through word and Spirit (cf. Acts 6:3, "full of the Spirit and wisdom"). Jesus remains the Chief Shepherd but installs under-shepherds who are responsible for the church's daily care. We might expect Scripture to describe in detail something as important as the form and function of leadership gifts, but this is not the case. Raymond Collins comments that "'overseers' and 'servers' appear together in Phil. 1:1, but apart from the etymological implications of the terms, Paul gives no specific indication of the role of the overseers and servers within the community."[1] This lack of specificity isn't limited to Paul's writings but

---

1. Collins, *1 and 2 Timothy*, 78.

applies throughout the New Testament. The form and function of any ministry role is never fixed or outlined, which impresses upon us just how wide open the potential and opportunities are in one's service to God.

Church historian Laurie Guy comments on the flexible dynamic of early church leadership: "Certainly there was leadership, but no determining template. The boundaries of specific leadership functions were not always clear, and there was a lot of overlap. Much of the shape of ministry was ad hoc response to particular situations. From a systematic perspective, NT leadership looked messy, but it was dynamic."[2] Leadership for the early church was dynamic and flexible, just as it is today, led by the dynamism of the Chief Shepherd himself through the supernatural gifting of his Spirit. It's not surprising that the Spirit who founded and inspired the early church would leave its structure open enough to encourage long-term dependence on him. Thus, our Shepherd-King has put certain ministry roles in place for our benefit, while leaving both form and function largely open.

Guy again observes that "the church's priority on preaching the gospel (2 Tim 4:1–2) meant that although matters of structure and organization were significant, it retained much ad hoc flexibility in its early life."[3] The purpose of ad hoc flexibility and the openness of ministry is to benefit the church's mission. Leadership and ministry roles are not open for the sake of being open but for the sake of allowing the lively, dynamic nature of God's Spirit to lead his church into thoughtful avenues of ministry, service, and mission. Together we discover creative methods and means for accomplishing our Spirit-filled tasks in order to release God's presence in the world.

INTRODUCING FIVEFOLD MINISTRY IN AN OPEN UNIVERSE

Every believer possesses ministry potential equally valuable and equally needed by every other member of the body of Christ (1 Cor 12:14–27). The assembly of saints is not the place for a one person show but for every gifted, Spirit-filled believer to minister to one another (14:26). Even though leadership roles exist within the church, there are not two classes of Christians, leaders and followers; rather, there are differing levels of responsibility within our ministries. Yet every believer is responsible to "love one another" by ministering to the needs around them. Although God does at times call a specific person to a specific area of ministry, that may be the exception rather than the rule. In an open universe, it has not been predetermined

2. Guy, *Introducing Early Christianity*, 85.
3. Ibid.

who will serve in what specific areas of ministry or what their final impact will be. Every believer should step into areas that stir their passion and skills. Rather than a strong distinction between laity and clergy, there is only one body of saints who depend equally on ministries of leadership and service.

Although detailed instruction is lacking on the exact how and what of performing leadership ministries, Scripture highlights the importance of those roles and the reality that we cannot function without them. The early church's mission of gospel proclamation was carried out under the express command and ongoing authority of Jesus Christ (Matt 28:18–20). It was also carried out within the context of numerous leadership *and other closely related ministries* designed to equip every believer for mission. Hence, our study will not focus merely on leadership offices but on the fivefold "equipping" ministry. Our Chief Shepherd has given the church "the apostles, the prophets, the evangelists, the pastors and teachers" for the express purpose of equipping the saints for mutual ministry until we all attain to maturity and the full glorification of God (Eph 4:11–13). Just as the early church thrived under this flexible, multi-faceted plurality, so can churches today.

First, we will briefly review the openness of the fivefold ministry and the potential that belongs to believers to fulfill those areas of service. God's plan for those gifts can be a useful paradigm for understanding his grace and guidance in all other *charismata*. Whatever openness applies to these ministries can also be applied to the full range of Spiritual gifts. After reviewing the openness of the fivefold ministry, we will see that leadership and other ministry roles are open to believers through sovereign design, by human appointment, by desire, by availability, and even at times by chance.

THE OPENNESS OF APOSTOLIC MINISTRY: BEYOND "THE TWELVE"

The ministry of apostle has always been of utmost importance to the church, *apostolos* meaning "sent one."[4] Apostles were sent out with a specific purpose, representing the one who sent them. The church was founded upon this ministry (Eph 2:20), with the initial "Twelve" being the first to make a significant contribution. Known simply as the Twelve, Jesus chose that number out of a much larger following of disciples (Luke 6:13), making it

---

4. Regarding apostleship in the New Testament, Hoke and Taylor observe that "the Greek term *apostello* emerges in two major categories: first, as a broadly used verb, meaning to send in one form or another and by different senders (132 times); and second, as a more specifically used noun connoting the apostolic person (80 times)" (*Global Mission Handbook*, 21–22).

appear for all intents and purposes that this number was forever closed.[5] According to Mark, Jesus chose the Twelve for a special purpose, "that they might be with him and that he might send them out (*apostello*) to preach and to have authority to drive out demons" (Mark 3:14–15; cf. 6:7; Matt 10:1, 5; Luke 9:1–2). Mark expresses that Jesus called these men for the purpose of being "with him" as *disciples* and for going out as *apostles* to preach and overcome the demonic kingdom. With such a calling, Jesus clearly placed priority on the fellowship of discipleship. Only after living "with him" in a lifestyle of discipleship were they then sent out to heal the sick and preach repentance as entrance into the approaching kingdom. Because Jesus is the chief "Apostle" and hence the ultimate Messenger from God (Heb 3:1; cf. John 3:17; 17:3), he sent the Twelve out as an extension of his own apostolic ministry (John 20:21).

One needs only to read the first few chapters of the book of Acts to see how important this ministry was to the early church. Jesus chose the Twelve not only to send them out on mission but also to prepare them for a larger foundational teaching and leading ministry to his church.[6] Beginning in Jerusalem, the Twelve did not go out with secondhand teaching but as "eyewitnesses" (Acts 1:21–22; 2:32; 3:15; 4:22) of the resurrected Christ who, seated on the Davidic throne at the right hand of glory, manifested the authority of his royal reign through them (2:43; 4:33; 5:12). The apostles bore powerful witness to the risen Christ while elaborating on his teaching and showing that Scripture bears witness to him (2:42; 17:2–3; 18:4). While going out, they established churches and installed local leadership, performing missionary activities while overseeing and ensuring that sound teaching and evangelism were occurring in the churches. There was considerable authority required to fulfill such a task, but that authority only extended as far as necessary to facilitate worldwide mission (cf. 2 Cor 10:8; 13:10; 1 Thess 2:6–12).

At the opening of Acts, we quickly learn that the exclusive Twelve was not in fact a closed ministry—they were taking auditions! Because Judas had betrayed Jesus and taken his own life, the other apostles don't hesitate to appoint his replacement in a man named Matthias (Acts 1:23, 26). If the Twelve wasn't a closed ministry before, surely it would be now, seeing it was necessary for Matthias to have been with Jesus and to have personally witnessed the resurrection (1:21–22). Even so, not far into the book of Acts, Jesus personally appoints yet another apostle, sending (*apostello*) Saul/Paul of Tarsus to the Gentiles (26:16, 17; cf. 9:3–16).

---

5. Jesus' twelve disciples are listed in Matt 10:2–4; Mark 3:16–19; Luke 6:14–16.
6. See Matt 11:1; 13:10–11; Mark 4:10–11; 8:31; 9:30–31; 10:32; Luke 18:31.

Paul clearly recognized himself as an apostle, informing the Galatians, "I did not go up to Jerusalem to see those who were apostles before I was" (Gal 1:17), and to the Corinthians, "I am the least of the apostles and do not even deserve to be called an apostle" (1 Cor 15:9). Not only was he a great leader to the early church, but his apostleship had the support of the Apostle Peter who placed Paul's letters on par with Old Testament Scripture (2 Pet 3:16, "the other Scriptures").[7] There should be no doubt that Paul was an apostle in the strictest sense, even satisfying similar credentials as the Twelve in that he had actually seen Jesus (1 Cor 9:1).[8] Nevertheless, the Twelve were required to be eyewitnesses in an even more restrictive sense than Paul, being with Jesus from the very beginning of his ministry, no doubt "to fulfill their roles as the proclaimers and protectors of the true story of Jesus."[9]

Paul is evidence that there are apostles beyond the Twelve, implying this ministry remains open to other believers. Important to our study are those apostles beyond the strict sense of the Twelve, others like Paul and James, the brother of Jesus (1 Cor 15:7). Examples of other apostles in Scripture include: Andronicus and Junia (Rom 16:7),[10] Apollos (1 Cor 4:6, 9), Barnabas (Acts 14:14), Epaphroditus (Phil 2:25, "your apostle/messenger"), and possibly Silas (Acts 17:10; cf. 15:40–41) and Timothy (1 Thess 1:1; 2:6–7). Donald Dent concludes that the New Testament identifies four different groups of apostles: (1) the Twelve, (2) other commissioned eyewitnesses, such as Paul and James the brother of Jesus, (3) missionary apostles, such as Barnabas (Acts 13:2–5), and (4) envoys of the churches, such as the church in Antioch that sent a financial contribution to Jerusalem (Acts 11:30; cf. 8:14; 11:22).[11] Each of these groups fits the New Testament definition of *apostolos* as one who is sent for a purpose.

7. Such apostles as Paul and Peter wrote inspired Scripture, but being an apostle was not prerequisite for writing Scripture; otherwise, both Luke and Jude would have been designated apostles.

8. Paul said to the Corinthians, "Even though I may not be an apostle to others, surely I am to you!" (1 Cor 9:2). His statement hints at some flexibility or openness related to being an apostle. In other words, my apostolic commission is closed to others but open to you!

9. Dent, *Ongoing Role of Apostles*, 36. See also Witherington, *Acts of the Apostles*, 125.

10. Andronicus and Junia are described as "outstanding among the apostles" (Rom 16:7), which can be interpreted two different ways: either they were outstanding *as* apostles or highly esteemed *by* the apostles.

11. Dent, *Ongoing Role of Apostles*, 34. Though Dent has identified these four groups to describe the New Testament usage of *apostolos*, he briefly summarizes other categorizations that have been suggested: "One traditional view is that only the Twelve and Paul were the only real apostles. Others have noted two groups of apostles, such as the Twelve and others or apostles of Christ and apostles of the church or eyewitnesses and missionaries" (ibid., n. 102).

Finally, there are two unnamed apostles (2 Cor 8:18–23). These two people are described as "apostles/representatives of the churches" (8:23). Just as they are unnamed and their identities unknown, suffice it to say the apostolic ministry is one that remains open today. Although today's apostles do not produce inspired Scripture, they must nonetheless be sensitive to supernatural revelation. They do not have the authority of the Twelve, but they do have responsibility over their spheres of ministry, often very large ministries. Today, in addition to being commissioned and sent to minister outside of one's local church with a message or gift, the apostolic ministry is fulfilled primarily through missionary enterprise, extending the kingdom of Christ throughout the world. A close reading of the New Testament reveals there are no other clear examples of missionaries other than the ministry of apostle.[12] The authority and function these apostle-missionaries assume remains somewhat open, as the degree of their authority will be determined by the scope and sphere of their church planting and discipleship activity.[13] Nonetheless, missionary activity does not exhaust the calling of apostles today.

These men and women will meet the same requirements as other church leadership (cf. 1 Tim 3:1–7; Titus 1:5–9). They will maintain humility as servant-leaders, they will assist in establishing other permanent leaders, and they will be examples of sound teaching with a reputation above reproach. Were apostles only men, or was this ministry open to women as well? Current application of the missionary aspect of apostleship rarely restricts God's call of missionaries to men. We should also be aware of the possibility that the first-century believer Junia was a female apostle (Rom 16:7). It seems, therefore, that a man or woman can faithfully fulfill the role of an apostle.

THE OPENNESS OF PROPHETIC MINISTRY

The prophet is another gift listed in the fivefold ministry in Eph 4:11. Prophets may or may not fill leadership roles,[14] so there's no need to imagine that a formal ordination or laying on of hands is required to designate someone a prophet.[15] Prophets simply fulfill the role of relaying divine revelation to the

---

12. See Turner, *Biblical Bible Translating*, 16–19; and Hesselgrave, *Paradigms in Conflict*, 215–16.

13. For a charismatic perspective on apostleship that advocates more apostolic authority and less missionary function, see Wagner, *Apostles Today*.

14. Although the role of prophets is not primarily to lead, this doesn't keep them from occasionally exercising leadership in the local church (cf. Acts 13:1; 1 Cor 12:28; Eph 2:20; 3:4–5).

15. Grudem observes that "there is no hint in the New Testament about any

church. Although some make a distinction between an *office* of prophet and those who occasionally prophesy, Wayne Grudem observes that "'prophet' appears to be not an office but a designation of function in the New Testament. Those who prophesied frequently or appeared to have the gift of prophecy were called 'prophets.'" Grudem goes on to explain just how open this gift is: "It probably was generally recognized by the believers that 'prophet' simply meant 'someone who prophesies.' Such a non-technical definition fits well with all the New Testament data."[16] Following Grudem's conclusions, the church could recognize any person as a prophet if God spontaneously reveals something to him that's intended to be shared with the congregation.

Jack Hayford remarks that, according to the New Testament and especially Paul's instructions to the Corinthian church, "there aren't any restrictions on when, where, or how prophecies may be delivered.... God has been willing to open the door quite wide."[17] Although Hayford points out the openness of prophecy, Scripture places limitations on how and when prophecies can be spoken to the congregation. Paul instructs the churches that anyone in the congregation may prophesy if they receive a revelation from God, but only two or three in turn; each one must be conscientious and open to interruption if God reveals something to someone else. After they're done speaking, the congregation must thoughtfully evaluate what was said (1 Cor 14:29).

When prophets step out to minister, they do so as an extension of the universal prophethood of believers. Every believer is privileged to possess the prophetic Spirit that was poured out at Pentecost, the Spirit who inspires us to understand and share the full gospel of Jesus Christ: "Even on my servants, both men and women, I will pour out my Spirit in those days, and they will prophesy" (Acts 2:18).[18] This emphasis, however, is not what Paul has in mind in the fivefold list to the believers in Asia Minor. Paul is referring to those who receive a direct, spontaneous revelation from God to foretell future events or forth-tell truth for a present occasion. These men and women possess the prophetic gift that we described earlier in chapter 8.

---

ceremony of recognizing or installing someone in a prophetic office or to perform some specific prophetic tasks (as with apostles, elders, and deacons in Acts 1:23–26; 6:6; 14:23; 1 Tim. 4:14; 5:22; Titus 1:5; etc.)" (*Gift of Prophecy*, 165).

16. Ibid., 165, 167. Donald Gee of the Assemblies of God expresses similar thoughts as Grudem: "Although there appears to be a distinction between official prophets and those who prophesied, it is arbitrary to claim for the prophets anything more than that they were those who exercised a frequent and proved gift of prophesying" (*Spiritual Gifts*, 43–44).

17. Hayford, "Despise Not Prophecy," 80.

18. This passage presents an *a fortiori* argument: If God's Spirit is poured out on the least (servants), it is certainly poured out on all!

Just as both men and women functioned as prophets in the New Testament, there will also be male and female prophets today. The prophet Agabus had "four unmarried daughters who prophesied" (Acts 21:9). Paul exhorted the believers in Corinth that "every woman who prays or prophesies" should do so with her head covered (1 Cor 11:5). This passage suggests that prophesying could be expressed just as regularly and naturally as prayer in the public gathering!

As believers "keep in step with the Spirit" (Gal 5:25), the divine presence uses us to share gospel truth under the Spirit's sensitive guidance, a benefit of being members of the prophethood of all believers. But does every saint have the ability to prophesy? Thankfully there's no need to speculate because Scripture anticipates the question and answers in the negative. Paul asks, "Are all prophets?", and the implied answer—no (1 Cor 12:29)! We could say the same about any ministry. Even though all believers have the prophetic Spirit, not all believers have the ability to prophesy. But for those who are gifted in this way, the Spirit commands the church throughout this age to remain open to their ministry: "Therefore, my brothers and sisters, be eager to prophesy" (14:39), and "do not treat prophecies with contempt" (1 Thess 5:20).

THE OPENNESS OF EVANGELISTIC MINISTRY

If the New Testament locates the missionary role in any gift, it's most likely the apostle rather than the evangelist. Evangelistic ministry is much broader in its application than missionary service. In a generic sense, this gift is open to every believer, yet there will be some who are especially gifted to promote the gospel. As an equipping ministry, the evangelist will equip other believers to become more effective evangelists themselves. As with most gifts, the task of equipping others is flexible enough for the evangelist to use her natural talents, creativity, and common sense, while always remaining sensitive to the Spirit's inner voice.

Whereas Eph 4:11 uses the plural *euangelistas* ("evangelists"), the term occurs in only two other places in the New Testament, both singular (Acts 21:8; 2 Tim 4:5). Timothy was one such "evangelist" who was obligated to "fulfill" this ministry (2 Tim 4:5), just as Paul had done (4:6–8). Known simply as "the evangelist," Philip is the other person this ministry is associated with in the New Testament (Acts 21:8). Philip was not an apostle but was indeed a man "full of the Spirit and wisdom" (6:3). He was a man who couldn't keep quiet but "proclaimed the Messiah" (8:5) and "preached the word wherever [he] went" (8:4; cf. v. 40). Philip "proclaimed the good news of the kingdom of God and the name of Jesus Christ" (8:12). Not only was

Philip an effective communicator of the gospel, but he was quick on his feet and adapted to circumstances as they presented themselves. When Philip encountered a traveling eunuch who was reading from the scroll of Isaiah, Scripture says that Philip "began with that very passage of Scripture and told him the good news about Jesus" (8:35).

THE OPENNESS OF PASTORAL/TEACHING MINISTRY

The phrase "pastors and teachers" in Eph 4:11 can be understood as "pastors and *other* teachers (*didaskalous*)," meaning the pastors are teachers but there are also other teachers besides them.[19] For simplicity's sake, we will treat teachers here under the same heading as pastors. The teaching ministry throughout the church extends to anyone who is an able communicator willing to faithfully explain and apply God's word, a ministry open to men and women alike. In Titus 2:3 it is specifically the women who are encouraged to be *kalodidaskalous*, teachers of what is good.

Turning our attention to pastoral ministry, Gerald Bray in his systematic theology offers a helpful, abbreviated definition of the practical function of pastor, stating, "The specific duty of a pastor is to shepherd those who have responded to the preaching of the gospel and to guide them along the pathway to spiritual maturity."[20] As an equipping ministry, the role and involvement of pastoral elders remains somewhat open and flexible. The earliest reference to elders in Acts mentions them receiving a relief-gift because of a famine (Acts 11:30), identifying those leaders with the unified church in Jerusalem. In Asia Minor, Paul beseeches the elders to protect the flock of believers and practice church discipline (20:28–31). Church leaders are also said to "direct the affairs of the church" as well as "preaching and teaching" (1 Tim 5:17), being people who are "able to teach" (3:2) and lead (Heb 13:7). There is some dispute over whether a teaching elder can be distinguished from an elder who leads.

---

19. A cursory glance at various Bible commentaries shows that many scholars interpret the ministry of pastor and teacher (*tous poimenas kai didaskalous*) in Ephesians 4 as one gift, the "pastor-teacher." A closer look, however, reveals that this is a misuse of Granville Sharp's Rule. According to the Rule, in the TSKS construction (article-substantive-καὶ-substantive), the second noun refers to the same person mentioned with the first noun *when neither noun is impersonal, plural, or a proper name*. In Eph 4:11, the construction *tous poimenas kai didaskalous* is disqualified due to containing plural nouns. According to Daniel Wallace, the plural construction in Ephesians 4 is likely an example of the first group being a subset of the second, "the X and [other] Y" (*Greek Grammar*, 271–72, 278–86). Other examples include Matt 5:20; 9:11; Luke 6:35; 14:3.

20. Bray, *God is Love*, 698.

It should come as no surprise that the New Testament is flexible in its recognition of church leadership. Elders were prominent in first-century Jewish synagogues where at least some overlap existed with the role, authority, and character requirements of the church elder. This could explain why that role was easily adapted to the church's organization, but there may have been other reasons as well.[21] Possibly most telling is the first-century Mediterranean conception of an elder. An elder was simply a mature man with seasoned judgment. Unlike the official office most churches recognize today, the early church elder/overseer may have been much less formal. In light of the multiple house churches that rose up throughout first-century cities and towns, elders were likely chosen from among the more mature and respected members of a household or community.[22]

On Paul's first missionary journey, he and Barnabas "appointed (*cheirotonesantes*) elders for them" (Acts 14:23). Luke uses the term *cheirotoneo*, which literally means to stretch out the hand (to vote). So were these elders chosen and appointed, or were they voted on? Moreover, we're not told what the criteria for selection and appointment might be until Paul provides a brief summary of qualifications in his letters to Titus and Timothy (Titus 1:5–7; 1 Tim 3:1–8). Paul was primarily concerned with an overall godly lifestyle rather than checking off a list of character qualities. Those who stood out were recognized as people of wisdom who were able to teach but not necessarily skilled at it.[23] They may not have been to seminary, but they knew God and manifested a godly maturity that others recognized.

Most references to leadership in the New Testament are plural. We're told that "elders" were to be appointed "in every town" (Titus 1:5). It isn't entirely clear whether that plurality refers to multiple elders per town or multiple elders per church. We're also told that "Paul and Barnabas appointed elders for them in each church" (Acts 14:23). This seems to suggest that each

---

21. Benjamin Merkle reviews the four most popular views on the origin of the elder in early church government. The office could have originated from (1) Old Testament leaders who were designated "elders" in the Septuagint, (2) the Sanhedrin, (3) the Jewish synagogue, or (4) the culture, as in a senior male within the community or family. Merkle concludes that the Christian office of elder was not directly borrowed from any of these, though the church borrowed the title and "defined for itself the specific duties that those who held this title performed" (*40 Questions About Elders and Deacons*, 72–74).

22. See Campbell, *Elders: Seniority within Earliest Christianity*. Reformed theologian and missionary Harry R. Boer suggests, "It may also be that the older members of the Christian community were automatically looked upon as the leaders" (*Short History of the Early Church*, 28).

23. Newton, *Elders in Congregational Life*, 38. Newton argues that not all elders are called to "pulpit ministry."

church was composed of multiple elders. But was that the city church, like Jerusalem, made up of multiple house churches, or something else? Perhaps each house church had only one elder, but since the "church of Corinth" or the "church of Jerusalem" could consist of multiple house churches, maybe that would explain the plurality?

Although most denominations acknowledge a plurality of leadership in the early church, others argue for a single elder or pastor to lead the church. They interpret the sole "angel" of the churches of Revelation as a single pastor leading each church (Rev 2:1, 8, 12, 18; 3:1, 7, 14). They highlight the singular "overseer" mentioned by Paul (1 Tim 3:2) and the sole "elder" that appears in the Johannine Epistles (2 John 1; 3 John 1). Most see James as a primary leader over other elders in Jerusalem (Acts 12:17; 15:12–13; 21:18; Gal 1:19; 2:9), forecasting the role the bishop would later take on. Some churches today hold that a bishop or presbytery is meant to oversee multiple churches, while others believe every church is autonomous and should be led by a single pastor or board of elders, while still others insist that final decisions are made by the congregation.[24] As important as church government is, the Spirit never directed the early church to formalize a doctrine. Instead, their forward progress for the kingdom of Christ was rather dynamic, more interested in action and growth than building governing bodies.

The flexibility of the pastorate is evident even in titles used of early church leaders. Among other things, the designations include elder (*presbuteros*, James 5:14), shepherd or pastor (*poimen*, Eph 4:11), overseer or bishop (*episkope*, 1 Tim 3:1), and leaders (*egoumenon*, Heb 13:7). Although there's disagreement on the matter, each of these titles likely refers to one and the same role, the pastor. By the end of the second century, extracanonical writings distinguished the bishop/overseer from the other elders.[25] This distinction is not explicit in the New Testament, however. Paul appears to use elder and overseer interchangeably (Titus 1:6–7).[26] Speaking to the elders (*presbuterous*) in Ephesus (Acts 20:17), Paul commands them to "keep watch over yourselves and all the flock of which the Holy Spirit has made you overseers (*episkopous*). Be shepherds (*poimainein*) of the church

---

24. For an introduction on the representative views of church government, see Engle and Cowan, *Who Runs the Church?*; and Brand and Norman, *Perspectives on Church Government*.

25. Ignatius, an early second-century bishop of Antioch, distinguished between a single bishop and a plurality of elders, likening the elders to the apostles (*Smyrn.* 8; cf. *Pol.* 6; *Trall.* 6). Other early extra-biblical sources describe only a plurality of elders or bishops (1 *Clem.* 42:4; 44:3; *Did.* 15:1; *Herm. Vis.* 8:3; 13:1; *Herm. Sim.* 104:2).

26. See Merkle, *Elder and Overseer*.

of God" (20:28). Peter enjoins elders (*presbuterous*) to be shepherds (*poimanate*) who submit fully to the authority of the Chief Shepherd (*Archipoimenos*), the Lord Jesus Christ (1 Pet 5:1, 2, 4). Although apostles were distinct from elders (Acts 20:17), they were also teachers, prophets (cf. Acts 13:1; Eph 2:5),[27] and other elders (cf. Acts 15:2; Gal 2:9; 1 Pet 5:1). Paul himself was "a preacher, an apostle, and a teacher" (2 Tim 1:11 NLT).

Regarding the question of women in pastoral leadership roles, this is somewhat difficult to answer from the New Testament alone. In 1 Tim 2:12, Paul says that he does not "tolerate" (*epitrepo*)[28] women "to teach or assume authority over (*authentein*) a man." He then grounds his logic, not in a cultural sensitivity, but in the biblical doctrine of creation, saying, "For Adam was formed first, then Eve. And Adam was not the one deceived" (2:13–14). While we consider Paul's intent, it should be in the back of our minds that the fullest New Testament picture of worship, ministry, and mission seems to emphasize a move toward ever-increasing liberation and freedom, whether for slaves or women's rights. It would also appear that the pastorate remains open to women largely due to the meaning of the Greek terms and construction found in 1 Tim 2:12. Linda Belleville observes that the specific manner of teaching that Paul's referring to is not teaching in general but teaching in a domineering way. She remarks that

> the Greek verb *authentein* . . . is not found elsewhere in Paul's writings or the NT. In the Greek of the day, the word meant "domineer." . . . Furthermore, in the Greek, we see a "neither—nor" construction: "neither teach nor domineer" (NLT, "have authority over"). Such constructions in the NT pair synonyms ("neither despised nor scorned," Gal 4:14), . . . In this context it seems that the Greek correlative "neither—nor" defines a single activity. . . . This means that women here are not prohibited from roles that involve teaching men. The issue is rather the manner in which they teach—that is, they should not teach in a dictatorial or domineering way.[29]

---

27. As with Eph 4:11 above, Wallace argues that "the apostles and prophets" (*ton apostolon kai propheton*) in Eph 2:20 and 3:5 are another example of the first group being a subset of the second, "the X and [other] Y." The apostles are prophets, but there are also other prophets besides them: "the apostles and *other* prophets" (*Greek Grammar*, 284–86).

28. Through personal email correspondence with Dr. Daniel Wallace, we discussed a nuance of the Greek ἐπιτρέπω that is not captured in lexicons; namely, *toleration*. For instance, Jesus stated, "Moses permitted (ἐπέτρεψεν) a man to write a certificate of divorce and send her away" (Mark 4:10). The nuance is clearly one of toleration; i.e., Moses *tolerated* divorce.

29. Belleville et al., *Cornerstone Biblical Commentary*, 55.

Finally, the elder is a servant-ministry intended to equip the saints. The experience of the first-century church was not a clergy-laity distinction but rather numerous complementary roles working together for God, bearing not even a hint of *lording it over your faith* (2 Cor 1:24). The leaders were ministers among equals, men and women who recognized that all believers are full-time ministers called to serve under the Headship of Jesus Christ. The church of Corinth never once mentioned an elder or other leader taking over the worship service. Rather, every member ministered one to another through the manifestation of divine presence and God's gracious gifts (1 Cor 14:26).

Another important area of openness is the manner in which a person comes into a leadership or ministry role in the church, which is where we'll turn our attention for the remainder of the chapter.

THE OPENNESS OF MINISTRY CANDIDACY

Much of what is expected in the fivefold ministry will first be identified by other believers instead of any self-identification as apostle, prophet, etc. The scene in the 1996 feature film, *The Apostle*, in which Robert Duvall baptizes himself and thereby appoints himself an apostle, is not by any means the norm for our churches! In fact, the person who must claim a title for himself should be approached with caution.

Ministry is an area in which God occasionally takes the sovereign prerogative to handpick his man or woman for a position, such as with King Saul or the Apostle Paul, but in the majority of cases it remains open to those who pursue service based on personal "desire" (1 Tim 3:1). The ideal is that other men and women of faith will recognize one's passion and gifting in order to then appoint, commission, or ordain that person to a particular area of service. This should be a freeing revelation to someone who's been hesitant to pursue a passion for the pastorate or other area of interest. We mustn't feel that we should wait for an epiphany or that "call of God" moment.

Although the ministries of prophecy and evangelism, perhaps even teaching, do not necessarily require recognition and appointment by other believers, others will be looking at how you use those gifts and should be respectfully evaluating your faithfulness to God's word and the benefit to the body of Christ. God desires that each of us take an active interest in pursuing service that will most build up his church. Believers should pursue ministries that will ignite a fire of passion to reach out to the lost and turn this world upside down for Jesus. To accomplish this, you should know that

God has gone so far as to call you his partner or "co-worker" (1 Cor 3:9; 2 Cor 6:1) and intends to take into account your passion and areas of interest. After all, you serve the God of an open universe!

It should be taken for granted that much of where people serve will be based on God-given motivation and God-given desire, because we are a Spirit-led people. However, that doesn't diminish the freedom we have to seek out ministries and ministry needs. It should motivate and encourage you to know that you are not ordained for one particular ministry or locked into one area of service but can pursue your passion through prayer and the burden that points you in a given direction. Of course, once a person makes a commitment to a given ministry, she or he is responsible within that sphere of influence to abide and *fulfill your ministry* (2 Tim 4:5).

As we consider the openness of ministry candidacy, we will see that leadership and other ministry roles are open to believers through divine or human appointment and on the basis of desire, chance, and availability.

Ministry by Sovereign Appointment

Even when God calls the minister of his choice, it doesn't always turn out for the best. We know from Scripture and from experience that God's will is not always done; otherwise, a prayer like "thy will be done in earth" would be in pretense only (Matt 6:10 KJV). This is the risk of being Lord and Creator over a world in which truly free choices are honored.

In an open universe, God will initially choose a person based on proven character and faith, which may ultimately turn out for good or bad. This was the case with men like Abraham, Moses, David, and King Saul. God chose Saul, not for just any position, but to be the first king of Israel! No doubt Yahweh had plans for Saul that were meant to bring about great blessing for Israel from generation to generation. Yet in the end, Saul's disobedience led to God's grim change of mind. Yahweh told the prophet Samuel, "I regret that I have made Saul king, because he has turned away from me and has not carried out my instructions" (1 Sam 15:11a). Although Samuel had always been a faithful prophet to Yahweh, he didn't take Yahweh's regret very well: "Samuel was angry, and he cried out to the Lord all that night" (15:11b). Scripture suggests Samuel wasn't happy with God's decision or perhaps with the cause of God's regret. So, by crying out throughout the night, it appears that Samuel was attempting to change God's mind, as Moses and others had done.

Jesus had selected each of his apostles, the ones he would send out to fulfill the post-resurrection, foundational ministry of establishing his church in the new age. Even so, Jesus' personal call didn't stop Judas from being influenced by Satan and using his freedom to pursue a path of destruction. Despite Judas's failure to represent the kingdom, the Lord didn't become apprehensive but later chose the Apostle Paul whose obsession had been to destroy the church (Acts 8:3). Even with a background of religious, murderous piety, Paul served Christ's kingdom as a true representative of the heart of God, sharing even the "affection of Christ Jesus" for God's people (Phil 1:8). In his infinite grace, God can call even the very *worst* to his service (1 Cor 15:9). If you have seen yourself in a negative light and struggle to accept that God would call you to minister, be certain that he truly is calling you to serve him.

God can call anyone at any time into any ministry in his church, but his "call" is not required. Many assume that church leadership is settled in God's mind and that all leaders must sense "the call" or experience some confirming event in their lives. This can of course be the case, as with men like Abraham, Moses, Samuel, and the Twelve, but surely this is the exception rather than the rule. Absent from Paul's instructions to Titus (1:5–9) for appointing elders "is any reference to appointing those who are, in modern jargon, 'called to preach.'"[30]

Ministry by Human Appointment

Throughout Acts and Paul's letters, people are appointed by Spirit-led leadership into positions of authority and other ministry responsibilities. This appointment can occur through election or by direct commission. Such a task takes a great deal of discernment but also rests upon the approval of a plurality of gifted individuals, whether that be a plurality of elders or the whole congregation. Many of the first-century leaders of the church were appointed by apostles, but as the churches matured, that responsibility necessarily fell into the hands of local churches. The authority of the first apostles did not continue indefinitely.

As an apostle, Paul had a unique gift and calling as well as a unique responsibility and authority over the churches. He was, in large part, responsible for all the churches. The apostles of the first century had a unique authority that cannot be duplicated today. For example, in order to replace Judas's position among the Twelve, they looked at men who had walked with Jesus since John's baptism and had been firsthand witnesses of Jesus' resurrection (Acts 1:21–22). This, of course, was not the case with all first-century apostles, as even the Apostle Paul did not meet that criteria.

---

30. Newton, *Elders in Congregational Life*, 38.

Nevertheless, there was something unique about their role and sphere of authority.

Without having those original apostles around today, local churches now bear the burden of prayerfully and thoughtfully considering who meets the qualifications of leadership (Titus 1:5–9; 1 Tim 3:1–7). Of utmost importance would be selecting men and women of high moral character while not ignoring other important qualities, such as the ability to teach and correct as well as having sufficient leadership skills. It's often the case that those gifted for leadership are already present in any seasoned congregation and can be discovered without having to search outside the local church. It can also be the case that some churches are young and immature and would therefore benefit from outside leadership. Regarding Paul's instructions to Titus, Samuel Ngewa provides a helpful observation:

> In instructing Titus to appoint elders, Paul is not making a theological statement governing all situations. It was simply the case that the church in Crete was young, and the best approach there was to appoint the elders. In some churches today elders are still appointed, while in others they are elected by the members. The method does not matter; what is important is that those who lead the church have the right qualities to be leaders.[31]

Whether churches appoint, elect, or even cast lots after selecting a person of character and ability, there is something awe-inspiring about God desiring that believers participate with him in the high calling and extreme responsibility of leading and ministering to his church.

As Chief Shepherd, Jesus once again demonstrates that he manifests his own power and authority through delegation and vice-regency. He does not think it best to sovereignly appoint leaders, as he did with Abraham or the Apostle Peter, but prefers to give his church a voice in the process. He takes into account our identification of gifted individuals and allows our choices to have real consequences as we experience a living church.

Other Aspects of Openness in Candidacy

If God is Lord over an open universe and desires to see that freedom played out in every area of church life, for leaders and non-leaders alike, the implications are profound and demonstrate a church more alive and more involved than many may realize. Because this becomes so apparent even in the leadership of the church, there are a few additional features of

---

31. Ngewa, *1 and 2 Timothy*, 338.

open ministry roles that would benefit us to touch on: ministry by desire, by chance, and by availability.

Ministry by Desire

God calls some into ministry more specifically than he calls others. The church must then identify those people by whatever thoughtful means it chooses. It remains open, however, that a person may pursue a certain ministry primarily on the basis of a desire or passion for it, even without sensing an inward calling. In many cases, *the desire is the inward call.*

There are few passages in the New Testament that address leadership selection. When someone is identified as a gifted person of high character, even before being appointed or elected, there must be some indicator to assist in knowing God's preference. The Pastoral Epistles suggest that a most revealing sign is that a person has the burden or passion to pursue the pastorate: "Here is a trustworthy saying: Whoever aspires (*oregetai*) to be an overseer desires a noble task" (1 Tim 3:1). Regarding the Greek root word *orego*, Raymond Collins comments that such aspiring "would connote striving after something good, even the kingship (see, e.g., Plutarch, *Solon* 29.3; *Phocion* 17.1; Josephus, Life 13 § 70, a passage that uses both aspire and desire)."[32] This striving is viewed in only the best possible light: not as a greedy or selfish endeavor but one that arises out of good and positive intent.

This is one of the most precious aspects of how God provides leadership and other important ministries within the church. His desire is to involve the church in the process. Not only does he take into account the desire and aspirations of a person's heart, but he also asks believers to thoughtfully consider the areas of ministry that interest them. If you have the desire to pursue a ministry, do so with confidence that the word of God is behind you.

Ministry by Chance

In an open universe, there's such a thing as chance. Although chance is never an absolute in God's world, it is a conditional reality in an open universe. We can't ignore the role that chance played in at least one scriptural instance of choosing leadership for the church. The situation I'm referring to is the

---

32. Collins, *1 and 2 Timothy*, 79.

replacement of the twelfth apostle, Judas Iscariot. After Judas's death, the Twelve were one short of their original number (Acts 1:17, 20).

The importance of the pioneering mission of the twelve apostles cannot be overstated, seeing that the household of the church was indeed "built on the foundation of the apostles and prophets, with Christ Jesus himself as the chief cornerstone" (Eph 2:20). The stakes were high, both to fulfill the mission Christ had laid before them and because they were so limited in number! The apostles didn't hesitate to narrow their search down to two qualified men, and then without wavering they "cast lots, and the lot fell to Matthias; so he was added to the eleven apostles" (Acts 1:26).[33] In the natural, it would appear they left the decision up to chance!

In his commentary on the book of Acts, F. F. Bruce adds some perspective to what took place: "It may well be that there was nothing to choose between Joseph and Matthias; in that case the casting of lots, which had very respectable precedent in Hebrew sacred history, was a reasonable way of deciding on one of the two, especially because they besought God to overrule the lot, in the spirit of Prov. 16:33: 'The lot is cast into the lap, but the decision is wholly from the LORD.'"[34] As essential as this apostolic position was to the early church, especially seeing what credentials were required of the person, to modern day readers it seems quite unusual that the apostles cast lots to make such an important decision. But as Bruce points out, they were confident that God would influence the lots in such a way that he would ultimately be the one choosing the twelfth apostle.

Although this is one possible interpretation, I must object. In an open universe with so many influential factors that impact prayer and God's response to it, it's never within anyone's power to *demand* that God intervene just because someone chooses to cast lots, whether he's an apostle or not. When lots are cast, the result is left to chance if God does not *directly* intervene. Chance often involves a certain level of risk, and it wouldn't have been any different for the apostles. Even so, in the case of choosing the twelfth apostle, it also wouldn't have been a problem for at least two reasons.

First, as Bruce points out, both candidates were probably more than qualified, so either would have excelled in fulfilling the role. This implies God never predetermined either man's potential for impact through apostleship. Truly, both were free to step into this ministry and to have a tremendous effect upon the Christian world. We should all be encouraged that our usefulness and potential are not predestined for good or bad, which at least

---

33. Throughout the Old Testament, the casting of lots was popular for decision-making. At one point, the LORD even *commanded* that they cast lots to assist in dividing up the land (Num 26:55–56).

34. Bruce, *Book of Acts Revised*, 46–47.

means none of us are doomed for failure!³⁵ Rather, believers can be exhorted to press on to accomplish the greatest impact in a universe designed with doors wide open with opportunity.

Second, God is infinitely resourceful. Had the apostles by chance made the wrong decision and Matthias later turned away from God (like Judas had), God could still redeem and make the most of the situation (cf. Rom 8:28). This was in fact the case with both Saul and David, two kings that God himself had chosen. Those men both failed miserably, but God raised up David to replace Saul and then redeemed David's kingdom after his mistakes.

Ministry by Availability

Being available when the need exists is also an important aspect of ministry in an open universe. Since God hasn't ordained every detail of human existence, including the details of leadership and other roles within the church, believers should remain available and prepare themselves for the opportunity to serve. God may be calling you into unexpected situations to accomplish unexpected exploits for his kingdom!

Deborah, a prophet and judge, is one example of a woman who had the right character and temperament to take on a significant leadership role in a culture dominated by men, and God used her mightily (Jud 4–5). Deborah even sang of the availability of God's people to be used by him. She sang, "My heart is with Israel's princes, with the willing volunteers among the people. Praise the LORD!" (5:9).

Every believer is expected to remain open and available to serve the needs around them. God calls us to minister whether it's convenient or not because the needs are always right in front of us. Paul exhorts Timothy, "Be prepared, whether the time is favorable or not" (2 Tim 4:2 NLT).

---

35. Jesus describes Judas as "the one doomed to destruction so that Scripture would be fulfilled" (John 17:12). This passage shouldn't give any believer the impression that they too might be doomed to failure since it's unlikely that even Judas was predestined for such loss. It's possible that Jesus only applied this notion to Judas *after* Judas himself chose a path of destruction. Jesus' statement doesn't imply that Judas's fate was predetermined or that an inevitable doom is applicable to any other human being in history. Besides that, Judas held a unique position during a unique time with a unique purpose within history.

CONCLUSION: CLOSING THE DISTANCE

We first looked at the fivefold ministry: apostles, prophets, evangelists, pastors, and teachers. This broad survey of the biblical material reveals there is no detailed outline for leadership in God's church or those ministries closely related to it. What we see is a biblical picture of godly men and women who lived out the flexibility of church life through the divine presence and his continual inspiring leadership. The church is never without the presence of the Spirit of Jesus to guide us. Because present-day pastors and other ministers are without a strict form or pattern to follow, we are all the more dependent on God's word and daily fellowship to lead us. Not unlike other gifts in the church, the form and function of the fivefold ministry remain largely open.

The *charismata* and the fivefold ministry are open in at least two primary senses. First, we are all part of the single universal church of God, but there remains freedom among local churches to determine by conviction and the full counsel of God's word exactly what expression (i.e., form and function) our ministries will have, while none are neglected. Every gift of the early church is available today for men and women alike to pursue and live out (though today's apostles look more like missionaries than popes or archbishops). There is also a second area of openness in the ministry, and that is the freedom of the local church to decide what form of church government it will preserve: congregational, presbyterian, bishop-led, single or plurality of elders, etc.

After looking at the fivefold ministry, we turned our attention to the openness of ministry candidacy. Believers enter various gifted roles through divine or human appointment and on the basis of desire, chance, and availability. All *charismata* are open to the degree that God waits for a person's initiative, input, and action, or at least awaits our response to his gracious, empowering initiative. Although our chapter didn't highlight the defeat of distance, it should be apparent that every ministry is a byproduct of the restoration of divine presence in people's lives. The involvement of God's presence, not to mention his creative genius, is put on display in all the great variety of ministries he gives the church, such as apostles, prophets, evangelists, pastors, and teachers.

Gifted leadership represents Jesus' authority and humility toward his church. In a profoundly humbling way, the Lord has invested his approval and authority into men and women who are now *little shepherds* called to represent the Master Shepherd. As God graciously shares his authority with mere human beings, divine humility is profoundly exemplified. The heart of God teaches us that every true leader is first a servant. As servants, may

God's gifted leaders set the tone for depending entirely upon the divine presence, and may we pioneer the way into the glory of a profound intimacy with Jesus Christ.

Each of us will fulfill our ministries through faithfulness to the gospel and through the kind of prayerful awakening that can only result from the mighty movement of God's Spirit.

10

Prayer and the Coming Revival
Open Impact

Our inquiry into divine absence and the openness of charismatic presence is behind us. We now turn to the devotional heart of God's presence on a most personal level, the intimacy of prayer and God's desire to awaken and revive his church. Prayer is the most natural expression of a life lived in God's presence and the indispensable driving force behind the *charismata*.

Prayer indicates to the church that we have been accepted and privileged to be partakers of the divine nature because we do not live and minister in word only but by words uttered in the very presence of God! Confession of Christ's lordship is one thing, participation in the vice-regency of cooperative prayer is quite another. Through prayer, believers move into the power behind effective evangelism and a bold testimony for Jesus Christ. We move into the nitty-gritty of knowing God personally through conversation that changes the world. Because we've been given the Breath of prophecy at Pentecost, which is the very person and presence of God the Spirit, we are now a community whose utterance is of a supernatural character and quality.

When believers speak to the world, they do so with supernatural enablement and the boldness of Pentecost. When I speak to the Lord, not even my frail human nature can hinder the dynamic engagement that takes place, for Scripture tells me that "the Spirit helps us in our weakness. We do not know what we ought to pray for, but the Spirit himself intercedes for us through wordless groans" (Rom 8:26). Just as the Spirit hovered over the chaos in the beginning, awaiting the spoken word of God (Gen 1:2), so now the Spirit personally broods over our hopeless situations. In an open universe, the Spirit waits in anticipation for us to speak out so that he can create new possibilities, new realities, new inevitabilities, and even a new future! Prayer in an open universe can truly enlarge future possibilities, much like the prayer of Jabez: "Jabez cried out to the God of Israel, 'Oh, that you would bless me and enlarge my territory!'" (1 Chr 4:10). Indeed, God did that very thing!

Perhaps the church hasn't yet grasped how much power there is in asking God to bring us into the best possible future. You might be just one prayer away from a world-encompassing revival! So in the spirit of revival, with distance defeated and God's Spirit all-in-all in his church, we will conclude this final chapter in a tone of devotion.

THE BEST POSSIBLE FUTURE

In the book of Genesis, we're first introduced to the "image of God," not through Yahweh's visible presence, but by his breath and through his spoken word: *Let there be . . . and indeed there was!* His spoken word is Scripture's first impression of his image, something humanity shares with him (cf. Gen 1:3, 27). Thus, it is through the indwelling Breath of prophecy and especially through our interaction with God in the earth-shattering utterance of prayer that the first account of God's image is restored to his people in a special way. With that image being restored in our words, we give life not only by proclaiming the gospel but also through the powerful practice of prayer. Since we were made in God's image and now possess the prophetic Spirit, like never before in history our prayers are intended to be the channel for God's creative life. In an open universe, our prayers create new future possibilities, including new possibilities for us, new possibilities for the church, and even new possibilities for God and his plan for people.

Just as God's own spoken word is creative, he wants to create through us. But our prayers have no creative power in themselves, not even by virtue of faith. Prayers are powerless apart from God's presence and the divine life settling upon them. But God uses our prayer relationship with him to create future reality that would not otherwise be possible. Even though prayers cannot change God's final purpose, the minute details of his plans are subject to revision in light of our input.[1] God's heart is open to our prayers; he actually listens and takes our requests and our perspective into account. This is no small thing! Listen to this remarkable account from the days of Joshua:

---

1. Tiessen, *Providence and Prayer*, 72.

> On the day the LORD gave the Amorites over to Israel, Joshua said to the LORD in the presence of Israel: "Sun, stand still over Gibeon, and you, moon, over the Valley of Aijalon." So the sun stood still, and the moon stopped, till the nation avenged itself on its enemies, as it is written in the Book of Jashar. The sun stopped in the middle of the sky and delayed going down about a full day. There has never been a day like it before or since, a day when the LORD listened to a human being. (Josh 10:12–14)

But is that really what the author means, that there's never been another day in all human history that Yahweh actually listened to someone? Of course not!

The precedent here is that God truly does listen to people. Joshua's prayer was simple, specific, and full of faith. Despite the fact that Joshua's request bordered on the absurd, Yahweh still heard his very special request and answered immediately and with precision. *There has never been a day like it?* Surely there has never been another day in which the sun stood still, but the author is also pointing out that Yahweh heard the specifics of an extremely unusual prayer and still answered! The NLT captures the sense: "There has never been a day like this one before or since, when the LORD answered such a prayer." The bottom line—God hears our prayers and values what we have to say. He mulls over our perspective and our arguments. God takes our requests seriously and wants us to be specific in our prayers. He plans for the future in light of them, changes course because of them, and delivers, saves, and heals in response to them! Pentecostal scholar Kenneth Archer puts it this way: "God encourages us to participate with him in creating the future."[2]

To put it another way, prayer not only rearranges the furniture in the room but actually changes the architecture of God's kingdom here on earth. This statement takes seriously Jesus' model prayer when he says to the Father, "Your kingdom come, your will be done, on earth as it is in heaven" (Matt 6:10). But we're not yet living in God's kingdom, are we? This world is a war zone filled with violence, hate, evil, and demonic devastation. A massive renovation is underway to transform Satan's earthly kingdom into the kingdom of God. Only believers can move hell and high water to accomplish this, and we will do so as bearers of the divine presence. As divine representatives, ambassadors even, his presence is always with us! *Charismata* are our world ministry, while prayer is the fuel and driving force. The church *will* transform this world through gospel and prayer for the sake of the kingdom of God.

---

2. Archer, *Gospel Revisited*, 86.

THE OPENNESS OF PRAYER

Almighty God not only responds to prayer but allows himself to be affected by it and therefore changed because of our thoughtful conversation with him. God has gone so far as to require prayer as an essential structural component in the success of his kingdom's establishment. John Wesley made the radical statement that "God does nothing but in answer to prayer."[3] This is only a slight exaggeration! Terrance Tiessen qualifies this idea and provides an excellent summary on the openness of prayer:

> There are many things that [God] will do for the good of his creatures, whether or not anyone prays, but there are also things that he will not do unless he is asked to do them. There are specific goods that people will not have if they do not ask for them and specific evils that will occur if the prayers of God's people are not offered for their prevention. This does not mean that everyone, even every obedient believer, gets what she asks for. God is free, as his creatures are, and may choose a better course than is suggested by us. But petitionary prayer has a real effect on the way things turn out and even on the actions that God takes to influence those outcomes.[4]

In an open universe, God experiences time and space in some sense at the pace of the world he created, so he remains open to fresh dialogue and often will not move forward with his plans apart from it. Prayer means that we are involved with God in a partnership to build his kingdom and push back the forces of darkness as we prayerfully open up to him about our thoughts, feelings, plans, and perspectives. In the truest sense, we are "God's co-workers" (2 Cor 6:1).

The openness of prayer is evidenced in nearly every communication that occurs between God and people in Scripture. Personal one-on-one communication occurred prior to the fall and after it. Adam's sin did not keep him from speaking up in the garden when God sought him out. When Yahweh searched for Adam after he ate the forbidden fruit, rather than continuing to hide, Adam depended on the gracious flexibility of God to meet him where he was. Consider the scenario: God had told Adam that he would certainly die if he ate from the tree. So after eating the fruit, what would Adam's immediate thought be? Is God approaching me in judgment to execute the death sentence, or perhaps he will be open to forgiveness?[5]

---

3. Wesley, *Christian Perfection*, 157.
4. Tiessen, *Providence and Prayer*, 72.
5. On the judgment language that pertains to God "walking in the garden in the

Instead of continuing to hide, Adam responded and entered back into a dialogue with his Maker. Adam's response implied a hope that God might help him in his desperate situation. Such hope is heard in the cries and prayerful pleas we find throughout Scripture. Many such cries appear in the form of lament, beseeching God to look upon the believer's situation and the attacks of the wicked and to intervene. The lament psalms are one category of prayer that would make little sense apart from an open universe.[6]

When God was looking for Adam in the garden, "[Adam] answered, 'I heard you in the garden, and I was afraid because I was naked; so I hid'" (Gen 3:10). The reason for Adam's hiding was not fear that God might strike him down, or even conviction over his disobedient act, but the entrance of a foreign, never-before-experienced sense of shame—Adam was naked. God's response resonated with frustration over what the man and woman had done, yet God did not immediately kill them as he said he would. Instead, he made the ground more difficult for humans to work (3:17), promising the man that he would return to that same ground, "for dust you are and to dust you will return" (3:19).[7] Adam and Eve were then banished as exiles from Eden just as we all remain today. But their dialogue continued—not only the dialogue between God and Adam but also with Adam's descendants.

Referring to Adam's grandchildren, Genesis records that after the exile from Eden there came a time when the "people began to call on the name of the LORD" (Gen 4:26).[8] No doubt this stirring of the social order was connected to Adam and Eve's example. Prior to Gen 4:26, only Eve had directly referred to God as LORD or Yahweh (4:1). It was the personal name Yahweh that people began to call out to, not some distant, ambiguous pagan deity. Moreover, calling on Yahweh "in Genesis is related to God's self-revelation to Abraham (12:7-8), Hagar (16:13), and Isaac (26:24-25)."[9] Calling on Yahweh is connected to God's initiative to personally reveal himself, something the people were beginning to appreciate. Because God had revealed himself by name, he was opening himself up to personal appeal.

For God to allow Adam and his descendants to call on his name, he initiated a certain vulnerability and accountability toward human relationship. God was covenanting himself to be attentive to their offered prayers, knowing that the people who used his name were depending on him for

---

cool of the day" (Gen 3:8), see Kline, "Primal Parousia," 244–80.

6. E.g., Pss 44; 60; 74; 79; 80; 85; 90.

7. The man's curse was to die and return to the ground, but the serpent (Gen 3:14-15), the woman (3:16), and the earth/ground (3:17-18) were also directly cursed.

8. The Hebrew literally reads without a stated subject, "It was begun to call . . . "

9. Mathews, *Genesis 1–11:26*, 294.

answers. Just as Adam's response in the garden implied at least the hope that God might bring man out of hiding and resolve the dilemma of a distance masked in shame, so Adam's descendants were awakening to the faithfulness of God toward those who call upon him, the God who reveals his name and covenant.

*Calling on the L*ORD also involved worship and living in the reality of a person-to-God relationship. By providing his name to the community, Yahweh made himself available, made their appeals personal, and made himself personally responsible to them. Adam and his children accepted the openness of prayer! The fact that men and women were calling out to Yahweh demonstrated that God does not demand to take all the initiative himself; instead, he places that responsibility on us. People are expected to know him as the open-minded God who welcomes our prayerful initiative, all because he revealed himself to Adam, Abraham, Israel, and the church of God today. God's heart is wide open to the prayers of his people.

We're at a time in church history when we can know, possibly more so than ever before, that God not only answers and requires prayer but even *depends* on it. This is not an offense to God but rather a joy for him to involve us so intimately in the plans he has ordained for human history. He wants to establish a grand kingdom, and he needs our involvement. There is a most evident openness in our opportunity to pursue the *charismata*, while within those ministries there remains the simplicity of prayer that seems to be the driving force behind it all. It's really up to each one of us to take advantage of such an unlimited anointing that consists of one glorious act of service after another, bearing in mind every step of the way that we must be a people continually crying out to Yahweh.

Every believer is called to work alongside God through prayer in order to change and transform this open universe for the glory of God. Our prayers actually mean something because of the divine presence at work in us. They are not merely ordained speeches that we utter back to God to accomplish what he already intended to do! In an open universe, our prayers literally change God's mind; they direct the power of God and enhance the ministries of God. My prayers set captives free!

Repentance and the Prayer of Salvation

One's first encounter with prayer is often a bedtime prayer as a child or a prayer quickly uttered at the dinner table. But when a person is struck with the conviction of her distance from God and the need for salvation, the prayer of repentance becomes her first genuine approach to an open-minded God. Knowing possibly for the first time the longsuffering grace of God, we beseech him to deliver us from impending judgment.[10] Jonah's message to Nineveh was honest, simple, and straightforward: "Forty more days and Nineveh will be overthrown" (Jonah 3:4). This prophet wasn't speaking from his own perspective but from God's. Yahweh himself determined that in forty days this city and its inhabitants would be destroyed, and his integrity depended on the trustworthiness and even the urgency of that message. God was not being held hostage by a foreknowledge that knew otherwise; instead, he proclaimed the truth from his perspective, thus a forty-day judgment was imminent. The integrity of God ensured the validity of his warning.

Of course, Nineveh was not destroyed. Even Nineveh's pagan king was able to perceive the personal responsiveness of God and remarked, "Who knows? God may yet relent (*nacham*) and with compassion turn from his fierce anger so that we will not perish" (Jonah 3:9; cf. 1:6). In light of the remote possibility that God may change his course of action and decide not to destroy the city, the people repented in hopes of *God's repentance*. The result: "When God saw what they did and how they turned from their evil ways, he relented (*nacham*) and did not bring on them the destruction he had threatened" (3:10). Make no mistake, judgment was threatened because God fully intended to carry it out. Rather than following a predetermined plan or succumbing to an exhaustive foreknowledge, the free and open-minded God changed his mind and reversed the judgment he was determined to bring against Nineveh. Rather than death and destruction, the people were saved and blessed! Rather than further distance, the prayers and actions surrounding their repentance brought God close. The people changed his mind through repentant hearts and by turning from their evil ways. Yahweh's thoughtfulness demonstrated that he is a God of personal relationship who responds to the hearts and actions of those who repent.

This passage and many others make us aware that God repents over matters of people's sin. One Hebrew term for repentance is *nacham*, which basically means a change of mind or direction. When *nacham* is used of God, it means the same thing. There are at least 35 uses of the term *nacham* in connection with God changing his mind, not to mention other passages that use different terms to describe the reversal of a previous divine

---

10. Today, the prayer of salvation is a simple one; most importantly, it's a matter of the heart. Do I believe what I am praying? "Father, thank you for sending Jesus to save me. I believe he died on the cross for me and that I can live because of him. I believe that Jesus rose from the dead, and I trust in him for my forgiveness and my future. Help me turn away from my sin to follow you with all my heart. This I ask in Jesus' name. Amen."

decision.[11] Based on Saul's disobedience, Yahweh regretted and repented (*nacham*) over appointing Saul as King (1 Sam 15:11, 35). He repented (*nacham*) over creating humankind because all the world's population became wicked (Gen 6:6–7). In those situations, God's hopes were shattered and he found himself at a distance, resulting in utter disappointment and a sorrowful regret. He repented over his previous choices, choices he expected to result in better things.

Because God changes his mind, we can be hopeful that he actually cares about and is concerned over our repentance and what we bring to his attention through faithful prayer.

Faith and the Openness of Prayer

One important question that often arises within charismatic and pentecostal circles is the place of faith in prayer. When I see my prayers go unanswered, is it because I don't have enough faith? Many believers limit the effectiveness of prayer to an exclusive kind of faith. It is a serious allegation to accuse fellow believers of remaining unhealed or undelivered because they simply don't have a strong enough faith. The real reason prayers are not always answered is far more complicated than this single variable. We will look briefly to Scripture for some of the reasons prayers seemingly go unanswered and the kind of faith that brings answers.

Prayer is not just a matter of faith. Gregory Boyd offers several variables that impact prayer's effectiveness. He first comments that "while prayer itself is as simple as talking to a friend, the actual mechanics of prayer are remarkably complex."[12] According to Boyd, the variables that impact answers to prayer include: God's will (Matt 26:39; 1 John 5:14; Jas 4:3), the faith of the person being prayed for (Matt 9:29; Luke 7:50; 17:19), the faith of the people praying (Matt 8:13; Mark 9:14–19; Luke 5:20), persistence in prayer (Luke 18:1–8; 1 Thess 5:17), the number of people praying (Matt 18:19–20),[13] human freewill (1 Tim 4:10; 2 Pet 3:9), angelic freewill (Dan

---

11. Regarding some things, God does in fact change his mind, while regarding other things, he does not. Of the numerous passages that utilize נחם (*nacham*) to indicate God's change of mind, there are other passages that use נחם specifically to say he does not. Regarding the former, see Exod 32:12, 14; Deut 32:36; Judg 2:18; 2 Sam 24:16; 1 Chr 21:15; Pss 90:13; 106:45; 135:14; Isa 57:6; Jer 15:6; 18:8, 10; 26:3, 13, 19; Joel 2:13–14; Amos 7:3, 6; Jonah 3:9, 10; 4:2. Regarding the latter, see Num 23:19; 1 Sam 15:29; Ps 110:4; Jer 4:28; Ezek 24:14; Zech 8:14.

12. Boyd, *Is God to Blame?*, 135.

13. Regarding the variable of the number of people praying, Boyd makes the point, "When dealing with an important matter, most people of faith instinctively ask others

10:12–13; 1 Thess 2:17–18),[14] the number and strength of spirit agents (Dan 10:12–20; 2 Kgs 6:16–17; Luke 11:24–26), and finally, the presence of sin (Josh 7:10–11; Ps 66:18; Mark 11:25).[15]

When we pray, we mustn't always be mindful of each one of these factors, but we also shouldn't lose sight of them as they do seem to work in tandem with each other. In every matter of prayer, we should first consider the will of God as revealed in Scripture. But even if God's will leans in one direction or another, he characteristically won't violate the freewill of human beings or of angels. The interplay of soldiers in the spiritual battle involves an entire world of free humans (seven billion and climbing), an innumerable company of free angels, and a remnant of praying saints. If we believe that battles in the physical realm are won or lost based on the size of an army, perhaps it is also the case in the spiritual realm. If so, it should be our regular practice to join the church for battle through prayer. Jesus said it like this: "Again, truly I tell you that if two of you on earth agree about anything they ask for, it will be done for them by my Father in heaven. For where two or three gather in my name, there am I with them" (Matt 18:19–20).

One of the most important factors in the effectiveness of prayer is persistence. Jesus told many different stories to encourage us in this:

> Then Jesus said to them, "Suppose you have a friend, and you go to him at midnight and say, 'Friend, lend me three loaves of bread; a friend of mine on a journey has come to me, and I have no food to offer him.' And suppose the one inside answers, 'Don't bother me. The door is already locked, and my children and I are in bed. I can't get up and give you anything.' I tell you, even though he will not get up and give you the bread because of friendship, yet because of your shameless audacity he will surely get up and give you as much as you need." (Luke 11:5–8; cf. 18:1–8)

Jesus describes a certain "audacity" that God accepts and expects in prayer. Jesus commends this attitude and wants us to approach God with the nerve to expect his response. As the passage states, audacity is shameless but it's also bold with its demands. Because Jesus is teaching us to pray in this way, we can be certain that God is not annoyed with our persistence but welcomes it.

---

to pray for them. The assumption is that with more people praying, it's more likely that this matter will be resolved in accordance with the prayer. This assumption is reasonable" (ibid., 139). Regarding the number of people praying, see also Neh 9:1; 2 Chr 7:14; Matt 26:36, 41; Acts 1:13–14; 4:24–30; Eph 6:19–20; Col 4:3–4; 1 Thess 5:25; 2 Thess 3:1; Heb 13:18; Jas 5:13–16.

14. Regarding the variable of angelic freewill, see Wink, *Engaging the Powers*, 310–11.

15. See Boyd, *Is God to Blame?*, 135–47.

As I am persistent in prayer, the simple act of opening my mouth to pray implies a certain level of faith, possibly even enough to qualify as a "mustard seed" of faith. Jesus says, "Truly I tell you, if you have faith as small as a mustard seed, you can say to this mountain, 'Move from here to there,' and it will move. Nothing will be impossible for you" (Matt 17:20). The mustard seed of faith that Jesus describes as moving mountains mustn't be any greater than the mere *existence* of faith that's demonstrated in the simple act of prayer. It is the Holy Spirit who makes our prayers effective in the spiritual battles of life. If we keep seeking, knocking, and asking, especially together with fellow believers, we will see mountains move (Luke 11:9)! And we'll be the ones telling them where to go.

In addition to persistence in prayer, my primary responsibility lies in the areas of personal faithfulness and holiness. As I approach prayer, I must bring a certain level of faith to the table, trusting in God both in his person and provision (Heb 11:6). But I must also be mindful of any sin in my life that has not been forsaken and left behind. Sin assaults the heart with a vivid reminder of distance (guilt) that must be overcome through repentance and the readjustment of my faith in God and in him alone.

But more than faith, what if the greatest release of answered prayer and even miraculous works is not great faith but heartfelt compassion? Before Jesus prayed or laid hands on the sick, he was often moved with compassion when he healed people. Remarkably, Scripture never once says that Jesus was moved by great faith, but it frequently says that he was moved with compassion: "When Jesus landed and saw a large crowd, he had compassion on them and healed their sick" (Matt 14:14).[16] Prayer that persists is prayer that joins thoughtful perseverance with *compassion*. If there's any key or formula that we can cite from Scripture to influence prayer and put into effect God's healing presence, it's compassion. In all your getting, get compassion! The greatest release of miraculous works is not great faith but true compassion (with mustard seed faith).

PRAYER, CHARISMATA, AND THE POWER OF REVIVAL

As we move into the topic of revival, we'll maintain a more devotional tone since revival itself resonates with devotion. Revival tends to break through the systematic approaches we're used to and bring us back to a simple dialogue with our ever-present Lord. It's so important that each of us find our personal language of dialogue with our heavenly Father. The traditional

---

16. On Jesus' compassion, see Matt 9:36; 15:32; 18:27; 20:34; Mark 1:41; 6:34; 8:2; Luke 7:13; 10:33; 15:20.

methods of folding hands and getting on your knees don't always fit. Find your own language of prayer and devotion. It may help you to draw or doodle, paint or pace, lie down or write down your thoughts, sing or yell. Find the language that best suits you and would be most conducive to your frequent return to the secret place of God's presence—our revival depends on it! As the writer of Lamentations says, your prayer life might even look like water: "Pour out your heart like water before the presence of the Lord!" (Lam 2:19 ESV).

While writing this book, it was my conviction that this was possibly the most important chapter to put to paper. It's no overstatement that compassionate prayer is essential if the church is going to once again enjoy the privileges and impact of revival. Prayer is the only choice for a Spirit-filled remnant! The prophet Isaiah once said, "The fortress will be abandoned, the noisy city deserted; citadel and watchtower will become a wasteland forever, the delight of donkeys, a pasture for flocks, till the Spirit is poured on us from on high, and the desert becomes a fertile field, and the fertile field seems like a forest" (Isa 32:14–15). This is what we've all been waiting for, the "fertile field" of revival to be ushered in by a fresh outpouring of God's Spirit in this generation! Even godless regions, the "wasteland," can become fertile fields.

Revival is the bow to tie up the loose ends of this inquiry. By revival we really mean *awakening*; it is the slumbering church that must be awakened, not only to a fresh zeal for the coming reign of God, but also to the current situation in our backyard—namely, the poor, the sick and afflicted, and the prisoner. The church must wake up to a renewed solidarity with those who are broken and hurting. Because God can wake us up, revival should be our painstaking, unrelenting prayer.

Revival and the Conviction of Distance

Historically, revival is known for the intense conviction of sin that comes over God's people and the lost. David Lloyd-Jones summarizes revival as bringing "a sense of the majesty of God, a personal sinfulness, [a sense] of the wonder of salvation through Jesus Christ and a desire that others might know it."[17] It seems to be the general consensus among historians and those who have observed or experienced revival that there is a heightened awareness and sensitivity to personal responsibility over one's sin, especially in the way it impacts and impedes the church at large. It is a profound conviction over any fault or failure to obey and respond to God in the daily Christian

---

17. Lloyd-Jones, *Revival*, 105.

walk. This conviction can be so overwhelming because sin, rooted in death and distance, is the one thing that can defeat and expel the divine presence.

Lloyd-Jones goes on to describe the purpose for revival: "God does this thing from time to time, God sends revival, blessing, upon the church, in order that he may do something with respect to those who are outside him. He is doing something that is going to arrest the attention of all the people of the earth. . . . This is the reason—the glory of God."[18] The reason for revival is clear, and it's not for the church to enjoy the personal, individual excitement and ecstatics of God's presence in our midst, though that is surely a glorious byproduct. The reason is that Almighty God might "arrest the attention" of those distant from him, those "outside him." In Scripture when God brought his presence near to the people to perform miraculous wonders, it was to benefit all the nations. Under the leadership of Joshua, after Yahweh split the Jordan River just as he had split the Red Sea, Scripture attests, "He did this so that all the peoples of the earth might know that the hand of the LORD is powerful and so that you might always fear the LORD your God" (Josh 4:24).

Revival is God's attempt to grab the attention of those who have so distanced themselves that nothing else could possibly reach them. Nothing, that is, except for the radical expression of his loving presence that comes to his people in the life-shaking, foundation-trembling manner of revival. The ultimate expression of love from the divine presence was the crucifixion of Jesus Christ, but the present expression is God's life within his people because of the victory of Christ's resurrection. The purpose of revival is to reach the lost while the motive is to glorify God and exalt the Victor of human history, the Lord Jesus Christ. God is glorified as people realize and experience that he has not abandoned the lost who have distanced him so severely. He continues to reach out to those who reject and neglect him; but in a very real way, he wants and needs the church's help.

Here is a definition of revival in light of divine absence: *Revival is the awakening of the corporate heart to accept personal responsibility over sin. This conviction emboldens the Christian community to battle against sin's distance by drawing near to God and wielding his presence as our greatest weapon.* As God draws near to his church and manifests his glory in dramatic and tangible ways during revival, a healthy conviction of sin reminds us not only that Holy God has drawn near, but that we are on mission to bring deliverance to those who live outside God's glorious, convicting presence. Conviction in the Christian life should be embraced as a gift of divine presence. Conviction is always a sign that God is near, bridging the gap,

---

18. Ibid., 119.

breaking the distance, offering his hand of fellowship. Hosea said it like this: "Come, let us return to the LORD. He has torn us to pieces but he will heal us; he has injured us but he will bind up our wounds. After two days he will revive us; on the third day he will restore us, that we may live in his presence" (Hos 6:1–3).

Even though believers can no longer experience any real distance from God, our personal sin can become an occasion to open our minds to Satan's kingdom. Satan uses the sins of believers to deceive us into sensing that a distance remains between us and God, despite the victory of the cross. Rather than leading us into *conviction* that results in freedom and closeness, deception brings *guilt* and shame, resulting in psychological and emotional distance from God that feels quite real in our experience. Hence, believers often live at an illusory distance from God, a distance of self-deception that does not actually exist. Jesus said to his people, "I am with you always," and he meant it (Matt 28:20). Revival shakes away the lies of distance propagated by "the accuser of our brethren" while bringing both believer and unbeliever to their knees in life-changing repentance and acceptance of the forgiving love of God (Rev 12:10 KJV).

Because revival is continually within the church's grasp, it remains our responsibility to take the initiative. The openness of revival means that the opportunity is ever-present and open before us to ignite the wildfire of awakening. God longs to grant the church an intensification of his presence if we will pay the price and continually draw near to him through prayer *and fasting* to release the fullness available to every generation (Isa 58:6–8). Although fasting can be painstaking, it's a necessary discipline to add to prayer. When we fast, we set apart time to deny the flesh its needs or privileges in order to focus our reliance upon a feast of spiritual sustenance and the nourishment of divine presence. In many ways, while we fast and pray, the church still behaves as if God is so close-minded that we must wait on his sovereign timetable before we can experience true awakening. But even the psalmist says, "You who seek God, let your hearts revive" (Ps 69:32 ESV). While it's true that revival is dependent on God, the opportunity is always open and available to God's people when we surrender and seek him with all our hearts.

God is waiting for you! "If my people, who are called by my name, will humble themselves and pray and seek my face and turn from their wicked ways, then I will hear from heaven, and I will forgive their sin and will heal their land" (2 Chr 7:14). God says, I will, I will, I will! God desires thoughtful, time-consuming *prayer* as we seek his face, and he commands us to turn from our wicked ways to embrace a profound *holiness*, the rebuttal and rebuke of sin's distance. The healing of the land means that renewal can become so widespread that it begins in the individual heart, spreads to the local church, is then unleashed without reserve into the community and every sphere of social, religious, and political life, and finally branches out into all the land. Genuine revival can affect the entire creation! In a radically open universe, revival can reach even godless regions of undisturbed evil.

Revival Recovers the Edenic Presence

The Old Testament portrays revival in terms of God making alive: "This is what the Sovereign LORD says to these bones: I will make breath enter you, and you will come to life. I will attach tendons to you and make flesh come upon you and cover you with skin; I will put breath in you, and you will come to life. Then you will know that I am the LORD" (Ezek 37:5–6). Long before Ezekiel prophesied these words for Israel's renewal, Adam experienced the first expression of the kind of creation-revival that God is capable of. In the garden, the Creator breathed his own sacred breath into Adam's nostrils, commanding that lifeless body, *Be alive! Live!* (Gen 2:7).

Today, revival comes when the breath of God enters his church in a fresh new way, reminding us of the paradise of Eden, as if to tell us that he's been here all along. But just as God gave Adam the greatest gift of divine breath and he soon rebelled against his Maker, we too can easily allow the truth of divine breath within us to slip from our minds and ministries. Through revival God reminds us that we are called to draw upon the sacred breath, even his Holy Presence, moment-by-moment. As Christians, we live with Sacred Breath inside us, which is another way to translate Holy Spirit. Paul reminds us, "Since we live by the Spirit, let us keep in step with the Spirit" (Gal 5:25). Even so, let us keep in step with the Spirit as he walks us back to Eden and keeps us in the near presence of God.

So I must ask you, dear Christian, *Do you know that the breath of God lives in you?* His breath is sacred, even holy; he is the Holy Breath, the Holy Wind, the Holy Spirit! The church must declare once again that we possess more than mere flesh and dust, not unlike Adam's body before God breathed in and commanded life. We must remind ourselves that we are the sacred representation of God, holy and set apart unto eternal life in the very presence of our Maker. As the people of God, we breathe in and release his sacred breath to a lost and dying world (cf. John 6:63). When we open our eyes to the reality of God restoring the Edenic fellowship to us, we can walk in the reality of Eden once again and expect the visible manifestations of the life of God who conquers all death and distance.

I'm not suggesting we should elevate the person of the Spirit above the Father and Son, but we must apprehend the reality that we are forever indwelt and infilled with divine breath, the triune fellowship of God. The first requirement of revival is knowing confidently that the distance is gone and God is in us, interpenetrating, infilling, intertwined, and embedded within and throughout our new nature. Paul says it this way: "Do you not know that your bodies are temples of the Holy Spirit, who is in you, whom you have received from God?" (1 Cor 6:19). If you aren't living in this knowledge, Paul also says, "Examine yourselves to see whether you are in the faith; test yourselves. Do you not realize that Christ Jesus is in you—unless, of course, you fail the test?" (2 Cor 13:5).

So what was so special about Eden? God's presence was with people, and he entrusted them with the responsibility to represent his presence throughout creation. In Eden the earth was not cursed but had to yield to the commands of human beings as God's vice-regents; nature was under the man's control in the garden. But never again did people enjoy such divine blessing until Jesus Christ restored the Edenic power of humankind in his own earthly flesh. Jesus rebuked the wind and rain and it obeyed him; he commanded nature and it fell into submission! Because Jesus remained under God's authority and power, he manifested that original human-given power of vice-regency that was granted in Eden. Jesus knew he lived in the supernatural—not mere flesh but endued with the sacred breath that was first breathed into humanity in Eden. Jesus now reserves the right to transfer that reminder of Edenic power to the church on certain occasions, on occasions of revival and renewal.

We must realize that we are the true church, the people of God redeemed for an inheritance of a new paradise with God, a new heaven and earth. The exceptional and extraordinary miracles and signs that we experience during revival remind us that the triune God truly is present with his church and that he's restoring to us a reflection of Eden, thy kingdom come. The miracles of revival are powers of the coming age, the experience of the church living in the "already, but not yet" foretaste of an imminent kingdom. During seasons of revival when we anticipate greater works and powers of the age to come, Jesus speaks to the human spirit and says, *Wake up! Live!* Remember that you are no longer mere flesh but have been baptized in the Sacred Ghost, the Holy Breath of God for new life. Revival comes to the church, not when we enter into something new, but when we surrender to Jesus and the word he's been speaking all along, since the church's inception: "And surely I am with you always, to the very end of the age" (Matt 28:20). Jesus was declaring that he had restored the Edenic presence of God to the people of earth once and for all. The church now forever bears a new breath, revival breath, even the revival presence of God!

Revival heightens our awareness of the manifest presence of God in our midst, but along with that presence comes boldness to declare that God truly is with us! Revival is not a new work of God but a refresher. Revival bestows a willingness and obedience to clothe ourselves with God's power for boldness to declare the good news. We are bold because he is near! During revival, he reminds us of what has always been true, that divine presence is in our midst both to enjoy and to accomplish his earthly mission. We might even say that the divine mission is ultimately the reason the church bears his presence. One scholar writing on pentecostal experience in Singapore captures the sober reality that God's presence is with us to continue the mission. Tan-chow remarks,

> Spirit-capacitated participation in the life of the triune God is polyphonic. It involves not just indwelling divine presence, but also continuing the divine mission begun by Jesus. The enabling operation of the Spirit is two-directional: witness and edification. Unlike the intermittent presence and activity of the Spirit in the OT, the coming of the outpoured Spirit-Paraclete will rest upon and indwell the disciples permanently ([John] 14:6f.). The sending of the Spirit-Paraclete to the disciples is for them to continue his work, even "greater works, . . ." (14:12).[19]

Right now, in this generation, the opportunity is open before us to say yes to God's presence with us, knowing that our ministries and gifts are two-directional: for the charismatic *edification* of the people of God, and to incarnationally *witness* the life of God's presence to a dying world.

God has removed the distance that preceded those dreadful words in the garden, *Where are you?* In principle, Jesus Christ has defeated the serpent and every enemy, even death. Every metaphor of the New Testament, from redemption to ransom, from propitiation to salvation, all point to the reality that the distance between God and his church is overcome. Now it's time for the church to live in that reality! We can be a bold witness because the testimony of Scripture is true: God is not absent, distance is closed, and God is forever open to giving us increasingly more of his experiential and even manifest presence. Jesus promised that believers, as incarnational representatives, would be the vehicles for such a powerful divine ministry: "Very truly I tell you, whoever believes in me will do the works I have been doing, and they will do even greater things than these, because I am going to the Father" (John 14:12). Because Jesus has ascended to his throne

---

19. May Ling, *Pentecostal Theology*, 107.

and poured out the divine presence for all time, we will experience those "greater works" even in the context of miraculous revival.

For the believer, God will never again ask the question, *Where are you?* We can now reckon dead this body of dust and declare that we are no longer the fleshly body that was cast out of an Eden guarded by "cherubim and a flaming sword" (Gen 3:24). We are a new creation, new in spirit, now living in the presence of divine life without distance. Armed with God's presence, we are his flaming sword to this generation, battling victoriously against death and distance. When the church becomes aware of this in any generation, we can experience the first-fruits of Eden and the fullness of divine life as revival is released upon the land.

CONCLUSION: SHOWERS OF REVIVAL AFTER THE STORM

Although pockets of revival exist everywhere in the world, the worldwide church may yet experience another great revival before Jesus returns to establish his kingdom. In both Mark 13 and Matthew 24, after the disciples ask Jesus essentially when the temple would be destroyed, he begins to describe great tribulation. Jesus prepares his disciples for the last days by assuring them of this, that "whenever you are arrested and brought to trial, do not worry beforehand about what to say. Just say whatever is given you at the time, for it is not you speaking, but the Holy Spirit" (Mark 13:11; cf. Matt 10:19–20). Jesus expressly warns his twelve disciples, not a future generation, to prepare themselves for the tribulation they will experience. But because tribulation is recapitulated throughout the history of the church until Jesus returns, every generation can rely upon the faithful breath of the Holy Spirit.

This passage assures us that even in the midst of a degree of tribulation, even *great* tribulation, the potential for revival always exists. Jesus was essentially promising his disciples that there will be periods of tribulation in which they will have a heightened awareness of God's holy presence. They will experience an elevated sensitivity to the fact that they are not alone in their suffering but dwell in divine presence, so they will not need to resort to the flesh for a defense. Instead, God himself will testify on their behalf! The Sacred Breath will anoint their breath to speak. The Lord will speak to them and through them, to us and through us. It is in the face of suffering for the sake of Jesus' name that we can be most assured that the Spirit will be at work. Perhaps one of the tragedies of Western Christianity is the comfort and convenience of being free from much persecution. This comfort relieves us of the need for power to persevere, but it can also steal from us God's glorious presence in revival, that gentle shower that comes after the storm. Whatever tribulation lies ahead for the church, there might yet be another great revival for us to experience in the midst of it.

At last, after the great revival of God's Edenic presence, he will soon return to establish a new heaven and a new earth, the true Eden forever restored to God and his community. The presence of God will never again be under assault! Until then, we agree with the words the Spirit still speaks: Ἀμήν. ἔρχου, κύριε Ἰησοῦ. "Amen. Come, Lord Jesus" (Rev 22:20).

Appendix

Origins of Pentecostal Tongues

The tongues phenomenon is a biblical teaching that's been revived in the church over the past few centuries. What many don't know, however, is how the teaching of both Spirit Baptism and speaking in tongues developed into what most Pentecostals believe today. Early Methodism and the Holiness movement provide insight into those origins. Though social overtones existed at the time, the foundation of Methodism was primarily theological. The theological root was John Wesley's contention that Christian experience is a road that travels away from willful rebellion against God to the place of an ever-increasing, perfect love toward God and people.[1] The Holiness movement was something of a continuation of Wesley and late eighteenth- and early nineteenth-century Methodism.[2]

Wesley contended that God delivers Christians into his perfect love over a *timely* process, all according to God's own sovereign timetable. In the nineteenth century, however, there were some within Methodism who embraced a subtle modification to Wesley's theology. Methodism started moving away from Wesley's perfection as an *end* in itself to a different kind of perfection that was the *means* to Christian life and service. Perfection was to be sought and expected at the beginning of Christian experience rather than the distant future. This new perfection model involved a second spiritual experience for believers as soon as willingly possible after their conversion. This post-conversion experience, known as Christian perfection or entire

---

1. Jones, *Guide to the Study of the Holiness Movement*, xvii.

2. "Most historians of Protestant 'holiness movements' of recent times would agree . . . that all of them in some way 'stem down' from the founder of Methodism" (Dieter, *Holiness Revival*, 15). For a list of those historians mentioned by Dieter, see ibid., 55.

sanctification, was based on personal faith rather than Wesley's emphasis on divine sovereignty.

By the 1830s and 40s the Holiness movement was well underway, and there were various networks of like-minded believers who committed their Christian practice to these fresh insights.[3] There were subtle differences that distinguished these informal groups. The primary differences included either the moral choice not to willfully sin or the complete eradication of all sin in one's life, but this notion of eliminating the sinful nature moved well beyond Wesley's view. The major adherents included Methodists; "German pietist groups such as the Evangelical Association and the United Brethren in Christ Church; Oberlin perfectionists and groups and institutions with ties to Oberlin College such as the Free Will Baptist Church, Hillsdale College, Berea College, and Wheaton College; and the related antinomian perfectionism associated with John Humphrey Noyes."[4]

Among all Holiness enthusiasts of the nineteenth century, it would not be an exaggeration to say that Charles Grandison Finney (1792–1875), president of Oberlin College (1851–66), left the greatest mark on pentecostal roots.[5] Finney heads the list of leading scholars and preachers who brought the language of Spirit Baptism into regular use by the Wesleyan/Holiness churches when referring to entire sanctification.[6] John Gresham, a scholar on the works of Charles Finney, states that Finney is "the most important figure to emphasize the Baptism of the Holy Spirit as a subsequent experience, and in at least some way, he influenced all of these various

---

3. Kostlevy, *Holiness Manuscripts*, viii.

4. Ibid.

5. Finney has been considered the "Second Awakening's most renowned preacher" in the western United States (Chesebrough, *Charles G. Finney*, xiii). During the 1820s, he vigorously preached revivals across Pennsylvania into New York and up into the New England states, literally bringing thousands into the churches (Hambrick-Stowe, *Charles G. Finney*, xi–xii). In subsequent years, Finney established himself as the most prominent leader of the revival movement in America because of the hundreds of thousands of people who are considered to have responded to his preaching. Today, his writings continue to exercise considerable influence upon Holiness and Classical Pentecostal churches. With his reputation preceding him, Finney continues to be labeled as the "grandfather of Pentecostalism" and the "father of American revivalism" (Kostlevy and Patzwald, *Historical Dictionary*, 102).

6. "While recognizing that, most probably, Finney developed his views in conjunction with his colleagues at Oberlin, and that Asa Mahan's ultimate influence upon the Holiness movement may have been the greatest, it does seem . . . correct in pointing to Finney as the one who initiated the shift within Wesleyanism to the language of Pentecost or Spirit Baptism to describe the experience of entire sanctification" (Gresham, *Charles G. Finney's Doctrine*, 65–67).

movements within late-nineteenth-century Evangelicalism thereby providing the source of Pentecostalism."[7]

Prior to the Civil War, the second blessing experience of perfection was most widely referred to as sanctification. Because Wesley's colleague, John Fletcher, had understood perfection as a baptism of the Spirit, there were some Methodists who conceived of the doctrine of perfection in terms of both sanctification and Spirit Baptism, two sides of the same coin.[8] After the Civil War, however, there was a subtle shift taking place to describe the second blessing entirely in terms of the pentecostal language of "baptism in the Holy Ghost," to use King James language, a shift largely due to the writings of Charles Finney.[9] That being the case, the definition of Spirit Baptism nonetheless maintained its Wesleyan/Holiness meaning of perfection.

Near the end of the nineteenth century, not surprisingly a three works model was promoted. A Wesleyan-Holiness preacher by the name of Benjamin Hardin Irwin was advocating a view that Spirit Baptism was actually a third experience that followed both conversion and holiness-sanctification. This development integrated *power for service* as a dominant theme along with the earlier motifs of sanctification that involved perfection, cleansing, and holiness.[10]

Not long after Finney helped to shift the language of entire sanctification to that of Spirit Baptism, the origin of the pentecostal movement as we know it can be traced back to a revival that took place in 1901 at Bethel Bible College in Topeka, Kansas. By the turn of the twentieth century, due to competing variations on the themes of sanctification, holiness, and a baptism for power, both the two-and three-separate-works models each had their own respective advocates.

Charles Fox Parham, a three-works advocate and the leader of Bethel Bible College, embraced the theme of power to define Spirit Baptism. He led students to search the Scriptures in order to discern any possible sign or evidence of the baptism. But even beyond baptism, he sought a sign of

---

7. Ibid., 78.

8. Fletcher wanted Wesley to call his perfection doctrine the baptism of the Holy Spirit according to the language found in the book of Acts. Wesley felt that this would be a compromise to the doctrine of salvation because Christians receive the Spirit at conversion and, therefore, Wesley saw the baptism as something that occurred at conversion. Wesley told Fletcher, "It seems our views on Christian Perfection are a little different, though not opposite. It is certain that every babe in Christ has received the Holy Ghost, and the Spirit witnesses with his spirit that he is a child of God. But he has not obtained Christian perfection" ("Letter of John Wesley to John Fletcher," 6:146).

9. Gresham, *Charles G. Finney's Doctrine of the Baptism*, 65–66, 78. See also Finney, *Promise of the Spirit*.

10. Synan, *Century of the Holy Spirit*, 26.

salvation itself. After a period of Bible study, prayer, and fasting, students of the school concluded that the Scriptures taught that speaking with special utterances ("tongues") was the initial evidence of the baptism of the Holy Ghost. This initial evidence was allegedly confirmed in the experience of Agnes Ozman when Parham laid hands on her. As one onlooker testified, she began speaking in Chinese!

The doctrine of the baptism of the Spirit is central to the origins of Pentecostalism. Moreover, just as the Holiness movement's transition from Wesleyan Methodism depended heavily upon the theology of Christian perfection, so did Classical Pentecostalism.[11] In terms of definition and description, the pentecostal baptism was mediated through Wesley's version of Christian perfection, then filtered through Holiness modifications, and finally resulted in the form it took at the turn of the twentieth century and today. Charles Parham, then, was the first to teach both that tongues are always the evidence of Spirit Baptism and that this baptism is the norm for Christian living, the foundation of pentecostal belief.[12]

---

[11]. Though the pentecostal movement can be traced back to the important doctrinal developments of Wesley's perfectionism, its uprising at the turn of the twentieth century involved a number of factors. For our purposes, it should suffice to simplify the matter and affirm that the pentecostal movement as a whole was derived from "Holiness churches, which in turn stemmed from nineteenth-century Methodism" (White, *Protestant Worship*, 193).

[12]. Synan, *Century of the Holy Spirit*, 43–44.

Bibliography

Aland, Kurt. *Did the Early Church Baptize Infants?* Translated by G.R. Beasley-Murray. London: SCM, 1963.
Alexander, T. D. *From Paradise to Promised Land: An Introduction to the Pentateuch.* 2nd ed. Grand Rapids: Baker Academic, 2002.
Archer, Kenneth J. *The Gospel Revisited: Towards a Pentecostal Theology of Worship and Witness.* Eugene, OR: Pickwick, 2011.
Aune, D. E. *Prophecy in Early Christianity and the Ancient Mediterranean World.* Grand Rapids: Eerdmans, 1983.
Barth, Karl. *Church Dogmatics.* 2/1: *The Doctrine of God.* Translated by T. H. L. Parker et al. New York: T & T Clark, 1940.
Barton, Stephen C. "1 Corinthians." In *Eerdmans Commentary on the Bible*, edited by James D.G. Dunn and James W. Rogerson, 1314–52. Grand Rapids: Eerdmans, 2003.
Basinger, David. *The Case for Freewill Theism: A Philosophical Assessment.* Downers Grove: InterVarsity, 1996.
Bauer, Walter, Frederick W. Danker, W. F. Arndt, and F. W. Gingrich. *Greek-English Lexicon of the New Testament and Other Early Christian Literature.* 3rd ed. Chicago: University of Chicago Press, 2000.
Baumert, Norbert. "'Charism' and 'Spirit-Baptism': Presentation of an Analysis." *Journal of Pentecostal Theology* 12:2 (2004) 147–79.
Bavinck, Herman. *Reformed Dogmatics.* Edited by John Bolt. Translated by John Vriend. Vol. 3, *Sin and Salvation in Christ.* Grand Rapids: Baker Academic, 2006.
Beck, Richard. *The Slavery of Death.* Eugene, OR: Cascade, 2014.
Beilby, James, and Paul R. Eddy, eds. *The Nature of the Atonement: Four Views.* Downers Grove: IVP Academic, 2006.
Belleville, Linda. "1 Timothy." In *Cornerstone Biblical Commentary*, edited by Philip W. Comfort, 25–123. Carol Streams: Tyndale, 2009.
Berding, Kenneth. *What Are Spiritual Gifts? Rethinking the Conventional View.* Grand Rapids: Kregel, 2006.
Boadt, Lawrence. *Reading the Old Testament: An Introduction.* Mahwah, NJ: Paulist, 1984.

Boer, Harry R. *A Short History of the Early Church*. Grand Rapids: Eerdmans, 1976.
Bonhoeffer, Dietrich. *Creation and Fall: A Theological Exposition of Genesis 1–3*. Minneapolis: Fortress, 2004.
Boyd, Gregory A. *God of the Possible: A Biblical Introduction to the Open View of God*. Grand Rapids: Baker, 2000.
———. *God at War: The Bible and Spiritual Conflict*. Downers Grove: IVP Academic, 1997.
———. *Is God to Blame? Beyond Pat Answers to the Problem of Evil*. Downers Grove: InterVarsity, 2003.
———. *Satan and the Problem of Evil: Constructing a Trinitarian Warfare Theodicy*. Downers Grove: InterVarsity, 2001.
Brand, Chad Owen, and R. Stanton Norman, eds. *Perspectives on Church Government: Five Views of Church Polity*. Nashville: B&H Academic, 2004.
Bray, Gerald. *God is Love: A Biblical and Systematic Theology*. Wheaton: Crossway, 2012.
Bruce, F. F. *The Book of the Acts: Revised*. The New International Commentary on the New Testament. Grand Rapids: Eerdmans, 1988.
Brueggemann, Walter. *Interpretation: A Bible Commentary for Teaching and Preaching: Genesis*. Louisville: John Knox, 1982.
———. *An Introduction to the Old Testament: The Canon and Christian Imagination*. Louisville: Westminster John Knox, 2003.
Bruner, Frederick Dale. *The Gospel of John: A Commentary*. Grand Rapids: Eerdmans, 2012.
Burgess, S. M. *The Holy Spirit: Ancient Christian Traditions*. Peabody: Hendrickson, 1984.
Burnett, Joel S. *Where is God? Divine Absence in the Hebrew Bible*. Minneapolis: Fortress, 2010.
Cahalan, Kathleen A. *Introducing the Practice of Ministry*. Collegeville, MN: Order of Saint Benedict, 2010.
Calvin, John. *Institutes of the Christian Religion: 1536 Edition*. Translated by Ford Lewis Battles. Grand Rapids: Eerdmans, 1986.
Campbell, R. Alastair. *The Elders: Seniority within Earliest Christianity*. Studies of the New Testament and Its World. Edinburgh: T & T Clark, 1994.
Campbell, Ted A. *Methodist Doctrine: The Essentials*. Nashville: Abingdon, 1999.
Chesebrough, David B. *Charles G. Finney: Revivalistic Rhetoric*. Westport, TN: Greenwood, 2002.
Collins, Raymond F. *1 and 2 Timothy and Titus: A Commentary*. The New Testament Library. Louisville: Westminster John Knox, 2002.
Cook, John E. *New Collegeville Bible Commentary: Genesis*. Collegeville, MN: Order of Saint Benedict, 2011.
Crofford, J. Gregory. *The Dark Side of Destiny: Hell Re-examined*. Eugene, OR: Wipf & Stock, 2013.
Curnock, Nehemiah, ed. *The Journal of Rev. John Wesley, A.M.* Vol. 2. London: Epworth, 1938.
Dent, Donald T. *The Ongoing Role of Apostles in Missions: The Forgotten Foundation*. Bloomington, IN: CrossBooks, 2011.
Dieter, Melvin Easterday. *The Holiness Revival of the Nineteenth Century*, 2nd ed. Lanham, MD: Scarecrow, 1996.
Dunn, James D. G. *The Acts of the Apostles*. Valley Forge: Trinity, 1996.

Duvall, Robert, Farrah Fawcett, John Beasley, and June Carter Cash. *The Apostle*. DVD. Written and directed by Robert Duvall. United States: October Films, 1997.

Ellington, Scott A. "Who Shall Lead Them Out? An Exploration of God's Openness in Exodus 32.7–14." *Journal of Pentecostal Theology* 14:1 (2005) 41–60.

Engle, Paul E., and Steven B. Cowan, eds. *Who Runs the Church? 4 Views on Church Government*. Grand Rapids: Zondervan, 2004.

Fairbairn, Donald. *Eastern Orthodoxy Through Western Eyes*. Louisville: Westminster John Knox, 2002.

Fee, Gordon D. *God's Empowering Presence: The Holy Spirit in the Letters of Paul*. Peabody, MA: Hendrickson, 1994.

Feuerbach, Ludwig. *The Essence of Christianity*. Translated by George Eliot. Amherst, NY: Prometheus, 1989.

Fiddes, Paul S. *Participating in God: A Pastoral Doctrine of the Trinity*. Louisville: Westminster John Knox, 2000.

Finney, Charles Grandison. *The Promise of the Spirit*. Edited by Timothy Lawrence Smith. Minneapolis: Bethany Fellowship, 1980.

Flood, Derek. "A Relational Understanding of Atonement." In *Relational Theology: A Contemporary Introduction*, edited by Brint Montgomery et al., 40–42. Eugene, OR: Wipf & Stock, 2012.

Fretheim, Terence E. *Abraham: Trials of Family and Faith*. Columbia: University of South Carolina Press, 2007.

———. *The Suffering of God: An Old Testament Perspective*. Philadelphia: Fortress, 1984.

Fudge, Edward William. *The Fire That Consumes: A Biblical and Historical Study of the Doctrine of the Final Punishment*. New York: Open Road, 2016.

Gabriel, Andrew K. *The Lord is the Spirit: The Holy Spirit and Divine Attributes*. Eugene, OR: Pickwick, 2011.

Garland, David E. *1 Corinthians: Baker Exegetical Commentary on the New Testament*. Grand Rapids: Baker Academic, 2003.

Gee, Donald. *Spiritual Gifts in the Work of Ministry Today*. Springfield: Gospel, 1963.

Glustrom, Simon. *The Language of Judaism*. Northvale, NJ: Jason Aronson, 1988.

Grant, Jamie A. "Spirit and Presence in Psalm 139." In *Presence, Power, and Promise: The Role of the Spirit of God in the Old Testament*, edited by David G. Firth and Paul D. Wegner, 135–46. Downers Grove: IVP Academic, 2011.

Gregg, Steve. *All You Want to Know about Hell: Three Christian Views of God's Final Solution to the Problem of Sin*. Nashville: Thomas Nelson, 2013.

Grenz, Stanley J. *Theology for the Community of God*. Grand Rapids: Eerdmans, 2000.

Gresham, John Leroy. *Charles G. Finney's Doctrine of the Baptism of the Holy Spirit*. Peabody, MA: Hendrickson, 1987.

Grudem, Wayne. *The Gift of Prophecy in the New Testament and Today*. Rev. ed. Wheaton: Crossway, 2000.

———. *Systematic Theology: An Introduction to Biblical Theology*. Grand Rapids: Zondervan, 1994.

Gundry, Stanley N., and William Crockett, eds. *Four Views on Hell*. Grand Rapids: Zondervan, 1996.

Guy, Laurie. *Introducing Early Christianity: A Topical Survey of Its Life, Beliefs, and Practice*. Downers Grove: InterVarsity, 2004.

Habets, Myk, ed. *Spirit of Truth: Reading Scripture and Constructing Theology with the Holy Spirit*. Eugene, OR: Pickwick, 2010.

Hambrick-Stowe, Charles E. *Charles G. Finney and the Spirit of American Evangelicalism*. Grand Rapids: Eerdmans, 1996.

Hamilton, Victor P. *The Book of Genesis: Chapters 8–50*. Grand Rapids: Eerdmans, 1995.

Hart, Larry. "Spirit Baptism: A Dimensional Charismatic Perspective." In *Perspectives on Spirit Baptism: Five Views*, edited by Chad Owen Brand, 105–80. Nashville: Broadman & Holman, 2004.

Harvey, Dean H. *Ransom: The High Cost of Sin*. United States: Xulon Press, 2010.

Hasker, William. "An Adequate God." In *Searching for an Adequate God: A Dialogue Between Process and Free Will Theists*, edited by John B. Cobb Jr. and Clark H. Pinnock, 215–45. Grand Rapids: Eerdmans, 2000.

———. *God in an Open Universe: Science, Metaphysics, and Open Theism*. Eugene, OR: Pickwick, 2011.

Hayford, Jack. "Despise Not Prophecy." In *Understanding the Fivefold Ministry*, edited by Matthew D. Green, 79–84. Lake Mary, FL: Charisma, 2005.

Hesselgrave, David. *Paradigms in Conflict: 10 Key Questions in Christian Missions Today*. Grand Rapids: Kregel, 2005.

Hick, John. *Evil and the God of Love*. 3rd ed. Glasgow: Fount, 1974.

———. "An Irenaean Theodicy." In *Encountering Evil: Live Options in Theodicy—A New Edition*, edited by Stephen T. Davis, 38–52. Louisville: Westminster John Knox, 2001.

Highfield, Ron. *Great is the Lord: Theology for the Praise of God*. Grand Rapids: Eerdmans, 2008.

Hill, David. *New Testament Prophecy*. New Foundations Theological Library. Atlanta: John Knox, 1979.

Hodge, Charles. *Systematic Theology*. Vol. 1. Grand Rapids: Eerdmans, 1952.

Hoke, Steve, and Bill Taylor. *Global Mission Handbook: A Guide for Crosscultural Service*. Downers Grove: InterVarsity, 2009.

House, H. Wayne, and Matt Power. *Charts on Open Theism and Orthodoxy*. Grand Rapids: Kregel, 2003.

Humphreys, W. Lee. *The Character of God in the Book of Genesis: A Narrative Appraisal*. Louisville: Westminster John Knox, 2001.

Hundley, Michael B. *Keeping Heaven on Earth: Safeguarding the Divine Presence in the Priestly Tabernacle*. Tübingen, Germany: Mohr Siebeck, 2011.

Inbody, Tyron. *The Faith of the Christian Church: An Introduction to Theology*. Grand Rapids: Eerdmans, 2005.

Jersak, Brad, and Michael Hardin, eds. *Stricken by God?: Nonviolent Identification and the Victory of Christ*. Abbotsford, B.C.: Fresh Wind, 2007.

Jones, Charles Edwin. *A Guide to the Study of the Holiness Movement*. ATLA Bibliography Series 1. Metuchen, NJ: Scarecrow, 1974.

Jowett, Benjamin. "On the Interpretation of Scripture." In *Essays and Reviews: The 1860 Text and Its Reading*, edited by Victor Shea and William Whitla, 477–594. Charlottesville: University Press of Virginia, 2000.

Kaiser Jr., Walter C. "The Pentateuch." In *A Biblical Theology of the Holy Spirit*, edited by Trevor J. Burke and Keith Warrington, 1–11. Eugene, OR: Cascade, 2014.

Keener, Craig S. *The Gospel of Matthew: A Socio-rhetorical Commentary*. Grand Rapids: Eerdmans, 2009.

———. "Power of Pentecost: Luke's Missiology in Acts 1–2." *Asian Journal of Pentecostal Studies* 12:1 (2009) 47–74.
Kline, Meredith. "Primal Parousia." *Westminster Theological Journal* 40.2 (1978) 244–80.
Kostlevy, William. *Holiness Manuscripts: A Guide to Sources Documenting the Wesleyan Holiness Movement in the United States and Canada.* Metuchen, NJ: Scarecrow, 1994.
———, and Gari-Anne Patzwald. *Historical Dictionary of the Holiness Movement.* Lanham, MD: Scarecrow, 2001.
Kydd, R. A. N. *Charismatic Gifts in the Early Church.* Peabody: Hendrickson, 1984.
Lewis, J. "Baptismal Practices of the Second and Third Century Church." *Restoration Quarterly* 26:1 (1983) 1–17.
Lloyd-Jones, David Martyn. *Revival.* Wheaton: Crossway, 1987.
Lodahl, Michael. "Sin in Relational Perspective." In *Relational Theology: A Contemporary Introduction*, edited by Brint Montgomery et al., 37–39. Eugene, OR: Wipf & Stock, 2012.
Louth, Andrew. *Introducing Eastern Orthodox Theology.* Downers Grove: InterVarsity, 2013.
Marguerat, Daniel. *The First Christian Historian: Writing the 'Acts of the Apostles.'* Translated by Ken McKinney et al. Society for New Testament Studies Monograph Series 121. Cambridge: Cambridge University Press, 2002.
Mathews, Kenneth A. *Genesis 1–11:26.* The New American Commentary: An Exegetical and Theological Exposition of Holy Scripture 1A. Nashville: Broadman & Holman, 1996.
May Ling, Tan-Chow. *Pentecostal Theology for the Twenty-First Century: Engaging with Multi-faith Singapore.* Burlington, VT: Ashgate, 2007.
McFarland, Ian. "The Fall and Sin." In *The Oxford Handbook of Systematic Theology*, edited by John Webster et al, 140–59. New York: Oxford University Press Inc., 2007.
Menzies, Robert P. *Empowered for Witness: The Spirit in Luke-Acts.* Sheffield, England: Sheffield Academic, 2001.
Merkle, Benjamin L. *40 Questions About Elders and Deacons.* Grand Rapids: Kregel, 2008.
———. *The Elder and Overseer: One Office in the Early Church.* New York: Peter Lang, 2003.
Migliore, Daniel L. *Faith Seeking Understanding: An Introduction to Christian Theology.* Grand Rapids: Eerdmans, 1991.
Miley, John. *Systematic Theology.* Vol. 1. New York: Hunt & Eaton, 1892.
Moltmann, Jürgen. *The Crucified God: The Cross of Christ as the Foundation and Criticism of Christian Theology.* Translated by R. A. Wilson and John Bowden. Minneapolis: Fortress, 1993.
———. *The Spirit of Life: A Universal Affirmation.* Translated by Margaret Kohl. Minneapolis: Fortress, 2001.
Newton, Phil A. *Elders in Congregational Life: Rediscovering the Biblical Model for Church Leadership.* Grand Rapids: Kregel, 2005.
Ngewa, Samuel M. *1 and 2 Timothy and Titus.* Africa Bible and Commentary Series. Grand Rapids: HippoBooks, 2009.

Osburn, C. D. "The Third Person Imperative in Acts 2:38." *Restoration Quarterly* 26:2 (1983) 81–84.

Outler, Albert C, ed. *The Works of John Wesley*. Bicentennial ed. Vol. 1, *Sermons I (1–30)*. Nashville: Abingdon Press, 1984.

Pannenberg, Wolfhart. *Systematic Theology*. Translated by Geoffrey W. Bromiley. Vol. 1. New York: T. and T. Clark, 2004.

Payton Jr., James R. *Light from the Christian East: An Introduction to the Orthodox Tradition*. Downers Grove: InterVarsity, 2007.

Pinnock, Clark H. *Most Moved Mover: A Theology of God's Openness*. Carlisle: Paternoster, 2002.

———, et al. *The Openness of God: A Biblical Challenge to the Traditional Understanding of God*. Downers Grove: InterVarsity, 1994.

———. *A Wideness in God's Mercy: The Finality of Jesus Christ in a World of Religions*. Eugene: Wipf & Stock, 1997.

Pool, Jeff B. *God's Wounds: Hermeneutic of the Christian Symbol of Divine Suffering*. Vol. 1, *Divine Vulnerability and Creation*. Eugene, OR: Pickwick, 2009.

Rosenblatt, Naomi H., and Joshua Horwitz. *Wrestling with Angels: What Genesis Teaches Us About Our Spiritual Identity, Sexuality, and Personal Relationships*. New York: Delta, 1995.

Ruthven, J. *On the Cessation of the Charismata: The Protestant Polemic on Postbiblical Miracles*. Sheffield: Sheffield Academic, 1993.

Sanders, John. *The God Who Risks: A Theology of Divine Providence*. Downers Grove: InterVarsity, 1998.

———. *No Other Name: An Investigation into the Destiny of the Unevangelized*. Eugene, OR: Wipf & Stock, 2001.

Schmitt, Harley H. *Many Gifts One Lord: A Biblical Understanding of the Variety of Spiritual Gifts Among Early Christians and in the Church Today*. Fairfax: Xulon Press, 2002.

Schreiner, Thomas R. *New Testament Theology: Magnifying God in Christ*. Grand Rapids: Baker Academic, 2008.

Skinner, John. *A Critical and Exegetical Commentary on Genesis*. New York: Charles Scribner's Sons, 1910.

Speiser, E.A. *Genesis: Introduction, Translation, and Notes*. The Anchor Bible 1. New York: Doubleday, 1964.

Stein, Robert H. "Baptism in Luke-Acts." In *Believer's Baptism: Sign of the New Covenant in Christ*, edited by Thomas D. Schreiner and Shawn D. Wright, 35–66. NAC Studies in Bible and Theology. Nashville: B&H Academic, 2006.

Stronstad, Roger. *The Prophethood of All Believers: A Study in Luke's Charismatic Theology*. New York: Scheffield Academic, 2004.

Swinburne, Richard. *The Coherence of Theism*. Oxford: Clarendon, 1977.

Synan, Vinson. *The Century of the Holy Spirit: 100 Years of Pentecostal and Charismatic Renewal, 1901–2001*. Nashville: Thomas Nelson, 2001.

Telford, John, ed. "Letter of John Wesley to John Fletcher." Vol. 6, *The Letters of Rev. John Wesley, A.M.* London: Epworth, 1931.

Terrien, Samuel. *The Elusive Presence: The Heart of Biblical Theology*. Religious Perspectives 26. San Francisco: Harper & Row, 1983.

Thielicke, Helmut. *Death and Life*. Translated by Edward H. Schroeder. Philadelphia: Fortress, 1970.

Thiselton, Anthony C. *The Holy Spirit—In Biblical Teaching, through the Centuries, and Today*. Grand Rapids: Eerdmans, 2013.

Thomas, Robert L. *Understanding Spiritual Gifts: A Verse-by-verse Study of 1 Corinthians 12–14*. Rev. ed. Grand Rapids: Kregel, 1999.

Tiessen, Terrance. *Providence and Prayer: How Does God Work in the World?* Downers Grove: InterVarsity, 2000.

Turner, Charles V. *Biblical Bible Translating*. United States: Lightning Source, 2001.

van den Brom, Luco J. *Divine Presence in the World: A Critical Analysis of the Notion of Divine Omnipresence*. Studies in Philosophical Theology 5. Kampen, Netherlands: Kok Pharos, 1993.

Von Rad, Gerhard. *Old Testament Theology*. Translated by D. M. G. Stalker. Vol. 1, *The Theology of Israel's Historical Traditions*. Louisville: Westminster John Knox, 1962.

Vos, Howard F. *Everyman's Bible Commentary: Genesis*. Chicago: The Moody Bible Institute of Chicago, 1982.

Wagner, C. Peter. *Apostles Today: Biblical Government for Biblical Power*. Ventura, CA: Regal, 2006.

———. *Changing Church: How God is Leading His Church into the Future*. Ventura, CA: Regal, 2004.

Wallace, Daniel B. *Greek Grammar beyond the Basics: An Exegetical Syntax of the New Testament*. Grand Rapids: Zondervan, 1996.

Wesley, John. *A Plain Account of Christian Perfection, As Believed and Taught by the Rev. John Wesley, From the Year 1725, To the Year 1727*. New York: Lane and Scott, 1850.

Westermann, Claus. *Genesis 1–11: A Commentary*. Translated by John J. Scullion. Minneapolis: Fortress, 1984.

White, James F. *Protestant Worship: Traditions in Transition*. Louisville: Westminster John Knox, 1989.

Wilkerson, David R., et al. *The Cross and the Switchblade*. New York: Pyramid, 1964.

Williams, J. Rodman. *Renewal Theology: Systematic Theology from a Charismatic Perspective*. Grand Rapids: Zondervan, 1996.

Wimber, John, and Kevin Springer. *Power Evangelism*. Grand Rapids: Chosen, 2009.

Wink, Walter. *Engaging the Powers: Discernment and Resistance in a World of Domination*. Minneapolis: Fortress, 1992.

Witherington III, Ben. *The Acts of the Apostles: A Socio-Rhetorical Commentary*. Grand Rapids: Eerdmans, 1998.

———, and Darlene Hyatt. *Paul's Letter to the Romans: A Socio-Rhetorical Commentary*. Grand Rapids: Eerdmans, 2004.

Wright, Christopher J. H. *Knowing the Holy Spirit through the Old Testament*. Downers Grove: InterVarsity, 2006.

Yong, Amos. "Relational Theology and the Holy Spirit." In *Relational Theology: A Contemporary Introduction*, edited by Brint Montgomery et al., 18–20. Eugene, OR: Wipf & Stock, 2012.

Young, Edward J. "The Interpretation of Gen. 1:2." *Westminster Theological Journal* 23:2 (1961) 151–78.

www.ingramcontent.com/pod-product-compliance
Lightning Source LLC
Chambersburg PA
CBHW050849230426
43667CB00012B/2217